BEYOND WHITE PICKET FENCES

BEYOND WHITE PICKET FENCES

EVOLUTION OF AN AMERICAN TOWN

CATHERINE SIMPSON BUEKER

Russell Sage Foundation • New York

The Russell Sage Foundation

The Russell Sage Foundation, one of the oldest of America's general purpose foundations, was established in 1907 by Mrs. Margaret Olivia Sage for "the improvement of social and living conditions in the United States." The foundation seeks to fulfill this mandate by fostering the development and dissemination of knowledge about the country's political, social, and economic problems. While the foundation endeavors to assure the accuracy and objectivity of each book it publishes, the conclusions and interpretations in Russell Sage Foundation publications are those of the authors and not of the foundation, its trustees, or its staff. Publication by Russell Sage, therefore, does not imply foundation endorsement.

BOARD OF TRUSTEES
Jennifer Richeson, Chair

Marianne Bertrand
Cathy J. Cohen
James N. Druckman
Jason Furman
Michael Jones-Correa

David Laibson
David Leonhardt
Earl Lewis
Hazel Rose Markus

Tracey L. Meares
Thomas J. Sugrue
Celeste Watkins-Hayes
Bruce Western

ROR: https://ror.org/02yh9se80
DOI: https://doi.org/10.7758/mpvu4414

Library of Congress Cataloging in Publication Control Number: 2024061102
ISBN 9780871540409 (paperback) / ISBN 9781610449427 (ebook)

Copyright © 2025 by Russell Sage Foundation. All rights reserved. Printed in the United States of America. No part of this publication may be reproduced, stored in a retrieval system, or transmitted in any form or by any means, electronic, mechanical, photocopying, recording, or otherwise, without the prior written permission of the publisher. Permission is not granted for large language model training. Reproduction by the United States Government in whole or in part is permitted for any purpose.

The paper used in this publication meets the minimum requirements of American National Standard for Information Sciences—Permanence of Paper for Printed Library Materials. ANSI Z39.48-1992.

Text design by Genna Patacsil. Front matter DOI: https://doi.org/10.7758/mpvu4414.9953

RUSSELL SAGE FOUNDATION
112 East 64th Street, New York, New York 10065
10 9 8 7 6 5 4 3 2 1

So we beat on, boats against the current, borne back ceaselessly into the past.
—F. Scott Fitzgerald, *The Great Gatsby*

The ship wherein Theseus and the youth of Athens returned from Crete had thirty oars, and was preserved by the Athenians down even to the time of Demetrius Phalereus, for they took away the old planks as they decayed, putting in new and stronger timber in their places, in so much that this ship became a standing example among the philosophers, for the logical question of things that grow; one side holding that the ship remained the same, and the other contending that it was not the same.
—Plutarch, *Life of Theseus*

Contents

LIST OF ILLUSTRATIONS		ix
ABOUT THE AUTHOR		xi
ACKNOWLEDGMENTS		xiii
CHAPTER 1	A Slowly Changing Town	1
CHAPTER 2	A Brief History of Wellesley and a Brief History of Immigration Theory	13
CHAPTER 3	Neighborhoods, Schools, and Places of Worship: Setting the Stage for Contact	39
CHAPTER 4	Multidirectional Influences on Individuals	65
CHAPTER 5	Community Organizations as Cause and Consequence of Change	97
CHAPTER 6	Durable Institutional Changes Across the Community	125
CHAPTER 7	A Variegated Process: Three Paths to Change and the Road Ahead	157
APPENDIX A	Methodology	165
APPENDIX B	Interview Protocol for Lifelong Residents	167
APPENDIX C	Interview Protocol for Diverse Voices	171
APPENDIX D	Interview Protocol for Organizational Leaders	175
NOTES		177
REFERENCES		189
INDEX		205

= Illustrations =

Figures

Figure 1.1	Demographics of Residents of Wellesley, the State of Massachusetts, and the United States, 2020	5
Figure 1.2	Variegated Assimilation	7
Figure 1.3	A Glocal Framework	8
Figure 2.1	The Hunnewell Topiary on Lake Waban, Wellesley, Massachusetts, c. 1902	21
Figure 2.2	Madame Chiang Kai-shek Tours the Wellesley College Campus, 1943	27
Figure 3.1	Map of Neighborhood School Districts, Wellesley, Massachusetts, 2024	42
Figure 3.2	Banner for the Wellesley Chinese Language School, Wellesley, Massachusetts, 2024	56
Figure 5.1	The Italo-American Educational Club, Wellesley, Massachusetts, 2024	112
Figure 6.1	Isaac Sprague Elementary School, Wellesley, Massachusetts, 2024	128
Figure 6.2	John D. Hardy Elementary School, Wellesley, Massachusetts, 2024	130
Figure 6.3	Multilingual Signs Posted in Wellesley High School, Wellesley, Massachusetts, 2024	141
Figure 6.4	Town Hall in December, Wellesley, Massachusetts	150

Table

Table 1.1	Changes in Race, Ethnicity, and Nativity in Wellesley, Massachusetts, 1970–2020	4

About the Author

Catherine Simpson Bueker is professor of sociology at Emmanuel College.

Acknowledgments

This book has been more than ten years in the making and is in many ways a perfect merger of my personal and professional lives. Sociologists begin every introduction to sociology course by teaching about the "sociological imagination"—the ways in which our individual lives intersect with larger global forces. This book is just that. As I sat in the Wellesley Middle School auditorium more than a decade ago, listening to my oldest son's concert, I was intrigued when the conductor invited my son's friend to give a solo performance. This sixth-grader, whose family originally hailed from South Asia, performed an amazing drumming solo on a traditional South Asian set of drums. I was struck by how his performance contrasted with, and complemented, the more traditional Western musical pieces that the orchestra played, as well as by how far this concert was from what one would have expected in Wellesley.

The question of how much Wellesley has changed through the decades stuck with me, although it would take another seven years, including a global pandemic, to get to some answers. The perception of Wellesley as exclusively White, Christian, and culturally monolithic did not match the experiences I was having in my neighborhood, at my children's schools, or in my friendship networks. This book is a testament to both the growing diversity of the town and the challenges that come with it. The story I tell here of Wellesley is intended to be read neither as one of complete harmony nor one of broad hostility and discrimination. Either framing would present an incomplete caricature of the town. As I say in the forthcoming pages, the story of how Wellesley has changed is a story of "both/and."

This is a story I could tell only by listening to the nearly one hundred town residents, both new and established, who spoke to me about their experiences in Wellesley. While I cannot list out your names here, you all have my tremendous thanks. This book is also heavily dependent upon the archival data from the *Wellesley Townsman*. The digitization of the historical record was funded by the Wellesley Free Library Foundation, and for that I am tremendously grateful. Piecing together nearly one hundred years of newspaper items about Italian, Jewish, and Chinese residents, totaling more than twenty thousand items, was possible only through the help of my many research assistants. My tremendous thanks to Deanna Bourque, Gabby DiPietro, Kiera Eubanks, Abigail Ganley, Erwin Kamuene, Shakira Ketant, M. Arielle Poudel, Grace Santana, and Olivia Wong. This was a Herculean task, and I hope I have not turned you off of research forever!

I owe tremendous thanks to the Russell Sage Foundation for its financial support of this project, to Suzanne Nichols for her commitment to it, to Jennifer Rappaport and all the people behind the scenes at Russell Sage who made this book come to life, and to the anonymous reviewers who made this a far better piece of work. I also need to reach way back to my undergraduate days at Cornell University and thank two very special professors from that time and through today—Mary Beth Norton and Glenn Altschuler. As Mary Beth's undergraduate researcher many decades ago, I learned that archives can teach us about the past and give us insight into the future. A deep dive into the archives also reminds us that the "unprecedented" and "extraordinary" events of today are rarely neither. Completely coincidentally, Glenn was working contemporaneously on a book using similar methods as this one, albeit in Brooklyn circa 1900. I greatly appreciate the feedback and support I received from Glenn on an early draft of what became this book.

To my many wonderful Wellesley friends, both new and established, thank you, thank you, thank you. Nothing quite binds people nor reveals a common humanity like raising children together. You have been a constant source of humor, love, and support. You have been my running partners, sounding boards, and my very own (sometimes literal) cheering section. I am forever grateful.

Finally, I would like to thank my family—John, Sam, Michael, and Rachel. They were forced to listen to every interesting piece of data I found in the archives, the details from interviews, and observations around town. In many ways, they know this book as well as I do. Thank you, John, for your meticulous proofreading. I know you had to walk a fine line with your red pen! My children are also the reason why this book came to exist. Without them, I would never have sat in that middle school auditorium, met parents at school pick-up, nor even lived in the suburbs. You introduced me to a much richer and more interesting place than I would have found on my own. I love you more than I can possibly put into words.

Chapter 1

A Slowly Changing Town

Wellesley, Massachusetts, is an affluent town of approximately thirty thousand people, situated at the midpoint of the famed Boston Marathon. The shopping district includes high-end independent boutiques (although there are fewer of these shops than a generation ago), stores that sell athleisure wear and preppy brands, and a mix of traditional American and ethnic restaurants, both chain and independent. The town has three colleges, two private schools, a state-of-the-art library, and a nineteenth-century town hall that overlooks a sloping town green and is on the National Register of Historic Places. Looming large in the center of town is the Village Church, established in 1798. A quick glance at Wellesley suggests an old-school, overwhelmingly White New England town. In fact, this perception is confirmed in interviews with lifelong residents from across the age spectrum, who almost universally describe the town as "White," "WASPY," and more than anything, "affluent"—this last descriptor the most accurate.[1] Interestingly, residents who identify as Black, Chinese, or Indian see an increasingly racially and ethnically diverse town.

Wellesley is indeed affluent; the town epitomizes the growing economic divide in American society. Wellesley is a concentration of 1 percenters. Historically it has been known for its strong schools—a reason many cite for choosing to live in Wellesley—and for its beautiful public spaces. Residents include presidents of national banks, owners of national sports franchises, entrepreneurs who have started widely known companies, heads of major law firms, well-known journalists, and private equity magnates who have been able to capitalize on the human capital that has long been found in Wellesley owing to its proximity to universities, research labs, and hospitals. The town has claimed federal judges and more than one Nobel Prize winner. With its whiteness, its history, and its concentrations of education and wealth, Wellesley has long suffered a reputation of being elite and unwelcoming to those who do not fall within the "right" racial, religious, and socioeconomic parameters. It is referred to derogatorily as "Swellesley" by residents and nonresidents alike, some using the term as a put-down and others as a tongue-in-cheek quip. A local radio station mockingly reads the Wellesley police blotter as entertainment for its listeners.

But both the quick glance and the shorthand descriptors miss a more nuanced story. Both those looking at Wellesley from the outside and those who live, work, and study in town largely fail to see, for a variety of reasons, its contemporary diversity, as well as the ways in which it has been shaped—and continues to be shaped—by that diversity.

The United States is often described as a "melting pot," a society that is the sum of its many mixed parts, melded together. However, social scientists have done little to examine what we mean by this metaphor. When, where, and how have these changes taken place? We often cite our foodways, pointing to the incorporation of tacos, pizza, and bagels into the typical American diet, but that discussion lacks depth. We are a beautiful, continually evolving, and multicolored tapestry, but understanding the processes that got us here and will continue to alter that tapestry requires a deep examination of each of the stitches that have made it.

In the absence of such a deep dive into the micro level, we give only limited recognition to the many groups that have made significant contributions to who we are today as a society. Further, our lack of deep introspection around who we are and how we got here—suggesting that we have always been what we are at this very time (be it 1875 or 1935 or 2025) and forever will be—makes the prospect of ongoing change terrifying. A look back allows us to see what we used to be, where we are now, and how we arrived here, recognizing that much of what we simply take for granted today as part of mainstream culture was not always widely accepted. In short, looking back makes going forward less scary, as it helps us recognize flux as a natural state.

The evidence suggests that new groups, with their varied racial, religious, and ethnic identities, have shaped the town of Wellesley in varied ways. In this book, individuals across groups discuss ways in which they have sought to maintain their ethnic identities for themselves, to honor prior generations, and to pass down traditions to the next generation, both historically and in the present day. These attempts to retain ethnic ties unintentionally reform the mainstream in myriad ways, be it by taking time off from work or school to honor holidays not (yet) on the calendar or by developing ethnic organizations to promote continuity. In these and in many other ways, *ethnic retention results in mainstream reformation.*

Interviews, observations, and archival data also reveal, somewhat counterintuitively, the impact of assimilation on the mainstream. For example, as parents engage with schools and PTOs—practices foreign in their home societies—they are altering the very institutions into which they are assimilating by bringing into these settings their own backgrounds and traditions. In these and many other ways, *assimilation results in mainstream reformation*.

Immigrants and members of other minority groups also encounter distinct challenges when they arrive in Wellesley, beyond just the pains of leaving behind their home and traditions. Individuals and groups may experience racialization and other forms of "othering" by established residents; ironically, they are likely to have more such negative experiences the more they assimilate into the mainstream. But members of new groups are not passive recipients of such hostilities. *Newcomers' reactions to racialization results in mainstream reformation*.

In short, new members of the community become incorporated into the mainstream over time, to varying degrees, and through varying channels, inevitably changing what the mainstream looks like through "neo-assimilation." Sometimes this overarching process is put in motion by the *retention* by individuals and groups of their ethnic identities and traditions, sometimes by the *assimilation* of individuals and groups into the mainstream, and sometimes by the *reactions* of individuals and groups to racialization. This book is about these processes and the changes that have occurred within Wellesley; it looks at how actions beget reactions as new ethnic, racial, and religious groups enter a historically homogenous community, and how those reactions, in turn, reshape the established community. All of these individual and small group interactions, reactions, and reformations are embedded within a larger and constantly evolving local, national, and even international framework. The process is dynamic, multileveled, multidirectional, and continuous.

The story of Wellesley is more nuanced than the stories of other communities across the country, probably not because it is so unique demographically speaking, but rather because researchers have tended to focus on communities whose demographics have changed more profoundly.[2] So, while Wellesley seems distinct in many ways, the processes unfolding here may be more representative of what takes place in communities that have diversified more slowly than has been described in the research on more extreme cases.

At the same time, Wellesley is its own form of an extreme case: an extremely educated, wealthy, and still disproportionately White community compared to the larger American society. Why would anyone focus on it? Given that it is so far outside the norm in various ways, why would we study that which cannot be generalized?

What happens in towns like Wellesley, Massachusetts, or Greenwich, Connecticut, or Highland Park, Illinois, matters because their outsize concentrations of income, wealth, and education have outsize effects on the larger society. Joe Feagin and Eileen O'Brien argue in their book on elite White men that racial attitudes largely trickle down from the top.[3] Just one example from the past is the case of the forced desegregation of

4   Beyond White Picket Fences

Table 1.1   Changes in Race, Ethnicity, and Nativity in Wellesley, Massachusetts, 1970–2020

	1970	1980	1990	2000	2010	2020
White	98.7%	96.6%	94.0%	90.0%	85.1%	75.8%
White (non-Hispanic)	NA	95.9	92.3	88.3	76.6	73.6
Black	0.7	1.1	1.6	1.6	2.0	2.1
Asian	0.4	1.7	3.9	6.4	12.4	13.3
Two or more races	NA	NA	NA	1.4	1.9	7.6
Latino	NA	1.3	2.2	2.3	3.6	5.3
Foreign-born	7.3	7.7	8.8	10.9	16.9	17.4

Source: US Census Bureau 1970, 1980, 1990, 2000, 2010, 2020.

Boston's public schools in 1974, a policy decision enacted by a federal judge living in Wellesley. A more recent example is a longtime resident in town who is the chair of the board of an Ivy League university. His views influence the policies that impact the tens of thousands of students who attend this elite university, many of whom will go on to take their places in the upper echelons of American society. A senior partner at a major law firm and longtime resident talks about the rise of diversity initiatives and programming at his firm, be it recognition of the Lunar New Year or providing kosher food options. Whether or not we view these initiatives as window dressing or marketing instead of genuine structural change, such initiatives touch both lawyers and support staff, straddling a wide range of racial groups and socioeconomic classes. Policies and practices in regard to race, ethnicity, and diversity often flow from the top.

Slowly Changing Demographics

Wellesley is still predominantly White, but much less so than it once was. While 99 percent of the town self-identified as White in 1970, that figure for White, non-Hispanic residents has dropped to approximately 73 percent today. Asian residents, most from China and India, and their American-born children now comprise 13 percent of the town's population and closer to 20 percent of the school district's student body (table 1.1).

As a point of comparison, according to the 2020 US census, just under 7 percent of the American population and just under 8 percent of Massachusetts residents identified as Asian or Asian American, as illustrated in figure 1.1. Approximately 17 percent of the town of Wellesley identified as foreign-born, whereas 14 percent of the US population and a comparable percentage of Massachusetts residents were foreign-born.

Further, the heavily Protestant and Catholic presence in the town, while undeniably still strong, has been moderated: the approximately

Figure 1.1   Demographics of Residents of Wellesley, the State of Massachusetts, and the United States, 2020

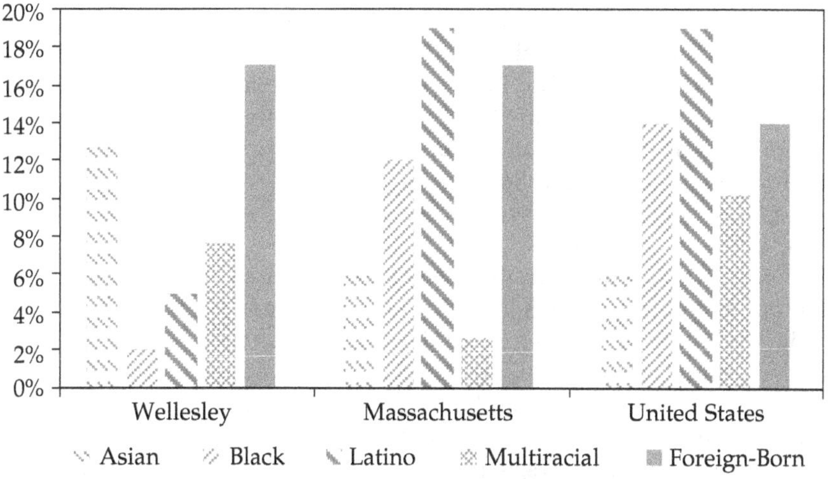

[Bar chart showing percentages for Asian, Black, Latino, Multiracial, and Foreign-Born populations across Wellesley, Massachusetts, and the United States]

Source: US Census Bureau 2020.

10 percent of today's residents who identify as Jewish represent a significantly larger percentage than is found nationwide or statewide. Those who are truly White Anglo-Saxon Protestant now comprise a minority of the community, as in the larger American society.[4] Just as the United States went from being overwhelmingly White, Black, and Christian to presenting a more diverse mosaic of residents in the period following immigration reform in 1965, so too has Wellesley experienced racial, ethnic, and religious shifts over the past fifty years. In some ways, Wellesley is more racially and ethnically diverse than the country and Massachusetts, but less diverse in other ways.

Those who consider these statistical changes in Wellesley's demographics inconsequential are being too quick to dismiss the implications. While few may notice these changes at first glance, the implications are playing out each and every day. The town has been altered and continues to be altered by the earlier waves of immigrant and ethnic groups that entered the community in the first half of the twentieth century, both while immigration to the United States was still open and after the country shut its doors in 1924. Although the community's more recent and largely unrecognized diversity makes sense given Wellesley's proximity to high-tech businesses, hospitals, and higher education institutions, the town's historic roots as a bastion of the old New England WASP, ironically, brought it into contact with new groups long before one would have expected. The historical record shows the presence and impact of Italian, Jewish, and Chinese residents in the community dating back to the early twentieth century.

The arrival of these three groups at different times in Wellesley reflected distinct immigration patterns and vastly different national and international climates. The Italian and Jewish residents largely came of age in the post–World War II era, when White ethnics were more easily assimilated as economic and educational opportunities expanded and anti-Semitism declined following the Holocaust. According to Richard Alba, these conditions allowed for socioeconomic mobility, personal contact, and moral elevation.[5]

Italian, Jewish, and Chinese newcomers came to Wellesley at different points in their group's immigration history and with distinct racial, religious, and socioeconomic profiles. All of these factors, at all levels of society, impacted their reception in Wellesley, the ways in which they were or were not accepted, and the ways in which their incorporation left marks on the larger community. Immigrants from each of these groups worked, in their own ways, to retain aspects of their ethnic identity, while also working to become accepted by those already established at the time in Wellesley. Although each group was sometimes marked as foreign, undesirable, and inferior through processes of racialization and anti-Semitism, each group changed as it became a part of the mainstream population and, through neo-assimilation, in turn changed the mainstream.

The process by which immigrants interact with established residents is often viewed as either racialization—the marginalization, stereotyping, and view of immigrants as undesirable until they perhaps become assimilated into the fold—or neo-assimilation, in which the new group enters the community and impacts the established population. The micro-level reality, however, is more nuanced. The story is one of "both/and" rather than "either/or." I put forth a theory of "variegated assimilation" (figure 1.2) that accounts for the multiple processes of ethnic retention, assimilation, and racialization to describe the reformation of the established community. This modified concept, in combining previously competing theories of racialization and neo-assimilation, speaks to the multidirectional and ongoing actions of individuals and groups and the reactions between them.

All of these interactions take place within a larger framework, influenced by the timing of the interactions, including the economic, political, and social conditions at the local, national, and international levels. The relationships between the new and the established are further influenced by the interactions *between* the local, national, and international levels. Thus, the processes that result in variegated assimilation play out at each level of a "glocal" framework (figure 1.3).

Figure 1.2   Variegated Assimilation

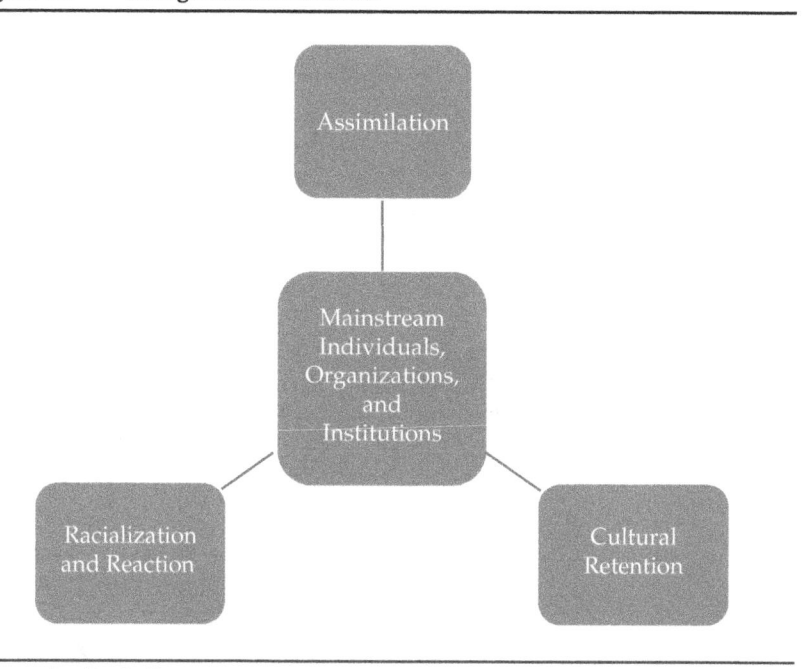

```
                    ┌─────────────┐
                    │ Assimilation│
                    └──────┬──────┘
                           │
                  ┌────────┴────────┐
                  │   Mainstream    │
                  │  Individuals,   │
                  │  Organizations, │
                  │      and        │
                  │  Institutions   │
                  └───┬─────────┬───┘
              ┌───────┘         └───────┐
      ┌───────┴──────┐           ┌──────┴───────┐
      │ Racialization│           │   Cultural   │
      │ and Reaction │           │   Retention  │
      └──────────────┘           └──────────────┘
```

Source: Author's diagram.

At the most micro level, individuals interact with each other in the neighborhood, at the bus stop, while checking out books at the library, and in the office. These micro-level interactions may become the basis for footpaths along which influence flows in both directions. Interactions resulting in footpaths can transform into ladders that lead new residents up to community organizations or even larger townwide institutions through implicit or explicit invitations from established residents or from their own sense of belonging and confidence. At times, bridges form between and among formal groups comprised of new and established residents.

Other micro-level interactions may be hostile, rooted in racial, ethnic, or religious discrimination, and lead to roadblocks. But roadblocks that develop from hostile experiences should not be assumed to end interactions, nor do they suggest a lack of influence. Negative experiences of racism, anti-Semitism, or xenophobia can be transformative for the entire community when targets of such discrimination push back as individuals and as formalized groups.

8   Beyond White Picket Fences

Figure 1.3   A Glocal Framework

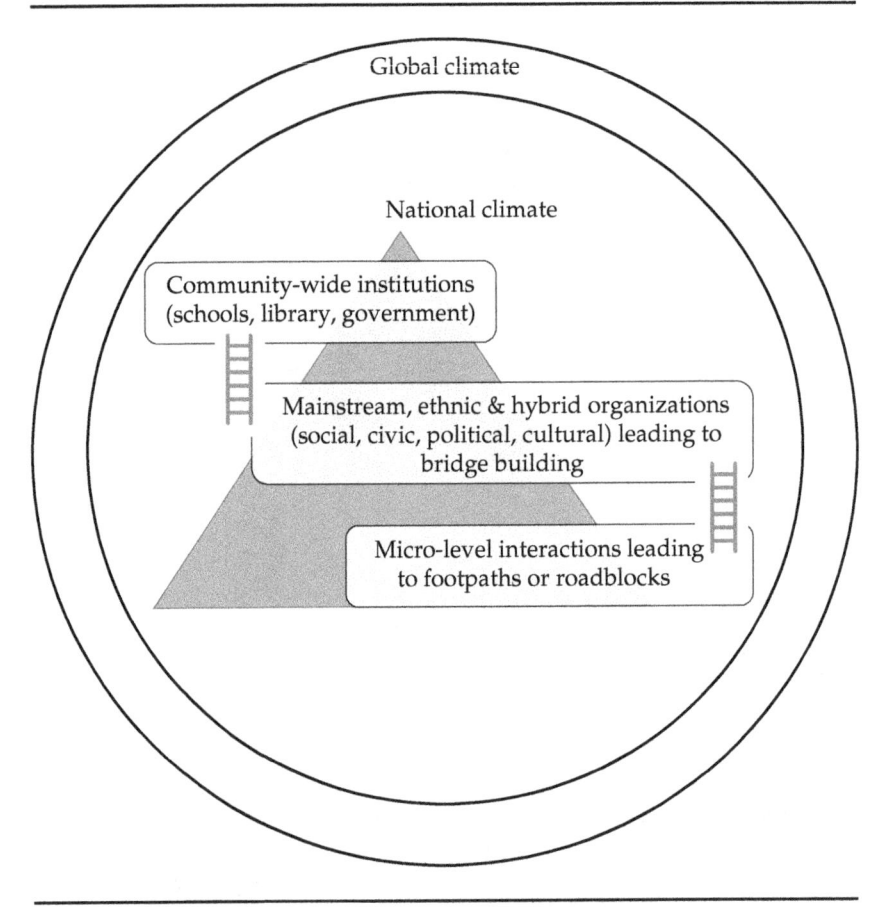

- Global climate
  - National climate
    - Community-wide institutions (schools, library, government)
    - Mainstream, ethnic & hybrid organizations (social, civic, political, cultural) leading to bridge building
    - Micro-level interactions leading to footpaths or roadblocks

Source: Author's diagram.

Methodology

To more fully understand the complex ways in which immigrant and ethnic groups have been folded into the Wellesley mainstream and have subsequently changed what is considered the mainstream, a multifaceted analysis is essential. Much of this project is based on eighty-five in-depth interviews with lifelong residents ($n = 47$), new residents ($n = 17$), and organizational leaders ($n = 21$). I have chosen to focus on lifelong residents, rather than those who have lived in the town for more than five, ten, or even twenty years, because moving into town, however long ago, suggests a level of selectivity ("I am choosing to move to Wellesley because it is diverse" or "I am choosing to move to Wellesley because it remains largely White"). Of course, focusing on lifelong residents presents its own form of selectivity, given that many Americans move, but this intentional choice allows for observations on real or perceived change over the course of a lifetime. I also interviewed a smaller sample of more diverse residents to include their voices, asking them specifically how they have experienced the community and how they have reacted to those experiences. These are individuals who identify as Black or African American, Chinese, Indian, and Sri Lankan and who have lived in the town for at least ten years. The overall resident sample ($n = 64$) approximates the population, with 72 percent identifying as White, 20 percent as Asian, 6 percent as Black or African American, 19 percent as foreign-born, and 9 percent as Jewish.

Hearing the viewpoints and experiences of newer residents is critical, as it allows us not only to see the extent to which the data triangulate or diverge but also to better understand the motivations behind the resulting processes of change. Established residents may, for example, discuss their exposure to new cultural or religious practices through learning about them within the schools, at the library, or through some other channel, without recognizing what may have prompted new residents to teach, request programming, or take on the role of cultural liaison.

At the same time, it is critical to recognize those who are not present in this case study because they do not live in Wellesley. We do not know who was prevented by discrimination from moving to Wellesley, who chose not to move there because they perceived Wellesley as a racially homogenous and discriminatory town, or who moved out of Wellesley after having hostile experiences while living there. We also lack the perspectives of those who could not afford to live in Wellesley in the first place. Although the absence of these individuals is largely in the nature of such studies, it is critical to acknowledge who does not show up in the data and would likely have more negative views of the town.

The participants were in various stages of the life course. I have divided the resident sample into three age categories (eighteen to thirty-four, thirty-five to fifty-four, and fifty-five or older), following Tomas Jiménez's methodology.[6] Among interviewees, nine are in the youngest category, twenty-seven are in the thirty-five to fifty-four age group, and twenty-eight are fifty-five or older. Ideally, established and new residents could be consistently compared across age groupings, but given the small numbers, such comparisons are made sparingly and cautiously when the sample is further divided. At times, I note obvious points of comparison by stage in the life course, but I have limited such discussion, since age comparisons are not the primary focus of the study. Certainly, future research on this topic is recommended.

The organizational data come primarily from the twenty-one interviews with current or past leaders of mainstream, ethnic, and hybrid institutions and organizations. I use the term "institution" to describe larger systems that structure the community and reflect and reinforce the formal and informal norms of Wellesley—the school system and town government, for example. "Organizations" are smaller in scale and have more clearly delineated membership and organizational structure. Examples include the Elks, Rotary, political clubs, and language schools.

Unsurprisingly, one-third of the individuals interviewed as community leaders have been highly involved in more than one of these groups, and they spoke at length about the various organizations and institutions in which they have held leadership positions. Because the interview protocol for residents includes questions on volunteer or civic participation, a number of interviewees, both lifelong residents and newer members of the community, provide insights into community groups in which they have served as leaders. As such, the data represent fifteen mainstream institutions, organizations, or committees, four ethnically focused organizations and three hybrid organizations.

Additionally, I conducted participant observations at townwide events over a three-year period and analyzed over twenty thousand items from the local newspaper, the *Wellesley Townsman*, which began publication in 1906.[7] These archival data are related to Italian, Jewish, and Chinese residents over the course of the twentieth century and include everything from articles to advertisements to wedding announcements to obituaries and beyond. By using these varied sources, both contemporary and historical, we can begin to piece together how new groups first appeared in the community (both literally and figuratively), how they were initially viewed by and interacted with established residents, how these perceptions and interactions changed over time, and the many ways in which the entire community has changed and continues to change. Although the interview data are cross-sectional in that participants are being interviewed only at one point in time, extensive use of the archival data provides a critical longitudinal component that allows us to examine how the past shapes the present—an often assumed but underexamined process.[8]

These multiple forms of data also allow for an examination of the impact of immigrant and ethnic groups at the individual, organizational, and community levels and within one particular case. Although case studies are arguably limited in their generalizability, their strength lies in enabling us to deeply understand a singular context—the ways in which the organizational structure of a town, its history, and its "culture" influence the process of multidirectional assimilation. Ideally, we are then better able to refine the theory and identify mechanisms that can shed light within other settings. These data allow for just such a deep understanding. Beyond the methodology and the depth of the data, this case has a further appeal in the diversity of the three groups under study: Italian residents as a group now racialized as White and Christian, Jewish residents as a group racialized as White but not Christian, and Chinese residents, both Christian and non-Christian, racialized as Asian. This demographic variety allows for tests of distinct theoretical frameworks—theories of racialization versus theories of neo-assimilation. Although this study focuses on one particular town, both the means of study and the findings can be more broadly applied to towns and cities across the United States.

The Roadmap

Chapter 2 begins with a history of Wellesley's development, the process of suburbanization, and the intentional shaping of the town racially, ethnically, economically, and religiously. The chapter explores the major, sometimes competing, theoretical frameworks of the past two decades that have sought to explain the interactions between the established population and newcomers: neo-assimilation, racialization, and variegated assimilation theory, a hybrid version of prior theories. Throughout the book, varying aspects of racialization, neo-assimilation, and variegated assimilation theory help make sense of what takes place in Wellesley as a result of differing group demographics and resources and local, national, and even international dynamics.

Chapter 3 examines the backdrops or stages—the neighborhoods, schools, playing fields, and myriad other settings that reflect, reinforce, and sometimes alter the patterns of relationships between members of new groups and established residents. Settings that historically did not allow for social mixing are also included in these backdrops or stages.

Chapters 4 through 6 examine how interactions and influences play out across the individual, organizational, and institutional levels. Chapter 4 explores the micro-level interactions that take place on the stages discussed in chapter 3 and identifies the small-scale footpaths that sometimes develop between individuals as well as the roadblocks that sometimes develop instead. Nascent ladder-building—the one-on-one relationships that lead individuals to higher levels of community engagement—also appears in this chapter.

Chapter 5 explores the presence and roles of mainstream, ethnic-specific, and hybrid organizations in Wellesley. Ethnic organizations are direct outgrowths of the new immigrant and ethnic groups settling in Wellesley as coethnics organize in response to unmet needs and a sometimes hostile environment. Hybrid organizations are preexisting groups that may alter their practices or goals in response to changing demographics; such changes speak to the impact of new groups. Bridges are built across formal groups and ladders reach up to decision-making bodies. Chapter 6 examines interactions and influences at the community-wide level. It is here that new groups have their greatest impact on established residents and the biggest pushbacks occur.

Although the forthcoming chapters are organized in terms of levels, it is critical to recognize that nothing happens in a vacuum. Individual interactions are shaped, and even made possible, by policies that grow out of town meeting, a governor's initiative, a federal mandate, or even an international crisis halfway around the world. These numerous, interrelated factors ranging from group-level demographics to international events combine in a "glocal" framework.

Today, as the levels of society have become increasingly flattened with the development of technology, it is more essential than ever to examine these multiple levels and their interactions in order to better understand smaller-scale interactions. The widespread schisms reported on the twenty-four-hour news cycle or on social media over issues of politics, education, race, immigration, the economy, and dozens of other issues do not stop when they reach the borders of Wellesley; they just appear as "local" issues. And in a town like Wellesley, these local issues, in turn, become national issues that are reported on cable news and in national newspapers, examples of which appear in the coming chapters.

The final chapter considers both the theoretical and practical lessons learned from the case of Wellesley and the application of these lessons more broadly in a period of increasing income inequality and extreme political polarization.

= Chapter 2 =

A Brief History of Wellesley and a Brief History of Immigration Theory

When English settlers first arrived on the land that would eventually become Wellesley in the mid-seventeenth century, they named it "Contentment."[1] This area—the home then and now of members of the Massachusett, Wampanoag, and Nipmuc communities—became incorporated into a larger area named Dedham. The town of Needham broke off from Dedham in 1711, with seventy-five British families. The local economy was based largely on sawmills, gristmills, and tanneries, taking advantage of the location on the Charles River, along with farming and, later, floriculture.[2] The Boston & Worcester Railroad line began in 1834 and shortly thereafter included three stops in the section of town that would become Wellesley.[3]

In April 1881, with the permission of the Massachusetts General Court, Wellesley officially declared its independence from Needham. The call for independence came from a small group of wealthy White men who were living and working in both Boston and the area that would come to be known as Wellesley. The families that worked to make Wellesley its own entity, providing political leadership and economic resources, included H. H. Hunnewell and Henry Durant. Hunnewell, a descendant of British colonists whose ancestors fought in the American Revolution, made his money through railroads and built his estate on Lake Waban. He named his home "Wellesley" in honor of his wife's family, the Welleses. As an amateur horticulturist, he developed the first-known Italianate gardens in the United States at his home and also funded the Arnold Arboretum in Boston.[4] To create the classic Italianate gardens Hunnewell arranged to bring Italian immigrant gardeners to Wellesley. Henry Durant, a close friend of Hunnewell's, provided the initial land for Wellesley College and named the school after his friend's estate. The town also took the name.

By the late nineteenth century, the town had multiple train stations, including ones designed by the renowned landscape architect Frederick Law Olmsted, as well as trolley service, but the town remained largely rural.[5] It would take decades longer for Wellesley to become a full-blown Boston suburb. Henry, one of the oldest participants in the study, recalls the history of Wellesley both before and after his birth.

> When I was a child, there was still a cattle drive through Wellesley, on Route 16, from Medfield to an abattoir in Brighton. The animals were driven on foot that distance. And they were accompanied by drivers, drivers who guided the animals so they wouldn't get onto people's lawns. And so it had quite a rural character. It was at about the turn of the century [that Wellesley was] known as the carnation capital of the world. There were 450 greenhouses in the town and 12 tracks on Linden Street to load freight cars with carnations daily for shipment all over the Northeast.

With these types of industries and a lack of easy transportation, largely unskilled laborers made up much of the Wellesley population in the late nineteenth and early twentieth centuries. These workers were concentrated in the area of Lower Falls, on the Charles River and near the mills and factories. The town grew in size over the summer, when wealthy Boston families would retreat to their summer homes in Wellesley and the "breadwinning" father would come on weekends.

The Growth of the Suburbs

Formal efforts to maintain Wellesley according to the wishes of elite residents began in 1914, when it was the first town in the country to establish zoning laws.[6] The current town website states, "Through the foresight of town fathers who in 1914 made Wellesley the first town in America to adopt zoning laws, Wellesley grew into a beautiful town. By the 1920s it was recognized as one of the leading suburbs of Boston."[7] Such zoning laws included minimum lot sizes, which had obvious implications for those of lower socioeconomic status. Zoning has been used in both the Boston suburbs and other wealthy communities throughout the country to ensure that towns remain off-limits to the majority of buyers.[8]

Additional forms of restrictive housing ensued. A real estate ad from February 1927 assured potential buyers that the featured house was in "the kind of community where you KNOW you will have good neighbors" (capitalization in the original).[9] The housing growth of the 1930s—across both the United States and Wellesley—was largely fueled by the New Deal programs enacted under President Franklin Roosevelt, including the development of the Homeowners' Loan Corporation (HOLC) and the Federal Housing Administration (FHA). These agencies enacted policies that were both implicitly and explicitly racist through the development and implementation of "redlining"—the refusal to authorize loans to finance properties in areas considered racially undesirable and economically risky.[10] Following World War II, the Servicemen's Readjustment Act, aka the GI Bill, only reinforced these trends. This federal law made it virtually impossible for Black GIs who had fought fascism in Europe to access home loans once they returned, and those who did often struggled to find a suburban home that they were able to purchase.

Wellesley participated in these types of racially restrictive housing practices, and as parts of the town began to transition from farmland to suburban neighborhoods, restrictive covenants began to appear. Approximately one hundred homes developed in the Boulder Brook neighborhood in the early 1940s had written into their deeds that no "non-white" person could live in or own these homes until 1970, with the exception of "domestic labor."[11] It is unclear who would be considered "non-white" during this period. Wellesley also engaged in less explicit forms of discriminatory housing in the form of unofficial "gentleman's agreements," as reported by both Lily Geismer and one elderly participant in this study.[12] In keeping with this practice, realtors steered potential Jewish buyers to one of the only neighborhoods where a builder would sell to them. Even with the passage of the 1968 Fair Housing Act, which prohibited housing discrimination along racial, ethnic, or religious lines, participants with whom I spoke, both on and off the record, felt that this form of steering continued through the late 1980s. There is little evidence of such housing discrimination today, and one of the rabbis in town said that when they first began working at the local synagogue in the late 1990s, they would often get calls about whether Wellesley was "friendly to Jews." They rarely got such calls today.

Unsurprisingly, given that the Black-White color line has remained fairly rigid in American society, racial discrimination in the housing sector has been far more intractable. Although Massachusetts had one of the most extensive and earliest sets of policies to guard against housing discrimination, such discrimination simply took other forms. As in many wealthy suburbs today, Wellesley's ongoing residential segregation and racial homogeneity is the result of a range of factors, including historical discriminatory practices, "snob zoning," and potential Black renters and buyers simply being priced out.[13] Until very recently, affordable housing in Wellesley has been primarily found on Barton Road, a former development for returning GIs that is now owned by the Wellesley Housing Authority. The ninety-unit development sits on the edge of the community, down a winding road that makes the development feel separate from the town. These two- and three-bedroom attached apartments are deemed family units, as opposed to the twelve low-income one-bedroom units owned by the town in the center of the commercial district and the approximately 125 one-bedroom units scattered throughout the town for the elderly and those with disabilities. Residents of Barton Road are disproportionately Black and Latino compared to the rest of Wellesley.

Massachusetts, in an effort to increase affordable housing across the state, passed 40B legislation in 1969. Known as "anti-snob" zoning, the legislation requires towns to strive to make at least 10 percent of their housing stock "affordable," but until recently, many towns have ignored the law or litigated attempts at development. Today towns that do not meet the requirement take the risk that developers will appeal directly to the state and thus avoid the town's zoning restrictions.

Wellesley has been cognizant of its legal obligations, and a portion of the town has also recognized its moral duties, but the town has been slow to meet both. In 2004, Wellesley passed inclusionary zoning bylaws, but affordable housing remained scant. It stood at just 6 percent as recently as 2018.[14] Public conversations are often framed around congestion, the impact on the schools, and, in some cases, the preservation of open spaces. For example, through debt exclusions placed on the ballot, the town has voted to purchase large swaths of undeveloped land that could have been developed. These purchases have included Centennial Park in 1982 and the North 40, forty-six acres of open land sold by Wellesley College in 2015.

Wellesley has recently met the requirement to make 10 percent of its housing stock affordable, reaching approximately 11 percent as of 2024. It has met its legal responsibilities largely through one large-scale rental property that was completed by developers through 40R, which has been described as a "kinder cousin" of 40B. Keeping towns partially involved in the process, 40R still requires 20 percent affordable housing. The large apartment complex was built by John Hancock, the insurance company, which owned the land and had underutilized office space sitting on it. With nearly three hundred rental units, the apartment complex includes studios as well as one-, two-, and three-bedroom apartments suitable for families. Approximately fifty children live in this new development and attend Wellesley Public Schools, according to a member of the Wellesley Zoning Board in 2024. Concomitantly to the complex's development, the governor's office enacted legislation known as the MBTA Communities Law to push for the construction of multifamily housing within half a mile of T stops. Serendipitously, this development meets the requirement.

Housing, Race, and Education

Their zip code plays an enormous role in other parts of people's lives, including their access to quality public education, as local real estate taxes are the main source of revenue for public schools in the United States. Schools in wealthy White communities tend to reflect those demographics. This has historically been the case for Wellesley: a town that reported being 99 percent White in the 1970 census had schools that were also 99 percent White.

In 1966, in response to the almost complete segregation of neighborhoods and schools in Boston, the Metropolitan Council for Educational Opportunity (METCO) was formed with the stated purpose of giving Black children living in Boston (and later Springfield) access to better-funded and higher-quality education in the suburbs and giving both Black and White children greater exposure to each other.[15] Geismer argues that the founding of METCO by educated White liberals in the Boston suburbs was really an effort to stave off more significant structural changes and maintain their own secure positions in their curated towns.[16] Wellesley was one of the seven towns that founded this voluntary desegregation program. In addition, the town started in 1970 a branch of A Better Chance (ABC), a national voluntary desegregation program that enabled high-performing young women of color to move to Wellesley, attend Wellesley High School, and live in a home run by the program.

The backdrop for both of these initiatives was rising racial tension amid ongoing housing and school segregation in the city of Boston. In 1974, the city of Boston was mandated by Federal Judge Arthur Garrity, ironically a resident of Wellesley, to enforce school busing to desegregate Boston's public schools.[17] Lucas, a man in his fifties, recalled that FBI agents were posted outside of Judge Garrity's home, owing to death threats. Clare, a woman a bit older, also discussed threats against Garrity and remembered people moving to Wellesley explicitly in response to the judge's ruling—a clear case of White flight. A slightly younger interviewee explained that the judicial ruling was *precisely* why her family moved to Wellesley from Boston. Her remarks about her parents' liberal Democratic politics and her father's concern that they had moved to a stronghold of Republicanism only underline Geismer's argument around the development and growth of liberal bastions in the suburbs of Boston.[18]

Wellesley's decision to participate in these voluntary desegregation programs might seem ironic, given its own hostile housing practices. It could also be read as a sign of the political and social divides in the town on issues of race and integration. Or in a more cynical vein, it could be understood as one way in which "good liberals" deal with historic racism in the United States, from the founding of these desegregation programs through to today.[19] Voluntary desegregation programs provide slow and controlled integration, without demanding real structural change. In a less cynical vein, it is one way in which individuals genuinely committed to greater racial equity can make a difference, at least in some small way, given the glacial and momentous nature of larger structural change. Prior research shows that students participating in such programs have a range of social and academic experiences, from very positive to very negative.[20]

From the very first discussions, the idea of participating in METCO was met with mixed responses from residents. An announcement in the "Church Services" section of the *Wellesley Townsman* urged readers to attend an upcoming panel with David Sargent, chair of the school committee, who was a champion of Wellesley signing onto METCO as a founding town.[21] The panel would also include a Mr. Wasserman of Sharon, Massachusetts, who had brought students from Boston to his town for additional educational programming. A letter to the editor from the same issue took a very different position:

> There is no law which says we must bus children in to our town for an education. This issue concerns neither private parochial schools nor Boston Latin. The issue concerns Wellesley PUBLIC SCHOOLS and TAXPAYERS pocketbooks. We are discussing Wellesley Public Schools, the property of every Wellesley TAXPAYER. . . . We are defending the right of men and women who work five, and perhaps more, days per week.[22] (capitalization in the original)

On the same page was another letter to the editor, signed by twelve clergymen in the community—including the sole rabbi, Jacob Lantz—saying that their primary concern was making sure the young people from Boston were welcomed in Wellesley. They stated, aware of their varied religious affiliations, that "if there is one deep element of faith common to all of us, it is that we are children of one and the same G-d. To us it follows directly that all men deserve our love and concern and that none are strangers."[23] These conflicting views speak to the various responses of established individuals and groups to new groups—either inclusion or racialization. They also illustrate how new groups quite quickly impact an established community, with a rabbi weighing in on the issue.

Nearly sixty years later, at the time of the interviews, the topic of METCO continued to be raised, and sharply different views were expressed. Abby, a middle-aged White Jewish woman, viewed the program as one of her few opportunities to meet people who were different from her.[24] She said, "The METCO program was in place when I was a kid. It's still in place, and that is really where the bulk of the diversity in Wellesley comes from, in my opinion. We participated as a family in the METCO program."

Gianni, a man of similar age and of Italian background, also cited METCO as the primary means by which there was racial diversity in the community: "As I went through school, you could see the town was becoming more diverse, and the METCO program helped a lot with that. I have three older brothers, they went through the tougher part of METCO, when there were some disputes about it, but I think we benefited from that." Gianni also told me about his relationships with the students who accessed the high school through METCO: "They used to sleep over. They would stay in town with the families, and they would be at our parties, and we would hang around them. There was zero racism when I was in Wellesley High School. I just didn't see it. We never thought that way. We had sports teams together." Students who lived in Boston may have had a different recollection, but sports have been identified in prior research as one of the main positive ways in which young White men come into contact with young Black men.[25] Decades later, Gianni remains friends with some of those men he met through METCO.

Clare, a slightly older woman who was in one of the first cohorts to go to school with METCO students, had the following to say: "We had a lot of racial tension. We had a lot of anger in the schools. METCO was very difficult. And as a student in the schools, it was scary." She remembered physical altercations.

The Black and Latino students who live in Boston and attend Wellesley Public Schools continue to be a significant percentage of all Black and Latino children in the system. As of the 2022–2023 school year, slightly more than 4,000 students were enrolled in the system. Of these students, 3.8 percent identified as Black or African American and 5.8 percent as Hispanic or Latino, for a total of just under 10 percent, or approximately 400 students.[26] The approximately 150 K-12 students in METCO annually and six young women at the high school through the ABC program account for nearly 40 percent of Black and Latino students in the district. The remaining Black and Latino students live disproportionately in Wellesley Housing Authority apartments.

Demographic Shifts

Although, based on this history, it would appear that Wellesley has changed little, in reality the town has indeed changed. These changes have been little noticed, however, because of both the groups now representing the town's diversity—its Italian, Jewish, and Chinese residents—and the time periods when they arrived in Wellesley. World wars, near-zero immigration, economic expansion, and civil rights legislation framed much of the Italian and Jewish experiences, allowing for the lowering of boundaries and the entry of ethnic groups into the mainstream during the 1950s and 1960s. This combination of factors allowed new groups to make economic and social progress, without established groups feeling threatened, resulting in what Richard Alba calls "non-zero-sum assimilation."[27] Late twentieth- and early twenty-first-century Chinese migration was shaped by post-1965 immigration policies, an expanding knowledge-based economy, and the growth of multiculturalism, while also taking place in a climate marked by rising political polarization and income inequality. What I refer to as "weather" events—passing but influential local, national, and international occurrences, such as the COVID-19 pandemic—further influence group relations. It is only within this glocal framework that the experiences of new groups can be fully understood.

The Need for Gardeners and Masons

When looking through the archives of the *Wellesley Townsman*, the town's love affair with Italian high culture is evident from the first decade of the twentieth century. The newspaper announced lectures on Italianate gardens and frequent exhibitions of Italian Renaissance art. The paper's "Neighborhood News" section regularly reported on couples taking an Italian liner to spend weeks and even months in Italy, and wedding announcements often noted that the young Protestant bride spent time at a finishing school in Rome or Florence.[28] This was all taking place long before international travel was commonplace. A street in town was named after Italian composer Gaetano Donizetti in 1853, shortly after he died but long before an Italian immigrant community had settled in Wellesley.

This attraction to Italian culture explains, in part, the presence of Italian gardeners and stone masons in Wellesley as early as the turn of the twentieth century, when immigration from Europe was still open. Somewhat surprisingly, Wellesley became a place of first settlement for Italian immigrants, single men at first, but later also wives and children. They came to design and cultivate Italian gardens on Wellesley estates owned by the most prominent families (figure 2.1). They also worked as stonemasons, in other aspects of the building trades, and for the town as manual laborers. Italian migration to Wellesley increased after a fire at Wellesley College in 1914, when significant labor to rebuild the structure was required. Many came to town through connections to Diehl's Hardware, a local company. Social networks are a common and dominant means by which migration self-perpetuates, as evidenced in both sociological and economic research.[29] The story of Italian migration to Wellesley is no exception.

While the WASP class was attracted to the highest levels of Italian culture, those who immigrated to Wellesley were pulled from lower tiers of Italian society and had come to the United States to earn a living. These early Italian immigrants who came at the turn of the twentieth century generally spoke regional versions of Italian or in dialect rather than the formal or classical Italian that emanated from Florence. That these versions of Italian were considered vulgar factored into how Italian immigrants felt about passing their language down to their children in Wellesley—they largely didn't. In contemporary interviews, residents of Italian descent discussed this early decision by the immigrant generation.

Figure 2.1 The Hunnewell Topiary on Lake Waban, Wellesley, Massachusetts, c. 1902

Source: Library of Congress.

For example, Christopher, a proud Italian American in his seventies, when asked whether he spoke any Italian in his home as a child, said:[30]

> My dad spoke Italian, but also spoke a regional dialect, which we refer to as "Bolognese." In our home, my mother spoke the dialect because her mother actually came for work. . . . She had to work all the time. And she [my grandmother] really wasn't as fluent in proper Italian, but both knew it in the dialect. The working class, they have their regional dialects. And they probably haven't had the opportunity for that formal education to speak the Florentine language, the proper Italian that you would communicate in correspondence. So she spoke in dialect. . . . My dad really, because he wanted to speak fluent in English and conduct his work in English, he didn't speak that much in Italian.

Similarly, Frank, a man in his eighties, explained, "So my dad, he could speak Italian, but it wasn't spoken at home because he spoke a dialect, and they didn't want us to learn not the real Italian." A much younger resident,

Anthony, who came from a "mixed" family of an Italian American father and a mother of western European descent, told the story of his mother taking him and his siblings into Boston to the Dante Alighieri Society and his Italian grandfather's reaction.

> My grandfather was not interested in talking about [Italy]. He just didn't see any value in discussing what it was like there. The place was a mess. I mean, there was no food. To him, it was all negative, right? And then my mother used to take us to the Dante Alighieri Society, and my mother's not Italian at all. Her parents both were born here. I think she had grandparents or great-grandparents who came here from more western Europe countries. But my mother was interested in having us learn about that history, and we used to go to the Dante Alighieri Society in Boston, and I remember when my grandfather found out, he was pissed, he just was pissed at my mother, who was trying to, I think, help us understand her father-in-law and trying to do a good thing, but he just, I think he was angry.... Again, to him, Italy was backwards and bad. And why would you want to engage with backwards and bad when the good future was here?

The historical record also reflects a split between, on the one hand, how Italian language and culture were viewed and experienced by the established class in Wellesley and, on the other hand, how the country of Italy was experienced by the Italian immigrants who needed to leave their homes in order to survive. Theirs was not the Italy of the Italian Renaissance, but an Italy of civil war, nation-building, and extreme poverty. Articles and obituaries occasionally discussed the premature deaths of some Italian immigrants (for instance, from heat stroke, a factory accident, or drowning),[31] alongside the many more pieces on wealthy Wellesley residents spending time in Italy.[32]

The majority of Italian immigrants and American-born residents of Italian descent were concentrated both geographically and economically in Wellesley. They clustered in two areas close to the business districts, near Isaac Sprague Elementary School and Wellesley High School, and began to build social, civic, and political institutions in and around those neighborhoods. The older Italian interviewees spoke of these neighborhoods as their community and of areas beyond them as "Wellesley," as if they were not part of the formal town. A classified ad listed by a Mr. George E. Saunders in November 1935 reads: "For the Italian Family we have an unusual rental value."[33]

The second- and third-generation Italian residents with whom I spoke were all college-educated and had a range of occupations; only one of them worked in the trades. Still, Wellesley residents of Italian ethnicity still have a strong presence in landscaping, masonry, hair salons, and other small businesses. The names of their businesses harken back three and even four generations to the grandfathers and great-grandfathers who originally settled in Wellesley and started them. Even as Italian Americans in Wellesley have been active in community affairs, serving as members of town meeting, the advisory committee, and other civic, political, and social service organizations, their Italian ethnic identity is not dead. The formal removal of Columbus Day in recent years led to a reigniting of interest among some members of the Italian American community, and the month of October has been dubbed "Italian Heritage Month" by the select board.

The Growth of the Jewish Community

Just as the established residents of early twentieth-century Wellesley had a perception of Italian life that may not have corresponded with the lived experiences of Italian residents in the community, so too did they appear to have preconceived—and less flattering—notions of Jews. Much of their contact with Jews in the earliest decades of the twentieth century came about through Americanization programs run by the major Congregational Church in Wellesley, which brought Jewish, Italian, and Syrian immigrant children and children of immigrants out from Boston for summer excursions.[34] Contemporary newspaper articles discussed the little "Rebekahs" and "Rachels" and "Hebrew maidens" who brought kosher food with them.[35] Such commentary reflected early forms of anti-Semitic views of Jews as a monolithic and distinct racial group. Besides the children visiting the town in the summer, Wellesley residents had regular contact with a man by the name of Henry Gideon from Temple Israel, who played the organ at the Wellesley Unitarian Church, and Rabbi Levi, also of Temple Israel, who came out to Wellesley throughout the 1920s to give talks to various groups and serve as a cultural liaison.

There was in fact a small Jewish presence in Wellesley, dating back to the early 1900s. Unlike the Italian immigrant community, Jews living in Wellesley were generally second-generation and had moved into town as families to run small businesses, such as markets and tailoring shops. Also distinct from the Italian community was their geographic spread throughout the town. In the early decades of the twentieth century, the fewer than one hundred Jewish residents lived in various neighborhoods, in contrast to the early segregation of Italian immigrants. This residential freedom would change as their numbers grew and Jewish residents came to be perceived as a threat.

Jews were distinct from Italian residents in other ways as well. Although the Jewish residents, unlike some members of the Italian community, were largely American-born and English-speaking, Judaism was clearly viewed as foreign. News articles in the *Wellesley Townsman* from the early decades of the twentieth century reported (sometimes incorrectly) on the annual High Holidays of Rosh Hashanah and Yom Kippur.

The newspaper seems to have kept almost a running tally, reporting, for instance, on the number of Jews celebrating the holidays and estimating the number of Jewish residents in the community. A September 1926 article entitled "Our Jewish Neighbors" discussed the approximately fifteen Jewish families "who shared their holiday celebration at Town Hall."[36] On September 30, 1927, an article began, "Our many residents of Jewish faith, among whom are some of our leading businessmen, celebrated their new year . . . ," again noting the celebrants' use of the town hall.[37] The article goes on to say that "Rosch Hoshana is observed in the United States on two days while in the Jews' native Palestine it is observed for only one day." It is unlikely that a single resident of Wellesley had ever stepped foot in Palestine, but the reference speaks to the view of Jewish residents as foreign, as not really American. By the 1928 Jewish High Holidays, the count was "in the neighborhood of fifty persons of the Jewish faith in Wellesley."[38]

That newspaper articles in Wellesley covered the High Holidays, or that the town allowed Jewish residents to use the town hall, should not be read as acceptance. Henry, an elderly man of WASP descent, recalled an experience from his childhood during the 1930s:

> I still own the house that I lived in. My parents gave me their house as a wedding present. So I've always lived in the same house in the same town. . . . And I would say that most adults would have preferred if there had been all Protestants living in the neighborhood. We had one Jewish family move into the neighborhood, and the house was pelted with eggs until the family left. So there was real unadorned anti-Semitism.

The Jewish community in Wellesley began to grow after World War II, and as a result, so did Jewish organizations. The approximately fifteen Jewish families in 1926 grew to seventy-two founding families of Temple Beth Elohim in 1960. Historian Gerald Gamm argues that Jews were more likely to leave Boston than their Catholic counterparts because the latter were tied to their parishes.[39] Others argue that out-migration resulted from housing policies that quickly transitioned the Jewish neighborhoods of Boston to overwhelmingly Black neighborhoods, stoking racial, religious, and ethnic tensions.[40] Regardless of what the primary driver was, Jewish Americans, like their fellow ethnic brethren who had also been able to cross the color line, benefited from the GI Bill, which enabled them to get a college education and buy a home in suburbia. Access to these benefits, combined with a growing economy created opportunities for White ethnics to fold into the mainstream.[41]

Jewish residents experienced surface-level inclusion throughout the 1950s and 1960s. The first rabbi of Temple Beth Elohim, Jacob Lantz, was an active member of the Rotary Club and even became its president, as well as giving the invocation at the Wellesley Club dinner and attending events at the Wellesley Country Club, an organization known to be restricted until late in the twentieth century. Unsurprisingly, however, the increasing number of Jews in the community was accompanied by increasing housing discrimination. The Jewish community was largely limited to the area on the edge of town where the synagogue opened its doors in 1960, next to the Schofield Elementary School. A 1960 letter to the editor from Jewish residents who had lived in Wellesley since 1951 wrote of their inability to buy a new home in a new neighborhood, owing to discrimination.[42] They left the town.

The theme of segregation was consistently raised by interviewees who were Jewish lifelong residents, as well as by some Christian interviewees. Virtually all of the former discussed either living in the Jewish neighborhood or not living in the Jewish neighborhood and how unusual that was. Anna, a Jewish woman in her late forties, talked about her parents attempt to move from the Jewish section to the estate area in the late 1970s:

> So my parents, you know, as they were able to, they were like, "Well, we should move, and we should find a more spacious home and a home that, you know, we could entertain in or whatnot." And my parents started looking in other neighborhoods in Wellesley. And they went to place an offer on a house. This is in the seventies, this is, like, late in the seventies. They went to place an offer on a house, and the realtor said, "Oh, I will put this bid in tomorrow." And they were like, "Well, we wanna put it in now. Like, we wanna be able to buy this house." And the realtor then, the next day said, "Someone's already bought the house, but I just wanna let you know that you don't want to live on that street. You don't wanna be in this part of Wellesley. They don't really like having Jewish families here, and I don't think you'd be comfortable."

Despite the discrimination, the Jewish community grew, the temple expanded, and in the last decade of the twentieth century the High Holidays—often inaccurately described in the *Wellesley Townsman* throughout the first decades of the twentieth century—became officially incorporated into the school calendar. The national increase in anti-Semitic acts, as well as a few local incidents, led the town government to issue a statement condemning anti-Semitism in November 2022. Nevertheless, the issue of taking the High Holidays off the school calendar continues to arise when discussions are underway around the inclusion of new holidays or the length of the academic year.

From Madame Chiang Kai-shek to the Growth of Biotech

The earliest mentions of Chinese people in the *Wellesley Townsman* alludes to them as a distant "other." The country and people of China were most often discussed by Christian missionaries returning home to their local

26   Beyond White Picket Fences

Congregational and Unitarian churches in Wellesley; they discussed the Chinese as a place and a people in need of aid owing to famine, floods, and, later, the civil war between the Communists and the Nationalist Party. These portrayals were almost exclusively from the vantage point of established residents.

Many of the earliest Chinese residents in Wellesley came for education and were generally Christian. Chinese women in particular arrived via a formal relationship that began in 1906 between Wellesley College and the Chinese High Commissioners of Education. Just one year later, in September 1907, as the new academic year began, the newspaper reported the arrival of three young Chinese women who would be attending Wellesley College, noting that two of them were royalty.[43] After China's Yenching University was founded in 1908, a merger of multiple Christian colleges, Yenching and Wellesley College formalized their relationship as sister institutions in 1919 and would exchange both faculty and students until 1949.

Even with high levels of education and wealth, Chinese people in town were consistently seen as distinct and racialized as exotic and foreign. A 1924 *Wellesley Townsman* article described an "unusual party when about 30 Chinese were the guests."[44] Otto, the pen name of the editor of the *Wellesley Townsman* from the 1920s through the 1950s, periodically discussed Chinese residents using racial tropes.

The Chinese students and longer-term residents living in and around Wellesley were overwhelmingly wealthy, well-educated, and Christian and were strongly on the side of the anti-Communist Nationalist Party as Chinese society moved toward civil war. Among these individuals was Mayling Soong, who would graduate from Wellesley College in 1917 and later become Madame Chiang Kai-shek (figure 2.2). The relationship she maintained with the town and the college throughout the years should not be underestimated, as it would influence local politics, fashion, and education.[45]

Dr. Tehyi Hsieh, a Cambridge University–educated economist, lawyer, author, diplomat, and representative of the Chinese Service Bureau, came to be a frequent speaker in town from the 1920s through the 1960s, serving as an important cultural liaison between the Chinese community in and around Boston and the town of Wellesley. His lectures covered by the *Wellesley Townsman* included, but were not limited to, the topics of religion in China, boycotting Japanese goods, Formosa (Taiwan), the overturning of the 1882 Chinese Exclusion Act, and memorials to various local and national figures. He spoke at the Congregational Club, the Kiwanis, the AARP, Babson College, the Wellesley Club, and various churches. His name appeared sixty times in the *Wellesley Townsman* from 1923 through 1972, often with commentary complimenting his English language skills, demonstrating that the racialization of Chinese residents as foreigners,

Figure 2.2   Madame Chiang Kai-shek Tours the Wellesley College Campus, 1943

Source: International News Photos. Photograph held by Wellesley College Archives, Library and Technology Services, Wellesley College.

even those who had been in the United States for decades and had earned advanced degrees from English-speaking institutions, was ongoing.

A handful of small Chinese-owned businesses in the community, including Mr. Wong's hand laundry, which opened in Wellesley in 1912, offered the few additional points of contact between established and Chinese residents. Chinese laundries were a common business venture for Chinese immigrants, who were largely excluded from the mainstream economy, and such businesses required little financial capital or English-speaking ability.[46] A Chinese hand laundry opened later in Wellesley and operated until it burned down in 1973. Chinese restaurants also began to advertise in the *Townsman* in 1928 and would grow in number throughout the 1930s and 1940s.

The absence of both Chinese voices in the newspaper and Chinese residents in the community was largely the result of the Chinese Exclusion Act, passed at the federal level in 1882 and not overturned until 1943.

Even at that point, however, the government distributed little more than one hundred visas annually to China. It was only after enactment of the Immigration and Nationality Act of 1965 (also known as the Hart-Celler Act) that country of origin was removed as a visa criterion and larger numbers of immigrants from Asia could gain access.

Public policies often experience a delay between implementation and real-world influence, particularly in the process of immigration. Accessing a work visa, completing the paperwork and screening process, and gaining approval can take months, if not years. Thus, even after the 1965 immigration act officially went into effect in 1967, the number of Chinese immigrants to the United States did not begin to increase significantly until the 1980s, only after immigration reform had passed in the United States and exit policies had loosened in China.

It was not until the 2000s that Wellesley began to experience any real Chinese presence. Highly educated Chinese immigrants began moving to the town, drawn by its close proximity to both Cambridge and Boston and the public school system's strong reputation. The Chinese immigrants in Wellesley today have various places of origin, with some migrating from mainland China, others from Hong Kong, and still others from Taiwan. There is also variation in their religious identities, largely based on area of origin. Those from Hong Kong and Taiwan often identity as Protestant, while those from the mainland most often identify as atheists. For some, Wellesley was the initial place of settlement, while for others Wellesley represented a secondary move.

Today approximately 13 percent of the town identifies as Asian, as does nearly 20 percent of the student body in the school district. The majority of Asian adults migrated from China, and many children are US-born. As a result of either family reunification policies or longer-term visitor visas, multigenerational Chinese families are common, with grandparents helping to raise the American-born children—a necessity particularly when both parents are in the workforce. There are also growing Indian and Sri Lankan communities in town.

Although Chinese residents do not face the residential barriers that Italian and Jewish residents before them experienced, they are disproportionately clustered in one section of town in the John D. Hardy School District. Lily, a lifelong resident in her late forties, said of her neighborhood, "You can walk down the street and hear Mandarin being spoken.... The whole street isn't Mandarin speakers, but there are enough that neighbors are having conversations in Mandarin." This clustering may have come about as neighborhood elementary schools offered certain programs to the entire community. For example, Chinese immigrant children and the American-born children of Chinese immigrants were placed disproportionately in neighborhood schools that offered English as a second language.

These neighborhoods were also more affordable, with smaller houses on smaller plots of land. Chinese residents of Wellesley have very high levels of education, and they pursue careers concentrated in biotech and academia. These are prestigious, knowledge-based careers, but they do not pay as much as private equity or "big" law, and often both parents in Chinese households must be in the workforce. There is also, of course, the role of networks in the distribution of Wellesley's Chinese residents. As more Chinese immigrants settle in the town, even more Chinese immigrants will be prompted to settle there too, and especially in neighborhoods where Chinese residents are concentrated.

Just as earlier Italian and Jewish residents began to build formal organizations, so too have Chinese residents, albeit much more recently. These groups serve as important bridges and ladders to established individuals and institutions. The town government issued a "Tolerance Pledge" in December 2016, in part a response to the election of Donald Trump. With the rise of Asian hate crimes across the United States during the COVID pandemic, and after a number of incidents in Wellesley, a rally was held at town hall in 2021 and the local government issued a statement on antiracism and anti-bias in February of that year. That statement is on the town government website, with links to two different Mandarin translations. The school district's launch of a committee to formulate a five-year strategic plan led to discussions about including holidays such as Chinese New Year and Diwali on the school calendar, and at a December 2023 meeting the five-member school committee voted to do so for the 2024–2025 academic year. The decision was met with significant pushback from some town residents.

Theories of Immigrant Assimilation

The seemingly subtle, but persistent changes that have taken place in the community over the past one hundred years have played out in various ways depending on the distinct demographics of each immigrant group, the timing of their entry, and the national and even international climates. The one constant with this variation, however, has been the impact on all sides.

From Straight-Line Assimilation to Segmented Assimilation

As individuals and groups brush up against each other, they invariably leave marks. As immigrants acquire the language, dress, culinary habits, and other patterns of the native-born, it becomes hard to distinguish those whose families have been here for hundreds of years from those descended from immigrants of just a few generations earlier.

The seven-stage straight-line theory of assimilation, developed by Milton Gordon, saw the process as beginning with cultural assimilation and ending with civic assimilation.[47] His theory of unidirectional and irreversible assimilation grew out of his observations of second- and third-generation White ethnics in Chicago—the children and grandchildren of those who had entered the country prior to the Immigration Act of 1924, which all but ended immigration to the United States for over forty years. Gordon's theory was based largely on the trajectories of "new" immigration flows from eastern Europe, Italy, and Poland, in contrast to the earlier waves from Ireland and Germany.

More significant demographic shifts, however, were on the horizon. The passage of the 1965 Immigration and Nationality Act removed country-of-origin criteria, resulting in large-scale migration flows of people of different skin tones and physiognomics from all around the world. If the Jewish and Italian immigrants of the late nineteenth century had seemed foreign owing to their religions, languages, and dress, the late twentieth-century migration flows brought people with new forms of difference into the country. These differences raised questions, both theoretically and practically, around the ability of these latest immigrants to assimilate.

Alejandro Portes and Min Zhou, in observing the outcomes of Asian, Latino, African, and West Indian immigrants and their children, developed a theory of segmented assimilation.[48] They posited three possible outcomes for the newest arrivals: (1) an upward trajectory toward White, middle-class America; (2) a downward trajectory toward lower-income Black America; or (3) a "middle-of-the-road" trajectory whereby they retain some aspects of their immigrant and ethnic heritage while becoming incorporated economically. The path taken would be influenced by racialization, coethnic resources, and federal settlement policies.

Theories of Neo-Assimilation

Although Portes and Zhou worked to correct the limitation of Gordon's theory from the perspective of race and skin tone, both models maintain a focus on immigrants and how they change. But established Americans (those born in the United States to US-born parents) are also altered in the process of immigrant assimilation. They are often thought of as a static marker by which to measure the assimilation and "success" of new groups, but many traditions and institutions that appear to have been part of American society for as long as people can remember came from immigrant and ethnic groups and were slowly woven into what has come to be viewed as the American fabric. This concept, developed by Richard Alba and Victor Nee and known as neo-assimilation, suggests a multi-directional process of change.[49] Our institutions are constantly in flux, being remade all the time bit by bit, but some changes take place so incrementally that we fail to see them.

The multidirectional changes that have been documented are significant. Nancy Foner, in a 2023 article and in her 2022 book *One Quarter of the Nation*, looks at macro-level changes in the course of extensively documenting the many ways in which immigrants and their children have shaped American society over the course of the twentieth century.[50] Foner explores everything from how newcomers have altered the economy to our racial hierarchy. Alba and Nee had earlier pointed out the inclusion of Italians, Irish, and Jews on the White side of the "color line" as evidence of expanded racial boundaries, as well as the acceptance of Jews and Catholics as part of the religious mainstream.[51] Racial changes continue today in response to immigration, reshaping ideas about not only who is considered White but also about what it means to be Black.[52] The academic success of Asian first- and second-generation Americans has also translated into a reconfiguring of the racial hierarchy, such that whiteness is now equated with mediocrity.[53]

There is also evidence of widespread cultural change, be it related to art and music, holidays, sports, or food. Historical work has tracked the impact of immigrants specifically in Brooklyn, including the removal of blue laws and the playing of baseball on Sundays.[54] Other work identifies the addition of Cinco de Mayo, Lunar New Year, and other holidays into the mainstream.[55] Foodways have also changed as Latino and Asian foods have been incorporated into American cuisine.[56]

Other research has also examined how immigrants have changed the face of communities, with studies of the East Asian enclave of Fort Lee, New Jersey, and the Korean enclave of Palisades Park, New Jersey.[57] The latter study identified a process of "immigrantification" to describe the growth of the Korean enclave and the increase in housing prices, with impacts on not only established residents but also other lower-income immigrant communities in the town.

Theories of Racialization

Another line of research has made sense of immigrant-established interactions through the lens of racialization as an organizing principle at all levels of modern society.[58] Racialization is the means by which racial categories are created, filled, and constantly reformulated and refilled over time; the concept speaks to the malleability of race and its status as a social construct.[59] As part of this process, society engages in "racial projects" that reflect and reinforce racial categorizations during a particular period of time, utilizing media, business, education, and other institutions to frame groups in relation to White America.[60] Values and norms are conceived as intrinsic to particular racial groups.[61]

Racialization takes different forms for different groups. For example, Latino immigrants disproportionately experience police stops and detentions because undocumented migration is viewed as a "Latino" issue, even though there are millions of undocumented immigrants in the United States from Europe and Asia.[62] Research explores the racialization of both documented and undocumented Latino immigrants and Black Americans in the United States, including how each group recognizes the other's racial situation vis-à-vis White Americans and law enforcement.[63] Undocumented Latino immigrants, for example, recognize that the particular form of racialization of Black Americans provides them with a form of protection: When police are in the neighborhood, their focus will be on Black residents rather than Latino residents. The racialization of Latino immigrants and Black Americans can also be seen in other institutions, such as the educational system.[64]

Asian immigrants and Asian Americans also experience racialization, but in a way that is distinct from the racialization of Black and Latino Americans.[65] Although this group is racialized as a "model minority" rather than as an undeserving burden on the system, consequences for individuals and groups can still be negative, such as elevated levels of depression and anxiety.[66]

Further, behaviors that challenge White, middle-class norms and White status are particularly likely to be racialized. Research has focused on the impact of immigrants on schools, identifying trends toward super-charged achievement and heightened competition.[67] In these studies, White respondents described Asian students and their parents as overly competitive and responsible for damage to the mental health of all students. Asian educational and parenting practices are viewed as racially inherent, rather than as the rational choice of a new group that lacks the social networks and dominant cultural capital of their White peers.

Complementary, Not Contradictory: Toward a Theory of Variegated Assimilation

Prior theories are often viewed as stepping stones, one building on another, or even pitted against each other as competing frameworks, as is often the case with neo-assimilation and racialization, but they need not be. Varied theories may all find support, even within the same setting. Individuals and groups, for example, may demonstrate patterns of acculturation, such as taking on the language and dress of the dominant group, Gordon's first step in his "straight-line" assimilation theory, but modify the way the dominant language is spoken, adding new words or phrases derived from their group's culture.[68] Behaviors can be racialized; for example, not only can the focus on academics be seen as an "Asian trait," but the established may change their behavior patterns and enroll their children in enrichment programs to keep up.[69] Latino neighbors may be racialized as "illegal" even as the established significantly alter their foodways to include tacos and burritos.[70] It can all be true.

While Alba and Nee and other proponents of neo-assimilation focus on lowering racial boundaries and expanding "whiteness," racialization scholars identify the ways in which new groups continue to be placed in inferior racial categories and to have their behavior patterns racialized.[71] Jennifer Lee and Dian Sheng argue that while statistical measures of assimilation—namely education, income, and residential integration—suggest that Asian Americans have assimilated, their individual and group experiences of racism tell another story.[72]

As with any sociological study, the data collected stem from the instrument used. Asking participants if particular traits are more common among particular groups of students may encourage racialized answers, just as asking participants if they engage in any "new" cultural practices may glean answers that lead to conclusions about neo-assimilation.[73] If a full range of questions were asked across such studies, the overall conclusions might be a bit different.

Some scholars have begun to push for incorporating multiple frameworks, both those anchored in race and racialization theories and those that utilize an assimilationist paradigm.[74] Even the strongest proponents of assimilation theory recognize the role of race and historic racial categories in the incorporation of groups into mainstream American society.[75] As Philip Kasinitz and Mary Waters point out, institutional barriers can be lowered and individual discrimination can still take place.[76] In fact, the lowering of boundaries and the entrance into previously restricted arenas may explain the "integration paradox": members of new groups becoming more exposed to discrimination while they are also becoming more integrated.[77] Concomitant inclusion and marginalization may highlight and reify ethnic differences and have the unintended consequence of reshaping the established population.[78] For example, Priya, an Indian resident of Wellesley for over thirty years, sums it up when discussing her sense of belonging in the workplace, a mainstream financial institution: "I think at first I was unaware of the fact that I'm not quite accepted the way I am, so I felt comfortable. The more I understood small comments, the less comfortable I felt."

Racialization, be it at the institutional level or the micro level, should not be read as individuals and groups passively accepting the status being given them or the conditions surrounding them. People can respond with agency, recognizing how they are viewed, pushing back against those perceptions, refusing to "relinquish the racial other," and working individually and in groups to alter the mainstream.[79] Priya, for example, volunteered in the schools to teach students about Diwali and other aspects of Indian culture.

Similarly, assimilation or acculturation, and cultural retention need not be at odds. Individuals and groups often engage in both, certainly in the second generation and possibly beyond.[80] For example, the president of a local ethnic organization that is charged with preserving the group's cultural heritage or even simply promoting an ongoing sense of identity may need to engage with mainstream structures.[81]

I put forth a new model, which I call "variegated assimilation," that recognizes the multiple ways in which new groups may respond to the established environment and alter it, consciously or unconsciously. For example, individuals may settle in a new area, taking on aspects of the established community, but work to retain their own culture and traditions; this is the "middle-of-the-road" path identified by Portes and Zhou in their theory of segmented assimilation.[82] Ironically, efforts to retain one's cultural heritage, especially those made beyond the private realm, require brushing up against the mainstream. For example, individuals may request that grocery stores carry certain items so that they can cook food from their place of origin, or they may coalesce into ethnic groups and rent space to teach language and culture classes for their children. Such acts to retain an ethnic heritage have impacts on the established community, be it the grocery store owner, the church congregation from whom the group rents space, or the neighbors who are exposed to new foods at the summer block party.

The process of assimilation, whereby individuals and groups come to look more and more like the mainstream, also alters the mainstream. New residents and groups may take on the habits and patterns of the established community, but by not leaving their own cultures at the door, they subtly alter not only the habits they acquire but the institutions they enter. For instance, as new groups begin to celebrate Thanksgiving or Christmas—a clear illustration of identificational assimilation—they may do so in distinct ways, such as having all-vegetarian meals. As parents volunteer with their local parent-teacher organization—a sign of structural assimilation—they bring their own backgrounds and experiences to the task, such as volunteering to help students make paper lanterns.

Some new individuals and groups are racialized by the dominant population, but even racialization can have a boomerang effect, influencing the established community. The behaviors of newcomers may threaten the position of the dominant, but in racializing those behaviors they may also emulate the newcomers. Another path to neo-assimilation is through reaction to racialization, such as when newcomers do not simply accept their racialized position but react to it and push back through individual action or by forming organizations. Housing segregation, for example, may be met with a push for desegregation.

Limitations

Contemporary analyses provide us with important insights into the ways in which individuals are influenced in real time—new neighbors appear, social networks diversify, grocery store shelves hold new international items, schools become more competitive. Both ethnographic studies and extensive in-depth interviews give insight into what is taking place in micro-level interactions in the moment. The limitation of this approach is that none of us can see beyond our own lives. With our human limitations, we often perceive changes as sudden, not recognizing the longer process leading up to them. Individuals remember when Chinese food "suddenly" appeared on a menu, or the first time a menorah appeared on the town green, without seeing each variegated stitch that went into creating a new pattern in the quilt.

An alternative and counter challenge is the seemingly glacial nature of these historic shifts and the absence of explicit connections mediating processes over time. As Julian Go argues, we often make assumptions about the role the past has played in shaping the present without interrogating the nature of the relationship or the processes involved.[83] For example, we assume that Wellesley's historically WASP past continues to influence the present without really examining where or how. Compared to surrounding towns, Wellesley does have stricter laws around alcohol, which are often explained away as a remnant of its "Puritan" past, but without real interrogation. Some aspects of a local community or larger society may appear to have been there "all along" but actually resulted from the long and sustained rubbing up of groups against each other. What has been retained from the past? Where and how do changes come about?

The extensive work documenting the many ways in which first- and second-generation Americans have shaped society is critically important, but much of it has taken a bird's-eye view.[84] Even while recent research recognizes that changes to established structures neither "have always been that way" nor "just suddenly happened," prior work in the field has done little to interrogate the processes by which those changes take place. The identification of these macro-level trends is critical, but incomplete.

Comparing and Contrasting Italian, Jewish, and Chinese Residents

Each of the immigrant and ethnic groups outlined in this book has its own unique story. The early Italian community, originally viewed as non-White, comprised unskilled male immigrant laborers who spoke little English and later brought their wives and children over from Italy over time. The Jewish community that settled in Wellesley was overwhelmingly second- and third-generation; they moved in as family units, and as their numbers grew over the course of the twentieth century they became increasingly well educated and wealthy. They too had slowly moved across the color line to land on the desirable side. Both Italians and Jews "came of age" in the post–World War II era of an expanding economy, advantageous governmental policies, increasing enforcement of civil rights, and declining religious discrimination.[85]

The much more recently arrived Chinese community is largely first-generation and highly educated; these immigrants either moved in with or quickly developed multigenerational households. Asian immigrants and Asian Americans today find themselves in the midst of the constantly churning process of racialization: amid questions around where to place them in the American racial hierarchy, the color line seems to keep moving.[86] What is the meaning of these expansions of whiteness, or "non-blackness," for groups within Wellesley?

In each case, some of their characteristics have benefited these groups, allowing them to more smoothly slot into the dominant culture, while other of their characteristics appear more challenging to the established community. Similarly, some changes take place almost passively in the form of cultural diffusion, regardless of the group from which the change emanates. These are modest cultural changes that have little structural impact; other changes appear more tectonic and cause ruptures.

For the Italian community, the established residents' fascination with Italian culture served as a small means of entry and could be used to their advantage by newcomers. For example, they were able to get Italian classes taught in town and included in the high school curriculum, in part, by playing up high Italian culture. Many of them were also Catholic, and while being Catholic in the early twentieth century in a Protestant community such as Wellesley brought its own challenges and discrimination, there was already a large Catholic community ready to incorporate coreligionists and make assimilation more of a possibility. Additionally, the Wellesley Village Church took under its wing a community in town of Waldensian Italians, a pre-Reformation version of Protestantism. Many Italian immigrants, however, had little formal education, worked in menial jobs, were relegated to a particular neighborhood, and had a lower status in the community. They did not embody the Italian culture so prized by the established residents of Wellesley, and they clearly experienced a form of racialization specific to Italian immigrants of that time.

The religion of Jews marked them as foreign from the beginning. The historical record suggests that Jews were viewed as racially and culturally distinct in the first decades of the twentieth century, both within Wellesley and beyond. However, those who moved into Wellesley spoke the fluent English of the American-born, had relatively high levels of education, and brought with them a history of institution building. They also benefited from the expansion of racial and religious boundaries and the implementation of civil rights laws.

Similarly, Chinese immigrants, the newest members of the community, arrived with a range of characteristics and tools that shaped their interactions with the established community—an established community that today is quite different from the community encountered by the Italian immigrants of the early twentieth century and by the Jewish American residents of the mid-twentieth century when they first arrived. Today's mainstream is neither exclusively White nor exclusively Christian, and "mainstream" is not a term that can be used synonymously with either demographic.[87] While Jews were marked as an "other" owing to their religion, Chinese immigrants and native-born Chinese were racialized and marked as "foreign" by the US system of racial classification—racialization that continues to this day. The Chinese generally entered Wellesley as speakers of English as a second language, but they also were very highly educated, and many worked in highly skilled professions.

Chinese migration has occurred at a time when the topic of race and ethnicity is increasingly fraught, but also at a time when racial diversity is increasingly welcomed in some arenas. For example, the rate at which respondents identified as multiracial in the 2020 census increased by nearly 300 percent from 2010. Although this increase in the rate was at least partly a result of how racial data were collected in 2020, both increased multiracial identification and the *possibility* of it through changes in data collection speak to changing views around race and ethnicity in American society.

A "Glocal" Approach

Lea Klarenbeek argues for a multilevel framework of relational integration, an approach that sees interactions as dynamic exchanges that take place between and among individuals, groups and organizations, and institutions.[88] Surprisingly little research on immigrant-established relations incorporates this multilevel approach. Micro-level interactions are critical to understanding the day-to-day experiences of both established and new residents, but they occur within a larger framework. Local organizations act as intermediary bodies between the individual and the larger community. Further, these intermediary bodies, depending on their presence and strength in the community, can respond to local manifestations of national and even international issues in ways beneficial to the groups they represent. If situated properly, intermediary bodies may be able to build ladders up to decision-making bodies and alter the community more broadly.

Research on issues of race, ethnicity, nationality, and even religion must be situated within a global context, given that the acceptance or exclusion of certain groups is influenced by larger-scale national politics and even international events. The formation of group identities may in fact be transnational in nature.[89] In short, understanding immigrant-established interactions must be examined within the larger glocal framework I lay out here.

I borrow the term "glocal" to name the multilevel influences that appear to be at play in the process of community change. The term "glocalization" first appeared in the 1980s in the business world to describe the ways in which international businesses modified their products to suit local markets (think rice being served at a McDonald's in Hawaii).[90] "Glocal" has also been used by geographer Erik Swyngedouw to describe the process by which national processes and policies shift up to supranational and global scales, as well as downward to the individual level.[91] Within this project, I am applying the term to describe the ways in which events at the local, national, and international levels may influence and animate individuals and groups within Wellesley, with these individual and group exchanges at times cycling back up to exert local influence and community change.

We now turn to the stages on which these exchanges occur—the neighborhood as housing barriers come down; the classrooms and school committee meetings as students and parents intermingle across ethnic, racial, and religious boundaries; and the local civic and social organizations and institutions, ranging from the Kiwanis to town government.

Chapter 3

Neighborhoods, Schools, and Places of Worship: Setting the Stage for Contact

For much of the twentieth century, contact between established residents and Chinese, Italian, and Jewish residents was limited in Wellesley. The dearth of contact between the dominant group and Chinese residents during virtually the entire twentieth century was due to the small numbers of Chinese immigrants and Chinese Americans living in town as a result of racially discriminatory federal immigration policies, as discussed earlier. This clear case of the macro influencing the micro highlights the glocal nature of both racialization and neo-assimilation. The limited contact that Italian and Jewish residents had with the established community was the result, however, of more local processes, including active and subtle discrimination and self-segregation.

Eleanor was a member of the oldest generation of Wellesley residents, a practicing Catholic, and a graduate of Radcliffe. Of Irish and German descent, she talked about her high school experience: "When I was in high school, the Catholic kids were the Italian kids who lived back in the town. They took Home Economics and Industrial Arts." The Italian residents were clearly viewed as lower-class and less academically capable when Eleanor was in school in the 1940s, but as can be seen from interviews with younger Italian American residents, these later generations continued to experience racialized othering throughout much of the twentieth century. Even though Eleanor shared a town, a high school, and a religion with these fellow students, she rarely found herself on the same stage.

Over the past several decades, as Jews and Italians have been folded into the Wellesley mainstream and Chinese and other Asian immigrants have grown in number, opportunities for individuals and groups of varied backgrounds to encounter one another across a variety of settings, from the neighborhood to the local elementary school to the ball field to the office, have increased. Gordon Allport's famous "contact" theory posits that one-on-one connections can reduce prejudice and improve group relations, in particular when four conditions are met: equal status between the groups in the setting, shared goals, intergroup cooperation, and the support of both informal norms and formal laws.[1] More recent psychological research on intergroup relations finds extensive empirical support for the theory.[2] Beyond simply altering relationships between individuals, such contact may also have primary transfer effects that alter attitudes toward all members of that group and secondary transfer effects that influence beliefs about other out-groups.[3] In short, social contacts, which may lead to the development of footpaths and close relationships, have been critical historically in the assimilation of groups.[4] The impact of such interactions partly derives from perceived similarity between both individuals and groups ("He's a doctor, and I'm a doctor," "That group values education, and my group values education"). But just as positive interactions between members of distinct groups can have positive effects, negative interactions can do the opposite.

Individual personality characteristics also appear to influence one-on-one exchanges. Research from the world of cultural psychology finds that those who value tradition and hierarchy benefit most from intergroup interactions.[5] Other research finds that native-born individuals with high scores on openness, sociability, and inquisitiveness are more likely to adopt the patterns and practices of new groups.[6] Research has also sought to understand how established residents alter their behaviors in response to increasingly diverse settings, their intrapersonal reactions to such changes, and the settings within which these changes occur.[7]

Sociologists tend to examine intergroup relations at a higher level than do cultural psychologists. Within the immigrant assimilation literature, Gordon identified seven steps on the road to complete assimilation.[8] The second step, which is structural, is inclusion in mainstream neighborhoods, workplaces, and organizations. Although Gordon focuses on the movement of the first and second generations into these settings, the groups already present there are also impacted. These are the physical spaces where footpaths may be built between individuals and where people's interactions with members of different groups may affect everyone.[9] Friendship circles may diversify and intermarriages may occur, but only *after* the sharing of spaces.

Not all settings are created equal in regard to intergroup contact and impact. Settings vary in the likelihood of intergroup interaction, the groups likely to appear, and the points of connection. Thus, relational inequality in a setting may have implications for the type or degree of multidirectional influence or assimilation that takes place there.[10]

Perceptions of who is "on the stage," based on the ethnicity and generation of the individual, also come into play. Older residents may see diversity more broadly, whereas younger residents seem to accept as the norm those members of groups who were deemed diverse by an earlier generation. Residents' own ethnic or religious background may also influence their perception of who is different from them and who is similar. White Americans may view Asian Americans as "just like us," as "honorary Whites," or as White-adjacent, but the lowest rates of feelings of belonging nationally are found among Asian Americans.[11] Similarly, Jewish Americans are thought to be fully included in the mainstream, but many continue to feel like outsiders. Racial appearance and socioeconomic status also factor into how difference is constructed in communities such as Wellesley and whether individuals and groups are viewed as contributing to the community's diversity.

Neighborhoods

As one of the primary settings that allow individuals and groups to come into contact with each other, neighborhoods play an important role in connecting individuals to each other and to resources.[12] Although zoning has often been the "polite" or legal way of keeping people out, housing discrimination in Wellesley was overt throughout much of the twentieth century.[13] Housing segregation affects not only the excluded group but also other groups with whom contact is limited.

Wellesley is a "town of neighborhoods," said Eleanor, the Radcliffe graduate, octogenarian, and grandmother. Each neighborhood—"The Generals," "The Estates," and "Poets' Corner," to name just a few—has a distinct feel. Eleanor, as a retired realtor, explained the "feels" of the different neighborhoods and how houses were historically marketed: "Real estate ads always listed 'such-and-such a district.' We sold houses by elementary school district. . . . It was telling people where and who they'd be living with." One neighborhood might be considered more serious and academic because it held a concentration of professors; another neighborhood might be more social and well known for its block parties.

Most of these neighborhoods, with their stately colonials and smaller Cape-style homes, were off-limits to various groups throughout the twentieth century. As such, certain neighborhoods—and thus schools—also became proxies for particular ethnic groups. For example, Sprague was the school serving the neighborhood where the Italian families historically lived (figure 3.1). Although hard to believe in the twenty-first century, Eleanor recalled being the only Irish Catholic family in her neighborhood of large homes and expansive lawns when they moved there in the 1940s. They were not particularly welcome. Henry, a man of similar vintage but of WASP extraction, mentioned his mother's complaints about their Irish Catholic neighbors; they had not moved to Wellesley, she asserted, to live next to Irish Catholics.

42 Beyond White Picket Fences

Figure 3.1 Map of Neighborhood School Districts, Wellesley, Massachusetts, 2024

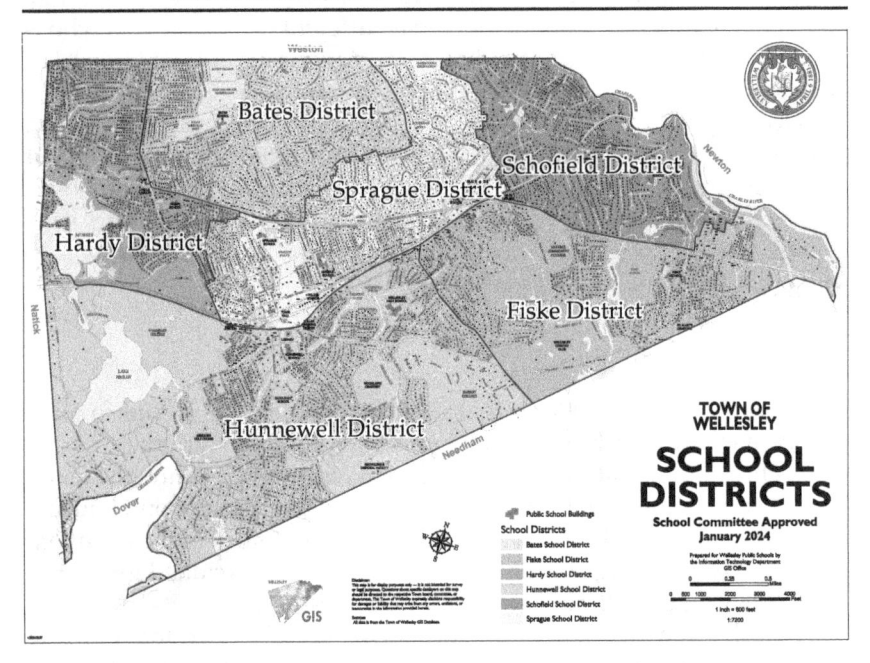

Source: Town of Wellesley 2024.

Small numbers of Jews lived in Wellesley from the early twentieth century, without obvious residential restrictions. As the number of Jewish residents grew in the post–World War II era, their access to Wellesley was limited to the neighborhood known as the "Bird Streets." This area, where the synagogue would eventually be located, was also in the Schofield school district. Alice, one of the oldest residents interviewed, discussed the "handshake" agreement with realtors to keep Jews in that one neighborhood. An initial forum discussed the "housing patterns of minority groups and the gradual integration of the suburbs" in 1958.[14] The Wellesley Fair Housing Committee was created during the same period, explicitly in response to anti-Semitism experienced by Jewish residents.

Anna, a woman in her late forties who grew up in that area, reminisced about the neighborhood: "And there was a little neighborhood group and we would walk to the temple together. And that's almost of a bygone era." Her memories of this tight-knit community were fond, but as discussed in the prior chapter, her parents experienced discrimination when they tried to move out of that neighborhood in the late 1970s and into another where, the realtor told them, they would not be welcome.

Noah, a slightly older Jewish man, recalled a similar experience in his childhood:

> They [my parents] moved to Wellesley in, like, '56. And you know, it's funny, I'll never forget my parents saying that when they looked at homes in Wellesley, the realtors would only show them one area, because that's where the Jewish families lived. So it's sort of wild to me to think that, you know. But it was a great neighborhood. You know, a lot of kids, we were all from the same sort of background. We all went to the temple and hung out down there.

Both Anna and Noah lived in other parts of town that would have been off-limits to their parents; now, they said, their neighbors were of varied racial, religious, and ethnic backgrounds.

The Italian community lived in two separate neighborhoods, both of which were near business districts; Italian social clubs also developed in each neighborhood. These neighborhoods were mentioned multiple times in interviews by both members of the community of Italian descent and those who came from other backgrounds. Christopher, a man in his seventies who still lived near where he had grown up, described his early life:

> We would have these great games of basketball, baseball, football, that we would all organize ourselves in the neighborhood with kids who probably wouldn't be on the honor roll, but they had street smarts and they had common sense, and we all became successful. The only common denominator is that we all came from families where if we weren't on the line, they would find out about it. We would make our own games, and then we'd play hard and try to beat the other guys. And then afterwards we'd walk down the street to—there used to be a little variety store on First Street. The owner of that store was best friends with my grandmother from their days in Italy.

Christopher talked about increasing diversity in his neighborhood, including his Chinese and Indian neighbors. This growing diversity speaks to both the changed migration flows in the post-1965 era and the enforcement of the civil rights legislation passed in the same era. He said, "I have a wonderful neighborhood," but noted the limited English of the elderly Chinese residents. Christopher felt that this language gap made it difficult to build relationships, although, he reported, they resorted to other means of communication—smiles, thumbs-ups, and the like. The lack of a common language is where the stage is not level for some residents.[15] Limited ability speaking the dominant language appears to have a particularly isolating effect on elderly immigrants, and even more so for those racialized as non-White.[16]

Even while the majority of the established residents interviewed described Wellesley as "White," "homogenous," "WASP-y," or lacking diversity, when they were asked specific questions about what their lives looked like and who their neighbors were, a more nuanced picture emerged. Gianni discussed his neighborhood:

> So, for example, I'm really good friends with Yen. He lives in my neighborhood. I have this retired doctor named Yoshi. [He] is a chronic walker. And so he walks by, I invite him in, you know, he brings bones for the dogs and stuff like that. He's a super-interesting guy. And, you know, there's an Asian couple that just moved in right across the street.... This is the big difference of when I grew up. There's just more opportunity to be neighbors with people of different backgrounds.

Clare, a married woman in her sixties who worked in management consulting, talked about her street. She described her neighborhood as being in transition, having gone from "very old and very White to very young and very Asian," mirroring changes in the larger community. She discussed the diversity in more detail:

> When we moved in, we had Indian neighbors on either side. One was a British Indian and the other was [from] India. The India Indian, they had parents living there and their little boy, and then the other side were older, like seventy-ish. Maybe they were younger when we moved in, but they traveled all the time to England, and they [the two Indian households] didn't know each other. Somehow the family in the middle had not connected the two Indian [households]. And so, I did my thing.

Clare "did her thing" by connecting the two Indian neighbors, who went on to develop friendships both with Clare and with each other. She was a highly engaged volunteer involved in various community groups, and her Chinese neighbors, she said, came to see her as their personal connection to learn about what was going on in town. Demonstrating the critical role of building footpaths between individuals and groups for the sake of resource distribution, she provided them with information on town affairs and local government. Such footpaths are also important for allowing multidirectional exchanges between individuals—as Clare's neighbors assimilated socially and civically, she was exposed to greater diversity—but they also have wider downstream effects (discussed in upcoming chapters). All such exchanges are made much more possible by first having a shared stage.

Kathy was of Irish descent and around Clare's age, but she lived in a different part of town and always had. She "grew up with a huge number of Italian families," she said. Although "you didn't have a huge variety" when she was growing up in the 1960s and 1970s, "at the time there were some Asian, probably a good number of Jewish families here. That was normal to me." Kathy also pointed out that what to her seemed like "some" or a "good number" was likely a very small percentage of her neighbors; her estimates, she clarified, were based on who she "hung out with." She told me that a number of these neighbors were connected to Harvard, MIT, Babson, or Wellesley College.

Upon further reflection or in passing, even many of those who did not initially describe their neighborhood as diverse mentioned Jewish, Chinese, Indian, Pakistani, and Black households in their proximate area. Eleanor, who had lived in the same neighborhood for sixty years, described what it used to look like: "My children, really, first of all, never saw a Black person, never saw an Italian person, and very few Catholics, which was really weird." She recalled that Jewish families slowly moved in. When asked if there was any diversity in her neighborhood today, her immediate response was "no," but she then talked about a Black family around the corner from her house and two Asian families living immediately behind her. There were also a number of Jewish families on her street. A trend emerged throughout the interviews that reflected established residents' construction of difference: Their limited recognition of neighborhood diversity was followed by examples of racially, ethnically, and religiously diverse households.

It is important to note, however, that the diversity recognized by interviewees tended to be forms that are White-adjacent (Chinese, Jewish) and generally non-Black, in keeping with the theory of a new twenty-first-century racial hierarchy in which a Black/non-Black color line has replaced the historic White/Black color line.[17] Black Americans continue to have a very small presence in Wellesley, most likely the result of a number of factors. Some Black families may be "priced out," but those with the financial wherewithal may choose other towns perceived as more open. Still other Black families may have moved out after hostile experiences in the town. Multiple Black residents with whom I spoke told me of their experiences of being misplaced, even in the twenty-first century; for example, some of their children were assumed to be part of the METCO program, or they themselves were assumed to be household "help." Their skin tone marked them as not belonging in Wellesley and they were racialized as outsiders, visitors, and employees rather than as homeowners, residents, and professionals. The concept of the racialization of spaces is nothing new, particularly in regard to neighborhoods.[18] In the long history of residential segregation, wealthy neighborhoods have been viewed as "White spaces"—a perception evident in Wellesley.

The topic of skin tone, beyond race, also arises in conversations with residents of color. Research finds that darker skin tones, regardless of racial classification, are associated with more negative outcomes.[19] Anjali, an immigrant from Sri Lanka, was married to an immigrant who was racialized as Black. Early on in the interview, she told me that their only child was dark-skinned, and she even sent me a picture. As discussed in upcoming chapters, her family's complexion raised questions about their belonging on various stages in the town.

At the same time, the Black and Asian residents interviewed discussed the significant changes they had seen in town. Adele, a Black woman in her seventies who had lived in Wellesley for nearly four decades and raised her children there, told me that her neighborhood had become much more diverse: "It feels like Cambridge." Sherry, a woman in her fifties who had lived in Wellesley for about two decades, described her neighborhood as having Indian, Chinese, and White families and two Black families within a few blocks. "That's very diverse," she said, "considering it's Wellesley." Priya, an Indian immigrant in her seventies, also discussed the variety in her neighborhood, ticking off the neighbors of many ethnic and racial backgrounds with whom she and her husband would have dinner. Newer residents, who identified as Black, Indian, and Chinese, were more likely to describe Wellesley as an increasingly diverse community, suggesting that while they were in the numerical minority, they were seeing change. Anh, a Chinese resident of fourteen years, described the town as "mostly White, but there are more Asians. Now I see a lot more."

Schools

As Eleanor told us, Wellesley houses for sale are listed with their school district. "When you said a school in the ad, it had a picture of what you're going to get." In a town organized around neighborhood elementary schools as Wellesley is, more diverse neighborhoods create more diverse schools and students experience diversity at earlier ages. For example, Kathy, the medical professional who grew up in a neighborhood with Italian, Jewish, and Asian neighbors in the 1960s and 1970s, would have had an elementary school experience distinctly different from that of Clare, the executive of a similar age and ethnic background. As with recollections of neighborhood diversity, difference within the school setting was subjective and filtered through interviewees' own demographics, including ethnicity, religion, and age. These factors, as well as others, influence residents' acceptance of some groups as normative but not others.

Although these data do not allow for a thorough analysis of the role of age in residents' personal experiences related to diversity, some initial trends emerge, particularly in regard to the school setting. Grace was in her late 30s, had three young children, and was the only lifelong resident who did not identify as White. Two of her three children were in the public school system. Grace made the connection between neighborhood and school diversity when she said, "I think Wellesley has become more diverse in some ways. I think that the diversity is maybe a little bit uneven across the different elementary schools in Wellesley.... I think that there are pockets of diversity in Wellesley and at the schools." She referenced one elementary school whose student body was heavily East Asian.

Courtney, who was about Grace's age and had children in a different elementary school, compared her experiences to those of her children: "It's definitely more diverse now. In my daughter's kindergarten ... I would say half non-White or a little bit more than half non-White, which was very different. There were a lot of kids of Chinese immigrants, American-born Chinese kids, or kids with one Asian parent." Kate, a professional woman in her fifties, similarly compared her experience to that of her children, concluding that they had known much greater diversity in the classroom setting. "I think Wellesley was much more homogenous when I was growing up. You know, 'ethnic' counted as Irish and Italian." Today, she explained, "I don't think my kids had a lot of Black students in their classes, but they did have a lot of Chinese and Indian families." The focus of diversity for Grace, Courtney, and Kate, women who attended Wellesley public schools in the 1980s and 1990s, was the presence of Asian children.

Emma, who attended Wellesley public schools in the 1960s, came into contact with diverse classmates in her public elementary school, but her marker of diversity was different:

> In elementary school, I remember kids being different because they went to temple. That's how I knew. They went to the temple, and we went to Sunday school. So, on Wednesdays, we had a half-day, and we all had to go do CCD [Catholic religious education]. And my friends who weren't Catholic went to temple, I think it was on the weekend. But to me that was the difference.

Mike, an architect who attended the Wellesley public schools in the 1960s, recalled not knowing anyone who was Jewish until he reached the one middle school everyone in town attended: "And it wasn't until junior high school that I think that I—that's kind of the first time I recall friends who were Jewish." Clare, only slightly younger than Mike, similarly explained that her son's friendship circles diversified once he entered the local middle school and discussed his new Jewish friends.

The recollections of those who attended the schools in the 1960s and 1970s, in contrast to what those who were in the schools in the 1980s, 1990s, and 2000s remembered, result from a variety of factors, including variation by elementary schools and how difference was recognized by individuals and over time. Emma, Mike, and Clare all attended elementary school in the 1960s and early 1970s, when Wellesley was just beginning to see larger numbers of Jewish residents. Housing discrimination was still present, the town maintained only a creche on the town green for the Christmas season, and the Jewish High Holidays were still more than twenty years away from being recognized formally by the school district. The American establishment was only beginning to see itself as a Judeo-Christian society.[20] Further, these interviewees did not live in the area with Jewish residents, and thus there would not have been Jewish students in their elementary schools.

In contrast, Grace was Asian American, Courtney was the product of a Jewish-Christian "mixed" marriage, and both were approximately twenty years younger than Emma, Mike, and Clare. Their idea of diversity was very different from how those who came of age twenty years earlier looked at it. Grace and Courtney were born and grew up in a post–1965 era America, after immigration laws had changed and migration flows had come to be dominated by Latino and Asian immigrants. Jewish Americans, who were now largely third- and fourth-generation, had taken on more public roles in American society and had pushed at the national level for greater equality and inclusion. Obvious demographic changes were well underway by the 1980s. These differing perceptions of race, ethnicity, and diversity speak to the critical role of timing in both racialization and neo-assimilation.[21]

The importance of timing becomes increasingly apparent in interviews with the youngest residents who attended the Wellesley public schools in the twenty-first century. I had the following exchange with twenty-year-old Josie, who identified as just "American" and had no religious affiliation (her parents were both Irish Catholic), when I asked about the backgrounds of her childhood school friends:

Josie: I would say many have, like, a similar background.

Author: So, Irish Catholic?

Josie: Um, no, I would say not. No, not really anyone's Irish. You know, I don't think religion is much of a factor, mostly Christian or Jewish. And yeah, that might be all the religions represented among friends.

For some residents, the presence of Jewish students in the elementary school classroom represented diversity; for others it went unrecognized because it was thought so commonplace. Further, this younger generation saw issues of race and ethnicity (as well as gender) as far more malleable. Individuals today exist much more as "free agents" in regard to their identity than had been the case with previous generations, for whom categorizations were external and legally binding.[22] As seen among these interviewees, larger national conversations taking place during critical junctures in the life course also shape their views around race, diversity, and immigration.[23]

Skin tone, however, and specifically darker skin tones associated with blackness, stands firm as a "bright" and "sticky" boundary, one not easily altered.[24] In a theme identified here, both racial classification and skin color have significant implications in the school setting.[25] A number of White residents discussed either the almost complete absence of Black students or the METCO and ABC students specifically.

The school as a setting for contact is experienced very differently by the Black residents interviewed, including Adele and Ronnie. They both said that teachers tried to put their children on the METCO bus to send them back to Boston, assuming they were not really Wellesley residents. Such assumptions and practices have been identified in prior research on towns with desegregation programs.[26] Sherry also talked about the low academic expectations for Black children in the schools, and Anjali shared her perception of similarly low expectations of her son during his early years in the Wellesley public schools. He would later go to an elite university.

These mothers of Black-identifying children were all pushing against long-established racial categories and racialized assumptions about intelligence, abilities and geographic belonging.[27] Such assumptions by the established significantly hinder the development of their relationships with newer residents. But as will be discussed in upcoming chapters, being racialized does not stop new members of a community from building footpaths to individuals and ladders up to organizations and decision-making bodies. Although some of these relationships develop spontaneously, others are instrumental reactions that impact individual members of established groups and even bring about structural changes to mainstream institutions.

Interviewees discussed other academic "stages" as well: private, parochial, and postsecondary schools. Some residents attended parochial or private schools growing up, or they opted to send their own children to these schools for a range of reasons, from seeking greater diversity to wanting to pass down their religious beliefs to prioritizing smaller class sizes. Because such schools are not limited to drawing students from a particular geographic region or town, they can cultivate a more diverse student body. Richard, who was in his sixties and a self-described WASP, attended private school and had sent his children to private schools as well. He felt that both he and they had benefited from the greater diversity of private schools than they would have experienced in the Wellesley public school system. Isabella, a surgeon in her forties, also attended independent schools and sent her children to private school as well, in part for the greater diversity. Marie discussed her experiences in both public and private schools:

> I was looking back at my class pictures [from public school] because I still have them. They had busing [METCO], so there were some kids who were coming from the city. But other than that, it was just White kids, there were no Asian kids. And then when I went to the other [private] school,

not specifically in my class, but there were absolutely other Asian families and certainly African American families and more Jewish families actually.

Mary Louise, a woman in her fifties who attended private school but whose children attended Wellesley public schools, felt that she had more contact with diverse groups than her children did, since her independent school had cultivated a more diverse student body. Henry, the oldest person interviewed, mentioned the tremendous variety of people he met as a result of teaching in a private school. The diversity discussed by the interviewees reflects a growing mission among many elite private schools, which view their responsibility as both to educate a more diverse cross-section of society and to teach their students how to operate in an increasingly diverse world.[28]

Connor, who both attended parochial school in Wellesley and sent his children there as well, compared Catholic school then to Catholic school now: "Growing up then, everyone was either a Murphy or an O'Donnell or some other Irish name, or a lot of Italian Americans. Now Saint Vincent's is quite diverse. We have Asian kids there, we have Sudanese families. Every name you could think of, but predominantly they're all practicing Catholics." Marie, whose grown child attended parochial school, said:

> When my daughter was at the parochial school, her specific class, funnily enough for us for a class in Wellesley, Massachusetts, she had two South African kids, a Lithuanian kid, a part-Chinese kid . . . and so I mean that in and of itself for a class of eighteen kids was pretty remarkable. And now where she's at school, she's got two Asian boys and three African American kids. One with a Ukrainian mother for one of the other children.

These micro-level parochial school experiences reflect numerous global processes, from the spread of Catholicism through colonization and missionary work to changing migration streams.

Responses from both established and new residents varied in how extensively and positively they experienced contact among individuals in school settings. Nevertheless, as illustrated in upcoming chapters, school is an important stage in the process of variegated assimilation.

The Most Segregated Hour of the Week

Wellesley has long been a community with high levels of religiosity, and in some ways continues to be today. One resident described the town as feeling a bit like the fictional town in the film *Footloose* when she was growing up, where dancing is prohibited on religious grounds. Numerous residents described the community as "religious" and their own upbringings as shaped by religion. Although, by their very nature, religious institutions attract coreligionists and therefore are largely segregated along religious lines, maintaining distance between groups, they have also provided a stage for "mixing."

The Village Church, long a prominent Wellesley institution, both physically and socially, interacted with the Italian community of the early twentieth century in a variety of ways. The church offered lectures and exhibitions on high Italian culture, in line with the interests of the established community. It also engaged with the Protestant Italian community in Wellesley, for instance by hosting Reverend S. V. Ravi to give sermons in Italian in 1908.[29] An October 1912 article excerpted a talk by Reverend Ravi in which he exhorted the Protestant churches to welcome the waves of new immigrants, who were just as Italian as their countrymen representing the high Italian culture so treasured by Wellesley's established residents. "The English do not speak of the races of Southern Europe as 'inferior.' It is because they are in constant contact with the cultured Italian, while we seldom meet such types. We see the peasant class."[30] Reverend F. T. Valdina, an Italian Protestant pastor from Hyde Park, formalized his relationship with the Village Church in 1926 and delivered weekly sermons in Italian to the Italian Waldensian immigrants of Wellesley.[31] In these varied ways, Italian immigrants had both a path into the established community and characteristics marking them as distinct and "less than."

The Village Church also engaged early on with representatives of the small Chinese community. Dr. T. Z. Koo, the head of the World Student Christian Federation (a Protestant organization), and Dr. Tehyi Hsieh gave talks at the church.[32] The church also held fundraisers throughout the early decades of the twentieth century in response to environmental crises and famines in China, often working with Wellesley College students from China. These interactions originated from the earlier Protestant missionary work to spread the gospel—a "reverberation of the past"—and illustrated the glocal nature of the neo-assimilation process.[33]

Although religious institutions in Wellesley and elsewhere were and continue to be focused primarily on their own members, the growth in ecumenical engagement among clergy has played a role in religious groups' interactions with each other. Throughout the earliest decades of the twentieth century, the interfaith contact reported in the *Wellesley Townsman* feels heavy-handed and unequal in nature. Jewish and Italian children were brought out from the Boston "tenements" for "fresh air excursions" by Reverend W. W. Sleeper of the Village Church, and missionaries returned to their home churches to discuss their work in China. The stage was there for interfaith interactions, but it was most certainly not a level one.

In formal interfaith interactions between representatives of different religious traditions in the early 1900s, individuals from immigrant and ethnic groups acted as cultural liaisons between religious groups.

Rabbi Harry Levi of Temple Israel in Boston was a regular speaker at Wellesley churches, and similarly, Henry Gideon, the organist from the same synagogue, periodically performed in Wellesley. Both served as representatives of Judaism to the then-dominant Protestant structure in the town.[34] Starting in the 1920s, churches and synagogues also engaged in multidirectional "pulpit swaps."[35] There were also instances of junior church and synagogue fellowship groups visiting each other's congregation. In September 1948, the Wellesley Unitarian Church even hung a banner in Hebrew, wishing Jewish residents a happy new year.[36] The Unitarian congregation continued to host Jewish clergy and other representatives of Judaism, and Jewish liturgy and tradition were taught within their own worship services. The Chinese community had their cultural liaisons as well. In October 1932, the Village Church hosted a lecture by Li Kai Ying about Chinese religions.[37] These "representative" interactions between groups of inconsistent and unequal status continued throughout the 1940s and 1950s.

Starting in the 1950s, the *Wellesley Townsman* would publish each September a welcome letter to new college students in the area, reminding them of the "many fine churches" in town where they could worship.[38] A letter to the editor in 1958 written by an established member of the town reminded the editor of the paper that, besides the town's ten churches, Wellesley also now had a Jewish community.[39] This letter foretold the changes to come.

Ecumenical activity changed the most after the founding of Temple Beth Elohim in 1960. It was then that representatives of religious institutions brushed up against each other more regularly, in more formalized ways, and on somewhat more equal footing. The Council of Religious Groups was formed in 1960, and Rabbi Jacob Lantz was elected a member.[40] Several other interfaith groups—including the Interfaith Forum, the Wellesley Interfaith Social Concerns Committee, the Wellesley Interfaith Youth Council, and the Wellesley Clergymen's Association—were formed and grew during the 1960s. Rabbi Lantz was elected president of the Wellesley Clergymen's Association in 1967.[41] A clergy member among the interviewees had the following to say about these historic interactions: Rabbi Lantz, he noted, "was invited by the ministers to play at Wellesley Country Club, where he would go often, and it aroused the jealousy of his congregants that he could play at Wellesley Country Club and they couldn't. And he felt that this was a big part of the job, that interfaith relations with the ministers and the town officials was necessary." This observation speaks to the unequal power relations at the time and the view that it was essential to build footpaths via personal relationships and bridges between the Jewish community and other religious, social, and civic groups in town.

It is important to note that the reach of Wellesley's religious institutions extended beyond Sunday morning and Friday night. Whether it was the sisterhood that developed at Temple Beth Elohim, the women's groups at the Village Congregational Church and St. Andrew's Episcopal, or the couples' dinners and dances put on by each institution, residents' social lives largely revolved around their church or synagogue. This dynamic, which started from a young age, with youth groups and social outings for teens, and continued into adulthood, when friends and romantic partners were largely chosen from religious settings, helped to maintain religious and ethnic homogeneity.

Leah, a lifelong resident in her fifties, confirmed the centrality of religion institutions in residents' lives, saying that she remembered her parents socializing only with other Temple members. The students she knew at school, Clare said, were also people she knew from church. Leah indirectly underlined Clare's point by saying that she often felt left out at school, as it seemed that many of her classmates knew each other through church as well as school. Henry, one of the oldest residents interviewed at age ninety and a lifelong Episcopalian, explained the impact of his religion on him compared to his children: "All of the children were much more willing to meet people of a diverse background than would initially be comfortable to my wife or to me. I mean, we met in our own church. And so, we never contemplated intermarriage and never had an idea of having to mix religions in any sense." Much of Henry's life revolved around his religious identity, from how he spent his Sunday mornings to who he married to the people he socialized with when he was younger. As will be clear in the next chapter, this fairly insular lifestyle changed significantly over time for Henry and his wife as they interacted with increasingly diverse residents on various stages in town.

Religious institutions divided people in other ways as well, even within the same religious tradition. Catholic residents historically attended the church in the parish where they lived. This religious practice based on geography historically played a role in the shaping of both Boston and its suburbs, including the slower movement of Catholic residents compared to Jewish residents, who were not tied through religious laws to particular physical spaces.[42] Eleanor, an active member of the Catholic Church, explained it this way: "We went to St. Paul's. Basically, it was also the Italian church. In those days they divided the parishes up geographically." She referenced Wellesley's Italian section, whose residents all went to St. Paul's. She also noted that this parish church was one of the few places where she interacted with "new" groups, as her neighborhood was almost entirely White Anglo-Saxon Protestant to begin with and, as a result, so was the local elementary school.

The elderly Italian American residents in the sample confirm this ethno-religious clustering. Frank, a man in his eighties, talked about his family's multigenerational involvement with St. Paul's and his grandfather's substantial gift to the rectory: "He came to this country when he was sixteen, and he made a promise and he kept the paperwork that he would give the chalice. It was cast in Italy. My grandmother raised some money, and they put some valuable [jewels] on the chalice." Christopher, an Italian American man in his seventies, was also a member of St. Paul's. Red Sox great and Wellesley resident of Italian descent Dom DiMaggio attended and was buried from St. Paul's, long after the practice of attending one's parish church had ceased.

Anjali's remarks demonstrated that religious settings can both unite and divide, that they can create footpaths as well as barriers. She discussed her connection with a neighbor, a woman who initially racialized Anjali's son as an outsider, as someone not from Wellesley, owing to his dark skin. Anjali, a devout Catholic, developed a very close relationship with this woman over the years; they attended mass together each week and participated in an annual cookie swap. Their shared religion bridged the racial and ethnic differences between them. At the same time, Anjali's grown child refused to attend church when he was home as a result of a number of racist experiences within the church. Sherry and her family, who were longtime Black residents and practicing Baptists, had not found their church in town, even though Wellesley is home to a Baptist church. She attended a Black Baptist church in another town where she felt a much closer connection.

Kate, a lifelong resident, discussed her interfaith interactions on a religious stage. She was of Irish and Italian descent, and her children had attended a mix of public and parochial schools. In discussing her experiences, she referenced the anti-Semitic attack that killed eleven people at the Tree of Life Synagogue in Pittsburgh in October 2018.

> After the shooting at the Tree of Life, my pastor had gotten an outreach from Temple Beth Elohim here in Wellesley, inviting everybody to come to a service. And I went to that. That was really heart-wrenching, but also heartening, because it was overflowing with people. And the rabbi said that night, "Look, we sent out this invitation. And we set up all these chairs, and we took down all these walls and we didn't really know if anybody would come." He was like, "Thank God people came." That was really tremendously moving.

Finally, religious institutions have literally made space for groups that are new to town or have historically been marginalized there. Until 1960, Jewish residents in Wellesley did not have their own space in which to meet and worship. Although the town did allow the Jewish community to hold High Holiday services in the town hall as early as 1926—somewhat surprisingly, given the generally anti-Semitic tenor of the time—they lacked their own space for regular meetings. But religious institutions as stages for interfaith engagement sometimes play a far more important role by stepping back. Starting in 1950, the Fells Community Church (also known as the Universalist Church) began to donate space to the newly formed Wellesley Jewish Community Group for the group's weekly Sunday School classes and other meetings and annually for High Holiday services. A 1955 letter to the editor of the *Wellesley Townsman* from Albert Sagansky of the Jewish Community Group read:

> We wish to acquaint the townspeople of Wellesley, through the good offices of your paper, of the great generosity of the minister and congregation of the Community Universalist Church in extending to the Jewish Community for the use of their church during the Jewish High Holy Days. It is not only an unparalleled act of neighborliness and friendship, but is all the more striking in that the Universalists cancelled their Sunday School sessions for Sunday, September 18th and postponed their regular Sunday services to Sunday evening.[43]

The church was literally and figuratively giving the Jewish Community Group the space to organize into a coherent entity that would eventually develop a physical, social, political, and religious presence in the town.

In the twenty-first century, the Village Church has engaged in these practices anew, this time with the Chinese community. The Wellesley Chinese Language School is housed at the Village Church and has been since its founding in the 2009–2010 school year (figure 3.2). A video with a message of welcome and partnership from an established member of the Village Church, primarily in English but using some Mandarin phrases, is on the home page of the Wellesley Chinese Language School. A banner in both Mandarin and English waves outside of the prominently located church, announcing the school's presence. An American flag and the church's sign are all nearby. The allocation of space to the Chinese community by the Village Church enables this new group to firmly establish its own cultural group, a necessary step to acquiring equal footing in town. Jing, one of the founders of the Chinese Language School, confirmed the openness and sense of welcome she felt from the Village Church. This reception represents a sea change in the interactions between the Village Church and the Chinese community a century ago.

Extracurricular Activities

Residents also commonly described Wellesley as "community-oriented"; this perception of the town as having high levels of civic engagement reflected Tocqueville's observations of nineteenth-century New England.[44] Although participation levels have declined to some extent from prior generations—in keeping with larger national trends identified by Robert Putnam in his now-famous book *Bowling Alone*—Wellesley retains an active citizenry and many formal organizations.[45] Wellesley also retains a town meeting structure, unique to New England. This is relevant as the

Figure 3.2 Banner for the Wellesley Chinese Language School, Wellesley, Massachusetts, 2024

Source: Author's photo.

high levels of broad-based citizen engagement required by this structure present additional stages on which participating individuals and groups interact. As Tocqueville noted in his observations of Massachusetts in the 1830s, administrative power in the town meeting format is "divided among many hands."[46]

A variety of factors enable the town to have and maintain so many volunteer organizations: high income levels, which have historically freed up women from working full-time; high levels of education, which provides a sense of efficacy; and a culture of community involvement that has been passed down through the generations. At the same time, at least some of Wellesley's organizations have historically been closed to "outsiders"—that is, those of distinct ethnic and religious backgrounds. For instance, a lifelong resident referenced one organization in town as one her Irish Catholic mother had been unable to join in the 1970s because she was not Protestant.

At the same time, many of these settings now provide a stage for the *possibility* of contact. The organization that would not accept an Irish Catholic woman in the 1970s has since then greatly diversified by the standards of the town; its membership now includes women of various racial and religious backgrounds, reflecting the expansion of its boundaries.[47] June, an Asian American community leader, decided to take on a leadership position in her organization because she thought it was important to have someone who looked like her at the helm of a group that had historically been viewed as quintessentially Wellesley—White, wealthy, and Christian, if not explicitly Protestant. Her organization was now quite diverse by the standards of Wellesley, with Jewish, Hindu, and Muslim members, some of whom were first-generation Americans. June had tried to encourage other immigrant women in town to participate, but as she told me, "If they're recent immigrants and language is a potential barrier, that would deter them. . . . I have a couple of friends who are recent immigrants from China. Their English is amazing, and I would ask them, 'Hey, do you want to come check it out?' And a lot of them were just too intimidated to come." Limited English ability or lack of confidence reinforces boundaries and uneven power relations.[48]

Multiple women, including residents of color, mentioned the League of Women Voters. Two Black Americans and one Asian immigrant spoke about their experience as members and leaders within the organization. Not only were they participating because of relationships with established residents in other settings, but the League was a setting in which they could build new relationships.

Recognition of what diversity means and who is diverse came into play in discussions around the broadening of these social and civic organizations—or lack thereof—just as it did in school and neighborhood discussions. One community leader contacted me after the initial interview to tell me that she had been thinking about my questions and wanted to amend her responses. She explained that she knew a number of foreign-born women in her organization who, because they were all highly educated, she had not thought of as immigrants or as having added diversity. A leader of another civic organization, when asked whether his organization had changed in regard to ethnicity or race, responded that there was only "one African American" member. It later became obvious that there were immigrants in his organization and that, as will be discussed in chapter 5, their varied backgrounds had significant implications for the organization's agenda. It is clear that at least some members of the Wellesley community defined diversity as the inclusion of people who had darker skin tones or were of lower socioeconomic status.

Ironically, various social justice organizations in town with the stated goal of improving racial equity did not always provide a stage for contact between racially diverse individuals and groups. For example, Kelly, who worked with a program focused on young people of color, said that African American and Latino students participated in the program, as did Muslim students. She also noticed that the majority of the students came from immigrant households. The board did not reflect this diversity. Emily, another leader in the organization, made a similar observation: "As far as the volunteers, I have not noticed a change and that's probably a negative on the board. I don't know how candid you want me to be, but on the board, for a program that is geared towards students of color, we usually have one woman of color, or one or two men." That situation, she said, sometimes felt very uncomfortable. At the same time, the program's outreach to local synagogues and churches for volunteers did bring some level of diversity to the organization.

Bonnie, who was active in the PTO, had noticed greater diversity in the schools in recent years compared to a decade earlier, when her older children were in elementary school. She recognized that elementary school PTOs were more neighborhood-specific, while the middle school and high school PTOs pulled from across the town. She was not sure if the community had become more diverse or if she herself had become more aware of diversity issues from her contact with those outside of her homogenous neighborhood. She also told me that since PTO meetings had started to go online and were held in the evening, she was seeing a much broader range of races and ethnicities among the attendees than she had seen in face-to-face PTO meetings. She further noted that questions, which were submitted in advance, seemed to be asked by a broader range of people, perhaps because non-native English speakers felt more comfortable submitting questions in advance than speaking impromptu. June, who was also involved in PTO, discussed the language barrier:

> I think it also comes back to a lot of the immigrant parents probably don't feel comfortable speaking English in a big group setting. A couple of the moms have told me that. I'm fluent in Mandarin, and so, a couple of the recent immigrant moms, I will speak to them in Mandarin because I feel like that just makes them feel more confident. And they have told me, "I so appreciate you doing that, because sometimes people are talking so fast, I can't actually understand what they're saying," and it does affect their confidence, right?

June was seeking to bridge the gap and bring in the newest parents.

Residents of Chinese background confirmed June's and Bonnie's sense that they were reluctant to speak in meetings. PTO is a stage on which multiple Chinese residents told me they did not feel comfortable. Anh explained that there were no PTOs in China, where schooling is the domain of the teachers and parents are contacted by the school only when a child is about to be expelled. Both Mei and Anh were concerned that Wellesley's established families and educators were unaware of this difference between American and Chinese schools, and so thought that Chinese parents were uninterested in volunteering their time or donating supplies. Mei and Anh also recognized and voiced worry about Asian stereotypes—that Asian children were all enrolled in Russian Math, played instruments from preschool on, and were focused exclusively on academics.

Mei's and Anh's recognition of how Chinese are viewed by American society reflects a version of W. E. B. Du Bois's "double consciousness."[49] At the same time, David Eng and Shinhee Han's argument that fitting the model minority myth is the only way for Asian Americans to gain access to the mainstream is not borne out here.[50] In Wellesley, we can see how Chinese and Indian immigrants have gained access to, and indeed shaped, the mainstream by appearing on school stages as parent volunteers, as will be discussed in upcoming chapters.

Cleo, a longtime Black resident of Wellesley, described how she felt when she first moved to town: "I didn't feel like I belonged because I wasn't married. I didn't feel like I belonged because I was a Black woman and I was usually the only one in the space. So I would attend [PTO] meetings, and I would be mistaken for the nanny." Cleo's response to this racialization was to become as involved in as many settings as possible. She volunteered in her children's school—in part to keep an eye on them—and she became a PTO member, helping to run the annual multicultural festival. Being racialized led Cleo to intentionally show up on these mainstream stages rather than retreat from them.

Children's extracurricular activities may also help to broaden their parents' experiences, though some activities attract more diverse participants than others. Although no longer affiliated with the Catholic Church, the Catholic Youth Basketball League, known as "CYO," is a longtime staple in the community. A 1969 article in the *Wellesley Townsman* advertised the start of the season and stated that "the League is open to boys of all faiths, and St. Paul's responded to the ecumenical spirit last year as they elected Rabbi Jacob Lantz's son Captain."[51] While the religious integration of the CYO was significant in the 1960s, interviewees generally saw little diversity on their children's sports teams today, and most described them as demographically similar to the population as a whole. Siobhan, who had four children, said that her boys were dedicated soccer and hockey players, sports she described as "predominantly White." However, Sarah, whose son played soccer and hockey in high school, recalled being surprised at "how international the sideline was."

Sean, a longtime journalist, when asked how changes in the town's demographics had impacted him, responded:

> So, for example in Wellesley, there's been a huge, well, I don't know if it's huge, but I think pretty big increase in the Asian population. And so that does sort of raise the profile of certain things that the Asian community in particular has gravitated to. Like with the younger people, a lot of them are in music, and I think that sort of raised the bar on how Wellesley does across the state with its music program. So in that respect we would probably cover some of this stuff more often because there are more kids that are getting awards and are getting recognized. So there are things like that.

A music concert program from a December 2022 participant observation suggests that approximately 40 percent of the musicians were Asian or Asian American. The remaining 60 percent had a mix of Italian, Jewish, Nigerian, Middle Eastern, Irish, English, and German last names.

The general observation that certain activities were more popular with first- and second-generation Americans was echoed in conversations with lifelong residents. Kate discussed the diversity of her children's dance teams, citing the presence of numerous Asian participants. Siobhan's two daughters were both heavily involved in dance, which she found to be quite diverse, in contrast to the sports played by her two sons. A number of Indian and Chinese immigrants interviewed discussed the role of dance in their culture, such as in Holi or Lunar New Year celebrations. In their remarks we see that retaining one's ethnic identity and cultural activities may be a form of variegated assimilation

Other extracurriculars also seemed to be more popular with Asian students. Lily said that in the science club at school, "most of the faces are Asian." She discussed the diversity of the students on a STEM team: besides her daughter, there were Chinese, Brazilian, and Indian children on the team. Avi, an Indian resident and father of multiple children, spoke of volunteering with a high school robotics team, and Anh, a Chinese mother, did the same at the elementary level. Similarly, Erin discussed the ethnic diversity of her son's Model UN team. These findings on the selectivity of after-school activities by ethnicity are in keeping with prior research on immigration and education.[52]

Scouting organizations also appear throughout various forms of data as a stage on which diverse groups meet. Articles about and advertisements for the Scouts throughout the twentieth century in the *Wellesley Townsman* cite it as an organization open to children of all faiths.[53] The Boy Scouts, for example, participated in the "Excursions" program as far back as 1912 when thirty-one Jewish boys from the West End of Boston joined the Scouts in Wellesley for the day.[54] A 1920 advertisement encouraging girls to enroll in Girl Scouts cited it as nonsectarian and noted that there were "Protestant, Jewish, Roman Catholic, Chinese, and Negro troops in larger cities."[55] Scout Weeks were celebrated at both churches and synagogues throughout the 1940s and beyond, and there was also interfaith representation at scouting events.[56]

Interviews also revealed scouting as a stage for the mixing of the established and the new that continues today. In noting the significant presence of Chinese American children in her child's scout troop, Kate's discussion of the values shared by Girl Scouts and the immigrant families spoke to the importance of common values to create connections.[57] Bonnie similarly noted that there seemed to be many second-generation scouts in her youngest son's troop—more than she had noticed in her older boys' troops—and that the children's families came originally from China, India, and Korea. Kathy, whose children were all considerably older, remembered diversity within her own scout troop, including a couple of children from Mexico, in the 1970s. Sherry, a Black resident of the town in her fifties, co-led her child's troop with a recent immigrant from Asia, and a number of Asian interviewees similarly discussed their participation in scouting.

Town Government

Town government, in its many forms, also serves as a stage for exchanges between established residents, members of old "new" groups, and the newest residents.

Clare talked about the friendship she developed with a Jewish woman with whom she served and the extension of that relationship outside of committee meetings. She also discussed her interactions with Jewish clergy through her involvement in town affairs:

> I don't remember the temple being a factor in town at all. Oh, now I would say the temple is a cornerstone in terms of driving things. Honestly, I call the temple and get the rabbi when I want help getting the religious group organized. I call either the minister at the church or the rabbi, right? We got to get the movers who are actually going to think through and be willing to engage in a social dialogue.... The rabbis and the ministers are amazing, because they're right out there.

Henry, one of the oldest people interviewed, talked about the historic segregation of the town and the opportunity he gained from his involvement in town government to be in contact with different groups. Decreasing segregation, he said, had been "one of the most notable changes that I think I've seen over a period of time in the town. I mean, I have to run for election continuously. And so I have a chance to say, 'How are you?' So I do meet quite a few people, including people in my own voting area as well as when I do run townwide for election." Courtney, a town meeting member, said, in noting the increasing diversity of her fellow members, "I have been happy that I think every year in town meeting it has seemed more diverse to me."

Elizabeth, a retired professional and a backbone of the community, also recalled the interactions with new groups she had experienced through her engagement in town government. She recalled an earlier era: "It was a very White community while I was growing up, very White, Protestant/Catholic community. When I was growing up, the Jewish population was limited and very, I think, very cautious about their involvement in town." A clergy member similarly discussed the Jewish community's historic desire to maintain a low-key profile and stay out of "the public square." In more recent years, however, Elizabeth had significant contact with Jewish residents as equal representatives on town committees and boards.

Remarks by three Jewish leaders in town affairs about their interactions with the newest members of the community on various public stages revealed something about the incorporation and impact of the next wave of Wellesleyites. In turn, Chinese, Indian, and Black women spoke about their participation in town meeting, their membership on the Wellesley School Committee and the Wellesley Housing Authority, and their experience serving in numerous other elected and appointed positions. The library now had a twice-elected representative who was a Chinese immigrant and the School Committee of five had Black, Asian, and Jewish members.

Although diversification is taking place in Wellesley's public square, and thus having an impact, the process can be daunting. Cleo said that when she first decided to become involved in town politics, she was not welcomed and was even told that people would "look into" her background. Courtney noted the trials of this sort facing newer community members:

> There was an Asian American woman who spoke at town meeting who had an Asian name, and when the moderator called on her, the way he was uncomfortable with her name was really clear, and I was like, oh, he could have just said, "How do you say your name?" But it was just so like, oh, "It's not, Mr. Williams who's speaking, it's Miss . . . ," and he just froze up. And I thought, English was her second language, and it just was interesting to me the more work she had to do to make space for herself to speak.

The scene at town meeting described by Courtney illustrates that people may share common norms (speaking at town meeting) but not equal status, as outlined by Allport.[58] The relational inequality resulting from limited language skills and less familiarity with the immediate cultural schema has implications for multidirectional assimilation, particularly when the individual or group is not viewed as White.[59] Language is a "privileged vehicle" that determines one's place in the hierarchy.[60]

Conclusion

This chapter has covered the main stages on which individuals and groups have had the opportunity to interact with each other in Wellesley, including neighborhoods, schools, religious institutions, extracurricular activities, and civic organizations. It is important to recognize that the collection of stages discussed here is not exhaustive. Myriad other stages have provided members of different groups with the opportunity to engage, from dog parks to running groups to one of the many immigrant-owned restaurants in town.

The extent of perceived diversification varies by both individual and setting. Some interviewees saw significant variety in their neighborhood, in their children's schools, or in various organizations in which they participated; others continued to perceive Wellesley as overwhelmingly homogenous. Some experienced greater diversity because they cultivated it—Isabella, Richard, Emma, and Marie, for example, placed their children in private schools where classes including students from a range of backgrounds could be purposefully formed. They may or may not have chosen private school for this reason, but an experience of greater diversity for their children was one of the outcomes, and one that all of them considered a positive outcome. Relatedly, children's interests or parents' interests for their children sometimes brought them into greater contact with more diverse populations. Participating in extracurricular activities such as dance, music, or STEM, as opposed to basketball or hockey, put their children on stages populated by more diverse players.

The more diverse members of the sample confirmed the impressions of established residents. Avi, who migrated from India and had been in the United States for decades, coached a STEM team in the Wellesley public schools, and Jing from China and Sherry, a Black American, were involved with scouts.

Interviewees who discussed attempts to diversify clubs, boards, and committees identified a number of challenges. Kelly, a woman who held a leadership role in a local educational organization, pointed out that "we mostly get volunteers that are a friend of a friend. And so then you end up kind of with the same type of people all the time." Other community leaders also identified this limitation—relying on networks for volunteers or membership tends to yield similar kinds of people. Another challenge in diversifying settings is language skills. Those who speak English as a second language may feel less comfortable speaking in public and taking on leadership roles, as discussed in the interviews with Courtney, June, and Frank. Some Chinese residents confirmed that their language skills kept them from participating in organizations like PTO and in town government. Finally, some interviewees, while established in their own right and lifelong members of the community, came from a historically marginalized group and continued to feel like outsiders in Wellesley. Some remembered housing discrimination, exclusion from club memberships, and exclusion from townwide rites of passage, and some had inherited stories of such experiences from their parents. As a result, they had no interest in joining clubs and organizations with a history of exclusion; they did not want to enter onto those stages. As a result, possible footpaths and bridges remained unbuilt.

From the perspective of more racially diverse residents, walking onto stages populated by established residents came with its own challenges. Anjali talked about the expectations associated with volunteering—the assumption, for instance, that one's home was big enough to host meetings and one's bank account was high enough to afford food and drinks for those meetings. "You know," she said, "there's just this dynamic of power. It just took me so long to f—ing understand what the hell's going on in these meetings, because there's so much not said. And so now I get it." Anjali was referring to the unwritten scripts, the cultural schema to which only those who have been socialized in a particular environment are privy.[61]

Now that the stages have been identified, the next chapter explores the ways in which established and new members of the community interact and mutually influence each other on these various stages. What are the implications of having a neighbor of a different ethnic background or a colleague with a different religious tradition? Does a more diverse team roster have any meaning beyond being a more diverse team roster? We now move from simply identifying the actors on each of the stages to examining the many ways in which the newest members of the community impact established members through three distinct pathways.

= Chapter 4 =

Multidirectional Influences on Individuals

Ben was in his forties and identified exclusively as American. He had little patience for the hyphenated identities of his friends, many of whom called themselves Irish or Italian American. He struggled to understand the connections they felt with countries that their great-grandparents left long ago and that they had never visited.

Ben's view of the world suggests that he had limited contact with new groups, as well as a fairly stagnant identity of his own, but any such assumption belies the effects of increasing diversity on his life: His wife was from Asia, and he spent a period of time teaching English as a second language to children. When asked what holidays he celebrated, Ben responded, "We celebrate the holidays that other people do, like on Saint Patty's Day, I'll drink Guinness, and, you know, Cinco de Mayo, we'll make tacos and things like that. . . . Just the regular holidays that everyone celebrates." Ben's experiences reflect the process of relational assimilation, or the day-to-day adjustments made by individuals in their own lives in response to increasing diversity.[1] Where and when Ben chooses to make accommodations and changes in his life also illustrate the ethnic options available to some Americans.[2] At the same time, his wife's actions spoke to her own pattern of assimilation: She had married an established American and spoke English at home, but by not entirely checking her identity at the door, she had influenced him in a variety of ways.

Saanvi and Jing, both Asian immigrants, spoke about their desire to maintain their cultural traditions in regard to food, holidays, religious practices, and language and to pass those traditions on to their children. Although such attempts at cultural retention seem to be made independent of established residents, they nevertheless have implications for everyone in a community. For example, as new members of a community spread foodways at neighborhood potlucks or celebrate Diwali or

https://doi.org/10.7758/mpvu4414.2867

Lunar New Year and invite work colleagues, neighbors, and friends to join them, cultural retention for one side of the table is cultural exposure for the other side.[3]

Anjali told me that when they first moved to town, the neighbors were shocked that her husband, "this Black man," could afford to buy a house in Wellesley. Anjali worked intentionally to build relationships with established individuals, building footpaths despite and even because of her family's initial experiences of being racialized as individuals who did not belong. Anjali had formed close relationships with her neighbors who initially assumed that her child was the housekeeper's; with the teachers and administrators she thought had lower expectations for darker-skinned students; and the organizational leaders and policymakers she felt had racial and ethnic blind spots. Her experiences of racialization led her to transform the established community by engaging in it both at the micro level and organizationally.[4]

New residents take varied paths—sometimes working to assimilate, sometimes fighting to retain their cultural heritage—and encounter varied obstacles along the way, including racialization.[5] Their efforts—sometimes undertaken discretely, sometimes concomitantly—are not made in a vacuum.[6] The new and the established are in relationship with one another, as Jiménez points out.[7] Residents discuss, both implicitly and explicitly, the diversity of neighbors, work colleagues, friendships, and even romantic partnerships that have developed over time.

Although such close micro-level connections among individuals of distinct groups could be viewed as outcomes of growing diversity, established residents often regard them as a starting point for explaining their range of experiences. These micro-level footpaths expose established residents to new religions, cultural traditions, and foods, as well as shaping their political views and even their sense of identity. The established may not see that even just the possibility of contact arises through the various forms of assimilation being undertaken by the newest members of the community, or that their interactions with their newest neighbors may be partly shaped by those neighbors' attempts at cultural retention or responses to racialization. In contrast, members of newer groups, while also describing individual-level footpaths connecting them with established residents, are more likely to think of these micro-level relationships, which they have often intentionally built, as themselves the outcomes of the connections.

Individual Interactions and Friendships

The number of foreign-born residents of the United States has increased, as has the rate at which the foreign-born enter the country.[8] These increases give established residents greater opportunities for contact, particularly as immigrants settle outside of traditional enclaves. Further, barriers separating White ethnics from the traditional mainstream have long fallen away as ethnic, racial, and religious boundaries have expanded in the post–civil rights era.[9] It is therefore unsurprising to hear lifelong residents of Wellesley discuss neighbors, work colleagues, volunteers, and friends from distinct ethnic, religious, and racial backgrounds after not initially noting that diversity in their community. In short, established residents are developing relationships—at times very close relationships—with members of new groups who have become incorporated in a variety of ways, even in a town that continues to be viewed both internally and externally as "White" and "WASPY."

Throughout the interviews, participants often mentioned that their neighborhoods were predominantly White and their friends looked like them. Many continued to think of themselves, sometimes critically and a bit abashed, as living in a homogenous world, well aware that the world "outside of Wellesley" is increasingly diverse. The youngest residents interviewed tended to be the most embarrassed and frustrated by what they perceived to be the lack of diversity. This variation by age group is explained by the constantly changing world into which distinct cohorts are socialized.[10] That younger residents increasingly experience a global environment highlights the need for a glocal framework to more fully understand the process of neo-assimilation. For example, James, who moved back to Wellesley after attending college and graduate school in another state, said that the "bread and butter of Wellesley is Wonder Bread White people." He felt a bit cheated by the lack of diversity in his community growing up. Jackson is of similar age. When I asked Jackson about the backgrounds of his closest friends, he responded that they were "very similar, which is not great, but very similar."

Only with a bit more digging did a more varied picture emerge. Jackson eventually told me that, while he was growing up in Wellesley, he had a number of close Indian American friends whose parents and grandparents had immigrated. Luke, who similarly described Wellesley as White and homogenous, said that about half of his friends were Asian. Lucas, who was middle-aged and Italian American, told me that his closest friends were those he grew up with in town and that their backgrounds were similar to his. As the interview continued, he told me about some very close Jewish friends of his. Courtney had White friends from both town and college, as well as Filipino and Chinese friends. Grace, who identified as Asian, had friends who were White, Chinese, and Indian. One of Abby's closest friends was Latina. Connor talked about the diverse group of friends he made through his children's parochial school and sports league, including individuals from Asia and Africa. Lily discussed the Korean, Indian, Brazilian, and Chinese parents and grandparents she had met through her children's participation in STEM activities.

Emma didn't tell me that one of her best friends was from Lebanon until I asked about the spelling of her friend's name, which was not traditionally Western. Emma had met this person through a work-related event, she said, and they both lived in town. She also discussed other close friends—a couple who were Japanese and English, and another couple who were Middle Eastern. She said, "I find I got to know the parents when he [my son] was younger, because we'd hang out together when they were playing." She remained close friends with these parents and continued to socialize with them long after their children had finished elementary school and the children's relationships had largely faded away. Emma also told me about a Syrian man she dated.

Residents from more newly arrived groups also discussed a diversity of social networks. Avi, an Indian resident, when asked if he felt a sense of belonging in his neighborhood, replied, "Oh, I think it's a great fit. We like all of our neighbors. There is an international group to it as well. There was a Norwegian couple who live on the street. There's also one from New Zealand. There's one from Croatia. And so there we are from India. There are several others, native-born. And so it feels very easy to fit in." Jing, from China, also reported feeling a sense of belonging in her neighborhood and described it as "very, very friendly." The neighborhood families got together for block parties and dinners, and they helped each other out. Priya also described warm relationships with neighbors and other town residents. Saanvi and Fang similarly reported that some of their closest friends were White established Americans. Saanvi talked about her neighbors as her "go-to people" whenever she was in need; those relationships had largely developed through her children.

This is not to suggest that Asian residents felt complete belonging or never experienced racism in the neighborhood or the workplace. Jing, for example, said that after experiencing racism during COVID, she was motivated to reach out to the larger community, both new and established. Her actions in reaction to those experiences prompted a townwide response.

More often, new residents, particularly Asian women, said that they had developed different types of relationships. In discussing her Chinese friends, Jing said, "They can just tell me they are coming in, they will ring the bell. So it's a different type of [relationship]." Priya similarly made a distinction between her established friends, with whom she had warm relations, and her Indian friends. This distinction bothered her, as it felt as if she could get only so close to her White neighbors. Lakshmi also had different relationships with her White friends.

> I got very close to the Indian friends, people from India, from Sri Lanka, like our ethnic group, and the White people, we would usually just talk, say hello. But we never went to their house for any celebration or anything like

that. We did not invite them home. We sometimes have invited a couple of White people home for dinner, but it was not the thing. But Indians are like family, even if they're friends. We always go to their house, and they come [here], and our kids, they take care of our kids, if there's a problem with drop-off and stuff like that.

There is an understandable level of greater comfort among newer residents who share a recent migration, a common culture, or a cultural schema.[11] The apparent mismatch in feelings between White established residents and newer Asian residents may reflect White Americans' view of Asian Americans as "just like us," even while Asian Americans do not feel that same familiarity.[12]

Black residents, including those whose families have been in the United States for centuries and who most certainly fit the definition of established Americans, tell a much more consistent story of racialization. Sherry said that town residents were surprised to learn that she and her husband were homeowners and not renters. They were also sometimes thought to be workers in the local grocery store, not patrons of it. Sherry, Adele, Ronnie, and Cleo, all Black women, discussed instances when their children were misplaced geographically and assumed to be part of the METCO program. They also had experienced teachers setting lower educational expectations for their children.[13]

Cleo discussed the diversity of her relationships across racial, ethnic, and religious lines but also stressed how intentionally she had built those relationships, taking into account the way in which she felt she and her children needed to present themselves in town. Sherry, in describing her close friends, said, "I actually have a very diverse group of friends in town." Sherry's and Cleo's relationships across racial and ethnic lines eventually led them both to sit on important boards and committees within the community. Even while experiencing significant racism, including assumptions around their intelligence, capabilities, and class, they had persisted and built footpaths to diverse relationships with far-reaching implications for themselves and the entire town. These women did not exit the stage but rather diversified the cast and rewrote the script.

Anjali had a particularly unique perspective as an immigrant whose child was racialized as Black. His skin tone influenced the family's micro-level interactions in town. When her son did odd jobs for a neighbor when he was younger, he was assumed to be from "elsewhere," not living across the street in a home that cost seven figures. Anjali did not let this interaction stop her from building intentional footpaths to established members of the neighborhood, including the woman who thought her child was from "elsewhere." Through a shared religious tradition, Anjali regularly attended church and social gatherings with this person and considered another neighbor to be one of her closest confidants. Her initial experience of being racialized led Anjali, like Cleo and Sherry, to react rather than retreat. In Anjali's story we see the varied paths to variegated assimilation for established residents as well as new residents: she and her family lived in the affluent White community of Wellesley, her child attended an elite college, and her husband worked in a sector of the economy that remained less diverse; she engaged in cultural retention in regard to food and language; and her family's experiences with racism inspired her to participate in and change mainstream organizations. In short, Anjali's decisions reached far beyond her household to impact established individuals, organizations, and the town.

So what is the origin of this mismatch between established residents' initial response of claiming to have homogeneous relationships and the actual diversity of those relationships? The inability to see difference may speak to our society's restructuring of the color line, from one defined by Du Bois as Black/White (the color line that prevailed in the twentieth century) to a Black/non-Black divide in the twenty-first century.[14] Although this change in racial categories can be read as a positive expansion of racial boundaries and one of the ways in which immigration and growing diversity have positively impacted society, it presents a variety of problems, both old and new. Asian Americans may now be on the "inside," having climbed to the non-Black side of the color line in the reformation of the hierarchy.[15] But they have ascended to this position because too often the simplistic view of them as a "model minority" and "just like us" (Whites) has not been challenged.[16] That view fails to see the unique needs and challenges of new Asian American groups, while continuing to construct boundaries around and problematize those who are racialized as Black and those of lower socioeconomic status. Some boundaries in American society remain remarkably "bright" and hard to overcome.[17]

Established residents also told me that they were "colorblind" and did not notice what their friends looked like or where they were from, a claim that is increasingly a part of the political discourse.[18] Clare told me that she was proud that her son was sent to school "quite colorblind—everyone is just the same." Clare's son had friends who were mostly White and Asian but also Latino. At least one of his close friends was Jewish. Emma similarly told me, when I asked about the ethnicity of her friends, "So that's not something that's forefront in terms of any kind of relationship." When discussing her closest friend, who was Lebanese, she said, "It's who I get along with." Nick, another established resident, told me about a close friend who was Iranian: "The number-one influence is that we're good friends, and we're like-minded, and the race and ethnicity just, to me, that just comes second or third. You know, I don't feel like I really see it."

The established participants' stated blindness to race and ethnicity also reflected a desire to *appear* colorblind in a time when race is a particularly sensitive issue for the White established community. Claiming colorblindness was how individuals felt they were supposed to view (or not view) race in the twenty-first century. One interviewee described having a colleague who was Black, interjecting, "If that's the right term to use." Joe Feagin has reformulated his theory of the White racial frame and Americans' historical socialization of Black Americans to incorporate other new groups that have entered the United States through migration.[19] This new framework has instilled in White Americans the notion of colorblindness, even while racialization still takes place and racial stereotypes hold firm. For example, cross-national research by Ann Morning and Marcello Maneri finds that both Italians and Americans have adopted the norm of avoiding "race talk" and not "seeing" race, but that, when asked to make sense of the athletic performances of racial groups, individuals in both countries fall back on biological stereotypes to explain the success of Black athletes.[20]

Vedran Omanović and Ann Langley, in studying how workplaces attempt to socialize immigrants, discuss the often-dueling societal-level discourses around equality and cultural diversity.[21] Eduardo Bonilla-Silva makes the argument that the refrain of colorblindness combined with an increasingly flexible racial hierarchy that now accepts individuals previously recognized as non-White on the non-Black side of the color line perpetuates systemic inequality, even while individuals may not be engaging in prejudice or discrimination.[22] Micro-level interactions between individuals, however, do not occur in a vacuum. As human beings, we are all socialized in particular ways, including the status, honor, or deference we give someone based on who they are and who we are, what they do and what we do, how they appear, what the setting or stage is, and how we have been taught to make sense of our surroundings.[23] We are also heavily influenced by local, national, and even international events and trends in regard to race and ethnicity.[24]

Moreover, it is important to recognize that *not* seeing color or difference in one's friendships and other relationships is a privilege held by members of the established population, particularly those who are lighter-skinned and Christian. Although Jewish, Asian, Black, or Latino Americans can very well be a part of the established population as multigenerational Americans, their perpetual differences make them more likely to recognize the difference in others, as *they* are the differences seen in many friendships. For example, Gianni, an Italian American and lifelong resident in his fifties, provided numerous examples of members of the established commenting on his appearance and skin tone. *He* was the difference. A Jewish woman of a similar age explained that her very close childhood friend would say things to her like, "It's too bad you can't come to the country club with me." She said it was just understood, even by close friends, that Jews were not permitted at the club.

Intermarriage

In the extreme case, micro-level contact leads to intimate partnerships and family formation. Indeed, rates of interracial and interethnic marriages have been trending higher, as have approval rates for such marriages.[25] Exogamy, or marrying outside of one's own group, is a frequently used measure to assess immigrant and ethnic assimilation and acceptance into the dominant society.[26]

The first obviously interfaith wedding announcement in Wellesley appeared in 1970 in the *Wellesley Townsman*, where the officiants were listed as Rabbi Uman and Reverend Harper.[27] That wedding was followed by additional marriage announcements of couples who identified as Jewish and Catholic, Jewish and Unitarian, or Jewish and various forms of Protestant. A 1976 interfaith wedding announcement between someone who identified as Jewish and someone of Irish Catholic identity discussed their upcoming honeymoon trip to both Israel and Ireland, an indication of their ongoing connections to their ancestral places of origin amid the mixing of the later generations.[28]

Under a November 1970 "Church Services" heading, Temple Beth Elohim announced a discussion on the relationship between the Jewish family and Christmas entitled "Saying 'No' to Our Children."[29] Rabbi Gendler, a local rabbi, spoke at Houghton Memorial Chapel on the Wellesley College campus in April 1972. The newspaper article reporting the event described him as known for "his controversial stand on interfaith marriages, many of which he has performed."[30] By 1980, a local social service organization in town, Jewish Family and Children's Services, was sponsoring lectures and running monthly discussion groups for both parents with intermarried children and those in interfaith relationships themselves.[31]

Within this case study, there is clear evidence of growing numbers of Jews marrying Christians: one Jewish participant was married to a practicing Catholic, four participants were the product of Jewish-Christian relationships, two were married to someone who was the product of such an interfaith partnership, and two had close relatives in such a relationship. The bulk of these Jewish-Christian partnerships had been formed among those in the youngest (eighteen to thirty-four) and middle-aged (thirty-five to fifty-four) cohorts. That there were no Jews or interfaith marriages in the oldest group of lifelong residents (fifty-five or older) was not a surprise, given the historic challenges that Jews—as well as other ethnic, racial, and religious groups—faced in trying to buy a home in Wellesley well into the late twentieth century. However, a number of the oldest residents discussed their children's interfaith and interethnic marriages.

Both established residents and members of new groups had engaged in other forms of intermarriage as well. Five lifelong residents were married, or had been married, to immigrants from a range of Latin and European countries. Frank, a man in his eighties who identified proudly as Italian American but also stressed the American side of his identity throughout the interview, discussed the marriages of two of his three children. Frank's daughter was married to a Venezuelan immigrant, whom she met through work at an international food importer. She had learned Spanish when she studied abroad in college. When his son married an Indian immigrant, they held two weddings—one in New England and one in India.

Still other unions would barely register by the standards of most Americans today, but they are worth noting as they speak to changing social norms over just a few generations.[32] Gianni was married to a woman whom he described as "the exact opposite of me. She is a mix of German and English and Scottish. I would consider her family a WASP family. So they were the exact family that I described at the beginning of the interview," referencing his response when I asked him to describe Wellesley to someone who had never been here before. As mentioned earlier in the chapter, his appearance was a point of conversation. His in-laws saw him through an ethnic lens—just as he did them—through which Italians were seen as an "other." Given his relatively dark complexion, in their view he occupied a peripheral position within the category of whiteness.[33]

Henry, the oldest participant in the study, who discussed in the prior chapter how limited his worldview had traditionally been, talked about the broader range of partners among his children: "My daughter is married to a Catholic. My son is married to a member of the Armenian church." Although many would not consider these partnerships illustrations of intermarriage, for Henry, Alice, and Gianni's wife they represented expanding religious boundaries and significant movements away from their WASP backgrounds.[34]

Finally, discussions with newer members of the community also reveal other forms of exogamy. Anjali, from south Asia, was married to an immigrant from Barbados. Cleo, a Black American, was married to a man from the Caribbean and converted to marry him. There is even a formal group in town for mixed-race families. Nearly 8 percent of the town identifies as having "two or more races," suggesting a growing number of intimate partnerships across racial categories. In short, there is movement in all directions and a blurring of racial, ethnic, and religious boundaries, in keeping with larger trends toward an increasingly multicultural society.[35] How those individuals will identify racially, ethnically, or religiously over the life course, however, remains to be seen.[36]

Religious Practices

Intermarriage reflects growing acceptance and assimilation and diversifies kinship networks.[37] For members of minority groups, however, the rise of intermarriage increases the fear of loss—loss of language, religion, food traditions, and other forms of cultural knowledge. The focus on interfaith marriage in the Jewish community speaks to the historic and, arguably, ongoing concern about fully assimilating into American society. This is the double-edged sword of greater acceptance for minority groups. The decline of housing segregation enables individuals to rightfully buy a home in whatever community they choose, but they are also more likely to find themselves living amid neighbors of other ethnic and religious traditions. Recall Anna's fond memories of the Jewish neighborhood of her childhood compared to how her children have grown up. "There was something nice about that, because you knew the Jewish kids in your school. I would say nowadays I would ask my kids, 'Oh, who's Jewish in your grade?' Which is probably creepy that I even ask them that, but they don't always know."

The concern about intermarriage also speaks to the larger relational inequality felt by many minority groups. Jews often sense that an interfaith household will be overwhelmed by one spouse's Christian heritage, given the societal tilt of the larger community toward Christianity. The 1970 lecture entitled "Saying 'No' to Our Children" was not about interfaith relationships, but about disallowing any form of Christmas celebration in the Jewish household, even the secular forms of Santa Claus and Christmas trees, given what those symbols represent. The feeling was that Jewish households must "hold the line," lest their children be absorbed by the stronger forces just outside the door. Similarly, some new residents insisted on speaking only Spanish or Mandarin in the home, while others cooked exclusively Indian food. Sensing that the American playing field was not equal, these residents decided that their children would absorb plenty of English and eat plenty of chicken fingers outside of the household.

The data suggest that members of newer groups are not without power or influence, however, and cultural retention and resistance can be practiced alongside growing assimilation.[38] Since individuals do not check their identity at the proverbial altar, their religious background may influence their partner, their children, and even extended family in a form of variegated assimilation for established residents in interfaith unions.

Three of the youngest participants in the study had one parent born Jewish and one born Christian; despite this similarity in their families, they had somewhat varied experiences growing up. Jackson, for example, experienced little religion in his household growing up, but his family did celebrate both Hanukkah and Christmas. These two celebrations could be considered, by Jews and Christians alike, the most accessible, widely celebrated, and, for many, least sacred of their holidays. This level of religious engagement suggests that religion was optional for Jackson in a way similar to the "ethnic options" that Mary Waters identified among

White, Christian, established Americans.[39] Without dietary restrictions, such as keeping Kosher, or particular garments of clothing, such as a yarmulke, there was nothing to mark Jackson as distinctly Jewish.

James similarly had one parent born Jewish and one born Christian. Although he described his household as "hard-core atheistic" and said that its "defining characteristic was the absence of any ethnic background," he noted that his grandfather did bring some small degree of Judaism into the household. Now having a partner who identified as Irish Catholic and attended church weekly, he told me, had "raised fun and challenging compromises" as they tried "to balance going to Church or listening to religious podcasts" with his irreligious upbringing.

Courtney, who claimed no religious affiliation, talked about her father, who was raised as a religious Jew but was lapsed by the time he married her mother. She described his background:

> And my dad is the middle of five siblings. He was raised Jewish Orthodox, but sort of ultimately like, lazy Orthodox, and then not Orthodox. My dad now, I make fun of him, because he always wants a ham for Easter. All of my dad and his siblings married non-Jews. But they were humanist Jews, even when they were within the Orthodox tradition when they were little, they would identify very strongly as humanists.

Her mother was from what Courtney called, "WASP descent, for lack of a better word." On the surface, her family seemed to have followed what sociologists historically considered the straight-line or traditional road of assimilation.[40] Her father's family intermarried with Christians, and some even married into the WASP class, the historical high mark of assimilation, but that was not the whole story. Courtney was exposed to Jewish holidays growing up and continued to engage in some ways. When asked about ethnic traditions, she said:

> And in terms of holidays, I was raised nothing, nothing spiritually. I mean, I'm agnostic at best, pretty much an atheist. But we did a Christmas tree, Santa Claus, Easter Bunny, and Hanukkah. Sometimes I would go with my dad when my grandfather was still alive, probably between the ages of like late elementary through middle and early high school until my grandfather died. I would go sometimes with my dad to High Holiday services.... The only time I ever had a Seder was when families invited me to one. Although interestingly, my dad is doing a Seder for my kids, which is fun, because I've tried to do it, but I'm not very good at it, and my dad has ordered the food. I'm sure there will also be an Easter ham.

Courtney had also tried to expose her children to other Jewish traditions, like lighting candles for Hanukkah. Both she and her child had retained some sense of connection to their Jewish past. "When people would ask when I was little, 'Well, are you Jewish or Christian?' I'd be like, 'I'm half and half.' And it's funny, because I hear my daughter saying that now, and I'm like, 'Well, you're sort of half and half, you're sort of neither.'" Like others whose ethnic identity waxes and wanes over the life course and across generations, Courtney had in recent years tried to reclaim some of her Jewish background.[41]

Raised Episcopalian, Lily was married to a man who grew up with a Jewish parent and a Christian parent. Because the original intermarriage led to a schism within her husband's family, Lily told me, her husband became very anti-religious. Nevertheless, Lily, her husband, and their children participated in some Jewish traditions. She said that her husband's family

> has some traditions that they've had from before. His mother makes blintzes and latkes, and when we go down over to her house for Hanukkah, you put napkins on all the women's heads and say, "Baruch atah Adonai . . ." [a Hebrew prayer], light the menorah. And when our kids were very young, before her daughter's daughter was born, she would involve us in some of the temple things, but as she kind of grew away from the temple, and she had a real Jewish grandchild, she gave us up, which was fine. I was a little offended at the point in time, but I'm not Jewish, so . . .

Anna strongly identified as Jewish, as did her children, and her husband, who came from an interfaith marriage, also identified as Jewish. Anna's contact with an in-law who once practiced another religion provided her with an insight into and compassion for those whose "brushing up" against other groups leads to a decline in their own ethnic practices. She said, "And I can tell that they still mourn the loss of some of the parts of their Christian upbringing. They love a good Easter dinner, or love Christmas decorations. I don't know if they miss it so much on a spiritual level, but they definitely have wonderful childhood memories of growing up Christian."

Connor was in his fifties and strongly identified as Irish Catholic, declaring in the interview that March 17 was the "most important day of the year." He, his wife, and his children had all been educated in Catholic institutions, from kindergarten through postsecondary education. However, Connor had "brushed up" against a close Jewish relative of his wife's through marriage, and this slight contact with an individual from a distinct religious background had influenced him and his family. They had celebrated many Jewish holidays together and continued to gather for the annual Passover celebration. Similarly, Gianni, an Italian Catholic, and his wife, a Protestant, had a Jewish in-law who gave them occasion to attend Jewish events.

Less intimate relationships—with neighbors, friends, work colleagues—can also lead to exposure to new religious traditions. Clare, a lifelong resident in her early sixties, was married with a grown child, worked in management consulting, and was a highly active community volunteer. Her background was Irish and German, although her strongest identity was Catholic, and she was highly engaged with her church. Still, Clare had developed close friendships with Jewish residents in town. Illustrating the changing religious demographics of the community, her son attended two Bar Mitzvahs by the time he was fourteen, and Clare attended her first Bar Mitzvah as a woman in her fifties. This invitation came about through a contact turned friend on a volunteer board in Wellesley. She had also become knowledgeable about other Jewish traditions, including keeping kosher, purifying silverware that has been used on nonkosher foods by burying it (although this practice stems from an old wives' tale, it is a Jewish old wives' tale), and sitting Shiva, the Jewish mourning tradition. Clare had a number of close friends who were Jewish, and she had paid numerous Shiva calls. She described the practice as "upside down Catholic": Catholics hold a wake where people gather, mourn, and eat prior to the burial, whereas Jews do so after the burial. She also talked of a Jewish friend from town who delivered a "Shiva" box to those who had lost someone, regardless of religious affiliation. It was filled with tissues, hand sanitizer, and Tupperware to hold all of the food people brought. Clare had replicated the practice for her friends in mourning. She wondered, she told me, how people who do not have these mourning traditions, be they Jewish or Catholic, got through such difficult times. The Jewish rituals resonated with her, reminding her of her own Catholic traditions.

Lucas was in his mid-fifties and of Italian background. His parents experienced significant ethnic and religious discrimination growing up as Italian Catholics in Wellesley, and as a result, Lucas explained, their world had remained narrow. His, however, was not. Besides the employees who worked for him, many of whom were immigrants, his friends came from a wide variety of backgrounds. Lucas had been to the local synagogue and attended the Bar Mitzvahs of his friend's children. "In my adult life," he explained, "we have all kinds of Jewish friends. And I've been to Bar Mitzvahs, and I've been to their houses for every family event and everything." Kate, of a similar age and ethnic background, also discussed her contact with Jewish traditions: "I've gone to synagogue with a couple of my friends on Friday nights." She explained that her closest friends from various parts of her life were Jewish, and said that another close friend had converted to Judaism when she got married.

Like Clare, both Lucas and Kate emphasized the similarities between their own backgrounds and Judaism, using ethnicity as a bridge of familiarity. Kate explained, "I guess I've always felt like, there's a lot of cultural commonalities between Italian families and Jewish families that I know. You know, love of food, love of dining together, love of children." Lucas made a similar comparison when talking about his Jewish friends and his interactions with them: "And I'm looking around, and I'm like, these people are exactly like Italians.... Jewish people and Italian people are exactly the same." Such feelings of commonality and connection may stem in part from the level of distinction from the WASP class that both groups have retained. Allport's theory that increased connection and declining prejudice are predicated, in part, on feelings of similarity is reinforced by the affection for and connection to their Jewish friends felt by Lucas, Clare, and Kate.[42]

Alice and Henry, a married couple in their nineties, gave separate interviews. They both came from WASP stock, and they had met in church, as discussed in the previous chapter. Henry told of living in a highly segregated neighborhood growing up, a place where Catholics were unwelcome and the one Jewish family who moved in had their house egged on a daily basis until they moved out. Through Henry's job in an independent school, he encountered a wide variety of people, religiously, ethnically, and racially. He also had the opportunity to travel and study abroad as part of his work.

He and Alice both talked about a very close relationship with a Jewish work colleague who became a dear friend. Alice said, "She became as close as a relative to us over the last thirty or forty years, and we have learned, we've shared religious holidays and food, and we've learned a great deal from her.... Our Jewish rabbi friend always made sure that we exchanged the religious holidays by having dinner together." Confirming trends illustrated here, large-scale survey research finds that 72 percent of Jewish Americans cook Jewish food and that 62 percent share holidays with non-Jewish friends.[43]

Kathy, a medical professional of Irish extraction, discussed her diverse neighborhood growing up. She ticked off new religious and ethnic practices in which she had engaged as a result of her friendships in town, citing Lunar New Year and Hanukkah in particular. Siobhan told me that she attended Shiva when her Jewish friends experienced losses. Angela, who worked in health care in Wellesley, discussed a conversation she had with a patient.

> I live right down the street from a temple. So I see when all the Jewish holidays [are happening]. So I was telling him one day, and I said, "Yeah, I tried to get down the street, and apparently there's some Jewish holiday, and I'm Catholic." I said, "I don't know what it is." And then he proceeded to tell me what the holiday was ... and the history behind the holiday, and I thought it was fascinating. And not only that, I used to work in some assisted living places, and as activities, they would have the Jewish holidays and the Catholic holidays. And I'd learn from there too. I mean, I just celebrated them.

In these many instances, the established community was reshaped by the efforts of individuals from new groups to retain their religious and cultural heritage, even as the new groups were being folded into the established community.

Both Wellesley and the larger society are diverse beyond the Judeo-Christian tradition. In describing the increasing diversity of her neighborhood, Clare implicitly discussed the ways in which her Chinese and Indian neighbors worked to retain their cultural heritage and its impact on her. In addition to having Indian neighbors on either side of her home and introducing them to each other, she developed relationships with these households of distinct immigrant, ethnic, religious, and racial identities.

> We got all three of us [Clare, her husband, and her son] together, and we went over. Oh my God, my husband and son just thought this was the best, because they had Vishnu. They had all the statues in the house, right? He [the neighbor] told them about all the mythology. And their daughter got married a couple of years after we'd been here. She came by, and she wanted to tell us there was going to be a wedding, and could they park here? And I was like, "Oh, my God, are they going to have a horse?" And she said "A horse? How do you know that?" I'm like, "I have friends that are Indian." I had taken my husband when we were dating to a friend of mine who worked for me, his wedding. He went and picked his bride up on the white horse and the dress. So I started talking to her about all this. And my husband's like, "Oh, we're going to get the sticks to dance with it." I've opened my husband's horizons.

While Clare might have opened up her husband's horizons to encompass Hindu religious traditions and rites of passage, she had her own horizons opened by her contact with members of this new group, both in the work and neighborhood settings. Her experience illustrates how a small-scale footpath can develop through which new knowledge and experiences spread and then spread again.

Frank, a man in his eighties, also experienced an Indian wedding when one of his children married an Indian immigrant. In addition to having a Catholic wedding in a chapel in which three generations of the family had been married, the family also went to India for a traditional Indian wedding that lasted a week. Frank proudly showed me photos of the wedding, including one of him and his wife dressed in a sherwani and a sari, respectively.

Newer residents in the community also discussed how they both spread and experienced new religious traditions and knowledge, suggesting multidirectional flows across individual-level footpaths. Priya, an Indian immigrant who had lived in Wellesley for over three decades, had previously spoken of her feelings of marginalization and a lack of belonging in the workplace. The longer she was there, the more she had come to understand the ways in which she was not accepted, an experience that was in keeping with prior research.[44] Instead of working toward greater assimilation, she had tried to teach others about her heritage, both in her children's school and in Wellesley, more generally. By exposing others to her traditions, Priya was practicing a form of normative inversion.[45] She said, "We used to have a lot of celebrations around Diwali, lots of people gathering and all that. One time we decided to invite people of every other religion from Wellesley. And we had the Diwali celebration with a couple of friends who had a Jewish background, who had Catholic, all different religious backgrounds."

Saanvi, an Indian immigrant who came to the United States as a young adult, tried to attend her Hindu temple at least once a month, as well as for festivals. Sometimes she took her children and even their friends. She said, "I get some Indian clothes for my neighbor's kids, but unfortunately, they don't have an opportunity to wear them much. But I took them once to temple, and then for the event that's called Navaratri, where they do a lot of dancing after prayers. . . . You pray and do a lot of fun and entertainment there. So I take the neighbor's kids." Saanvi's personal attempts at cultural retention also served to move the established community toward variegated assimilation.

Similarly, Jing talked about organizing Lunar New Year celebrations for the public schools and local community organizations and inviting children from the established community whom she knew to participate in dance performances for the event. Kate, who primarily identified as Italian American, also mentioned that her children's involvement in dance had led to her family's participation in Lunar New Year activities.

Although both Avi and his wife were practicing Hindus, they incorporated a Christmas tree and a Hanukkah menorah into their celebrations because, he said, it just "feels right." Lakshmi and her family, also practicing Hindus, also had a Christmas tree, which helped her children feel like they were fitting in in Wellesley, she explained. New residents consistently discussed incorporating celebrations of both Thanksgiving and Christmas into their family holidays, even while holding fast to their own traditions related to holidays, dress, and food.

These accounts all speak to the move away from a Protestant society and toward a Judeo-Christian one, or even a society beyond that dyad.[46] But it is important to note that the relationships are not entirely equal, owing largely to numeric differences and institutional inequalities. For many established residents, these dynamics allow them to participate in alternative religious practices with little concern for protecting their own traditions. One woman, making a public comment before a school committee meeting, told a story of a teacher asking the children in her class to raise their hands if they celebrated Christmas. Then she asked who celebrated Hanukkah, and finally who celebrated something "other." As she told the school committee, "My son came home and said, 'Guess what, Mom? I am other.' He was ten. It would not have occurred to me that he, at ten years old, would come to understand the concept of being othered in such a literal way."[47] This micro-level interaction built a roadblock rather than a footpath, stymieing the potential for contact and understanding. But by making her child's racialized experience a matter of public record, this resident reacted in a way that led to variegated assimilation in the town by encouraging the reform of policies and practices. As will be discussed in upcoming chapters, footpaths are simply a starting point for impacting the established community.

Food

Food is one means by which ethnic, cultural, and religious ties are maintained or spread at relatively low cost to groups on all sides. Although seemingly minor in impact, culinary traditions should be neither minimized nor discounted, as they serve important emotional, educative, and even economic functions for new individuals and groups and can reshape the established community.[48]

Ironically, altering the foodways of an established community results through both cultural retention and cultural assimilation, sometimes simultaneously. Gordon discusses the process of identificational assimilation, such as adopting American holidays, whereby new groups come to see the history and traditions of the host society as their own.[49] For some new members of the community, celebrating a new holiday may mean adopting the traditional foods that often accompany it—turkey on Thanksgiving or beef on Christmas. Others adopt a modified version of a new holiday: they mark a societal celebration, but with foods from their country of origin. Still others from new groups not only retain traditional holidays and foods but also spread them along micro-level footpaths to the established community.

Christopher was an Italian American in his seventies, as was his wife, and his daughter was married to an Italian American. He explained the importance of carrying on food traditions, even within an ethnically homogenous household:

> We will never be able to cook as good as my grandmother did. That was the best. We try, and we like to think we do, but we don't. We still make homemade tortellini, which is a regional dish. That was a pride, a staple for us, and I buy the ingredients, and we make them from scratch. . . . So we spend a whole day as an extended family doing this so that we have enough tortellini to cover us for the Christmas holidays, or maybe New Year's. And it's a great tradition for us, because my parents used to do it. My wife was

taught how to do it, and she's passing down the tradition. My daughter loved the tradition. She will be doing that with her daughter.

Passing down this ethnic food tradition was clearly of great importance to Christopher, as it was to others of Italian descent who were interviewed. Kate said, "It never crosses our minds to have turkey for Christmas, you have turkey for Thanksgiving, you have, you know, gnocchi or some other kind of homemade pasta for Christmas, with a bunch of meats and things like that. There are a lot of traditions around Easter for Italian families and, you know, food traditions in particular." Nick, a man in his fifties who identified as "Irish/German/Western European" and Catholic and was married to a woman of Italian background, stated, "It's all the seafood routines on Christmas Eve. You know, there's not a holiday meal that doesn't have pasta and some kind of red sauce in it." Residents of Italian descent appeared to have an almost reverential view of the foods and traditions connected with Italian holidays, and of their traditions generally. Moreover, their family's assimilation to American religious and cultural holiday traditions changed those American traditions—for example, by celebrating New Year's and Thanksgiving, but with pasta. Such assimilation patterns have been identified before.[50]

The concurrent processes of assimilation and cultural retention are evident throughout this study's data in regard to food. Angela, an established resident, told a story of a modified Christmas celebration with a neighbor from India who had become a good friend:

> Well, he's a sweetheart. He really is. And he's an awesome cook. So we went over there last Christmas. And I'm not a fish eater, and it was Christmas. And to me Christmas is roast beef, mashed potatoes. You know, that's what I grew up with. So I go over to his house expecting roast beef. No, I get fish. So that's what he's used to, since he's from India. He's used to fish. He's a vegetarian. That kind of threw me for a loop, but surprisingly, I enjoyed it.

Echoing Angela's experiences, the Indian and Chinese residents interviewed all discussed their adoption of Thanksgiving in various forms; what they told me often reflected precisely what established residents were telling me. For example, Priya, a longtime resident of Wellesley, raised the issue of combining her Hindu practices and American traditions. She explained that the *"Wellesley Townsman* once had an article about this, because they were looking for vegetarian Thanksgiving, and they came to me to ask us what do we do for Thanksgiving if we are not eating turkey and all that." Lakshmi similarly discussed modifying Thanksgiving by "Indianizing" the feast with Indian gravy and Indian rice, such as biryani.

Avi, an Indian man who had been in the United States since his college days, talked about the importance of the holiday and the food aspects of it:

> Thanksgiving is one of the things that comes foremost. When I came to the US in 1993, to Georgia, that was my first introduction to Thanksgiving. I was at my host family's house for Thanksgiving, and so that left a deep impression on me. And so that's something that I've kind of continued. So we've made it a thing of our own. We enjoy doing turkey, we just basically do all kinds of cuisines, we choose a cuisine every year.

A Chinese resident disclosed that her family celebrated Thanksgiving, but because she disliked turkey, they cooked more traditional Chinese foods for the holiday. Her story and Avi's also speak to the spread of new practices through assimilation.

In a similar vein, Tammy, an established resident in her late sixties who had no religious or ethnic affiliation but was raised Catholic, told a story about a Jewish friend of hers:

> A friend of mine who is Jewish, who lives in Wellesley, was married to someone who was Protestant, but decided a few years ago that she wanted to, they always had a Christmas party, but she wanted to have something that she felt that she grew up with. And she isn't much of a cook. So she said, "You're a great cook. Will you make this brisket? You have to make it. It's got to have cranberry sauce." And you know, that was, I think, the only thing, so I found a recipe and I said, "Does this look like the right one?" And she said, "Yes." And, I don't know if you've ever made brisket, but it's fairly elaborate. It takes like three days to get all the seasonings and everything. I don't eat much meat at all, but you know, it's "Okay. I'll make this brisket for you." And everyone was like, "This is the most fantastic brisket" and you know, look who made it, you know, the little Catholic girl made the brisket.

Tammy's story speaks to her friend's assimilation—through intermarriage and some form of religious assimilation, even if only with a Christmas party—and it also illustrates the spread of ethnic food within that process of assimilation. Food, a relatively low-cost way of maintaining one's cultural heritage, is nevertheless symbolically important and can have deep cultural meaning for an individual or group. Tammy's friend desperately wanted to have a brisket at the Christmas party because it would be "something that she grew up with." Food represents both a particular and historical way of being, a marker of belonging and group membership, a statement that "I am still here," even while assimilating in a different culture.

Ironically, attempts at cultural retention, even retaining traditions like foodways, may bring about diffusion into the mainstream. Saanvi, an Indian resident, spoke about the importance of food in her household with as much conviction as Christopher did. To her, food was a major form of cultural continuity and a tradition she felt it was critical to pass down to her children as part of their ethnic heritage:

> Food plays a very important role in the culture, right? I don't cook any other food than Indian. Maybe it's because I'm not good in any other ethnic food than Indian food, because it's so easy for me. You ask me to cook, I can cook within half an hour and get it done. If you asked me to cook something else, it's going to take me time. I have to read about it, need to learn about it, and it's a long process for me to make it easy. The food is the first thing, and the other thing is the kind of clothes you wear, right?

Although it might seem that food and clothing, a topic Saanvi returned to later in the interview, had implications only for herself and her children, her efforts at maintaining her Indian heritage influenced others outside of her household. Her children complained about the food, but their closest friends in the neighborhood were not Indian, and they often came over for dinner. "My neighbor's kids love Indian food," Saanvi said. "When they come to my home, they just eat and relish it. I'm like, 'Kiddos, look at them. They love food.'" Her children's friends also loved the colorful, festive clothing that Saanvi wore on holidays, and she brought back clothes from India for them, even though her own children preferred to wear Western-style clothing. The established members of Saanvi's neighborhood were being influenced by her family, newer members of the community, as they worked to retain ethnic traditions.

In discussions around interfaith relationships, individuals often mentioned having been exposed to ethnic-specific foods. James grew up in an intentionally secular household and said that the only ethnic influence came from his Jewish grandfather, and that was in the form of food. Again, food was a low-cost form of ethnic retention that brushed up against the established in small ways. Lily, who identified as atheist, was raised Episcopalian, and married a man who was the product of an interfaith marriage, discussed going to her in-laws' to eat latkes and blintzes to celebrate Hanukkah. Frank's Indian daughter-in-law cooked them curry when they visited, and Frank had come to realize that he enjoyed Indian food. He and his wife now frequented an Indian restaurant in town.

Work colleagues and neighbors also introduced established residents to new foods. Connor, who strongly identified as Irish, celebrated Lunar New Year by going for lunch in Chinatown with his Chinese work colleagues. Kathy, the medical professional in her sixties who discussed the variety of neighbors she had as a child and the diversity of the friendships that developed among them, connected the celebration of holidays new to her with new foods. "We did Hanukkah, different foods with friends. And like I said, that was sort of part of our world." Angela, who was demographically similar to Kathy—in her sixties, working in health care, of Italian, Irish, and Catholic descent—also discussed how both her patients and her neighbors taught her about Jewish holidays and traditions. She learned "what the matzah ball was for, or what the honey was, or the latkes were for."

Friendships, including the friends of one's children, can influence whole households. Luke described Wellesley as "primarily White," but also said that "my friends are Asian, half my friend group is Asian." He also discussed the impact of childhood relationships on food:

> My dad really liked some Indian food, and one of my sister Sally's good friends is Indian. So Sally would go over there and sometimes cook Indian food with the family. And then Sally would come back to us and be like, "Oh, you're not supposed to do it this way. You guys are doing it completely wrong. You're supposed to use your hands," and all this other stuff, which is kind of cool.

Similarly, Lily had been exposed to more diverse groups—and thus to ethnic foods—through her children. She talked about one of her son's extracurricular activities: "We did a STEM team for Aiden, and Aiden's partners were Ping and Rahul. And we had it at Ping's house, and her grandmother lived there and only spoke Chinese and made us scallion pancakes."

A number of individuals in the sample discussed celebrating a range of holidays and preparing the foods associated with them even though they had no direct personal connection with the holiday or its traditional foods. Christopher, the man in his mid-seventies who identified strongly with his Italian ethnicity, discussed how his son-in-law, also Italian American, enjoyed cooking all sorts of food and had incorporated Saint Patrick's Day into their annual repertoire. Lily, who came from a WASP background, celebrated Thanksgiving in a modified way that seemed to have arisen, not from any singular relationship, but from her and her family's curiosity about other cuisines and the broader effect of an increasingly diverse society.

> Now there are two Thanksgiving celebrations, one with turkey and one with calzones. So my family always did some sort of wacky turkey thing. Although, after my dad was experimenting with all these other things, we used to have these big gatherings where they would say like, "It's Jamaican Thanksgiving," and we would have a Jamaican theme with sweet potatoes with ginger. You know that was crazy, but that was pretty good.

Ben, who began this chapter, identified as American and had no religious affiliation. His wife was born in Asia. When asked if they had incorporated any new ethnic traditions into their household, he mentioned celebrating Saint Patrick's Day and Cinco de Mayo, "regular holidays that everyone celebrates." As someone with a strong American identity, Ben knew "a lot of families that are still really into their Irish heritage. Well, they're like, third generation. So that's cool that you want to celebrate your forefathers but you're an American, you raise three generations of people here in America, being part of America." His household's celebration of both Saint Patrick's Day and Cinco de Mayo speaks to how he viewed these holidays and foods within the American canon of holidays.

Acquisition of the food habits of the established community has often been viewed as a measurement of assimilation and acculturation, one of the early signs of growing convergence. Unfortunately, such dietary assimilation is also associated with rising obesity rates and declining health outcomes the longer an immigrant group lives in the United States.[51] The data here suggest that changes in food habits flow in both directions and tend to be one of the earlier changes exhibited by established residents, even when confined to private domains.[52] Food habits change and the American palate diversifies through varied processes, including both the process of ethnic retention, whereby new groups work to retain cultural traditions, and the process of assimilation, whereby new groups adopt American holidays but modify them.

Food is an easy means of accommodation, in that established residents are not required to change their values or feel any threat to their identity or status when they enjoy the cuisine of other groups. Food is a form of exchange and acceptance that does not alter the power dynamics. Further, it reinforces a trend toward cultural omnivorism among established Americans; those in the highest tier of American society are especially likely to feel that an appreciation of other cuisines signals their cosmopolitanism.[53]

But neither should these new food experiences be dismissed as irrelevant. Research in the field of cultural psychology finds that individual-level contact with an aspect of a new culture by a member of the established community is the first step in its being incorporated into the mainstream.[54] Consider Avi's comment about his first Thanksgiving at his host family's house and the impression it made on him. Such encounters with new foods in the home of a friend or relative may encourage an individual to try a new restaurant in town or buy new items at the grocery store—possibly even to start a new business venture. Large-scale quantitative analysis has identified the spread of both individual ethnic restaurants and ethnic chains, such as Panda Express and Boloco, that are owned by established Americans, illustrating both relational and appropriative assimilation.[55] While these forms of exposure may not appear to have drastic implications for anyone's life, many of these food traditions have flowed into the mainstream from the ethnic margins.[56]

Local, National, and International Politics

In a number of instances, both the interview and archival data reveal ways in which individual relationships influence established residents' political attitudes. These data, again, speak to the push and pull between new and established groups and the multilevel effects on those interactions. They also reflect how influences and group dynamics change over time.

A *Wellesley Townsman* editorial from November 1943 made a political plea to Wellesley residents regarding the Chinese Exclusion Act.[57] As a conservative-leaning paper during a time of war when the United States was allied with China, the editor sought to overturn the discriminatory immigration policy for the sake of diplomacy. The writer explicitly reminded town residents of their personal relationships: "Otto hopes that the many friends of Madame Chiang Kai-shek in this town and throughout the country will wire their Senators and urge them to follow the good example of the House of Representatives" to vote to overturn the act, which had been in place since 1882. Even with this personal plea to residents to support overturning the law, "Otto" promised readers that any changes in the law would ensure that very few visas were given to those from China.

The impact of relationships between new and established residents was felt in local politics as well. Paul Chin, the longtime owner of Chin's Village, a local Chinese restaurant, placed a full-page political ad in the *Wellesley Townsman* in 1972, encouraging residents to vote on a ballot initiative to allow alcohol to be served in restaurants with fewer than one hundred seats.[58] While Chin's ad suggests a form of civic assimilation, there is also evidence that he influenced the political attitudes and engagement of established residents. Chin ran more political advertisements, in both English and Chinese, and an established resident and friend of Chin's, Leslie Madden, took out an ad on the restaurateur's behalf. Madden told the story of Chin's migration and his contributions to Wellesley and beseeched his fellow townspeople to vote for Chin's position. "I have known Stanley Chin and his family over the entire 23 years that they have been in Wellesley," he wrote in the ad. "I urge my fellow voters to recognize and reward the efforts of one of our fine citizens and businessmen."[59] When the ballot initiative passed and Chin's position won, the impact was felt by individuals and businesses across Wellesley. Although many residents in the town may have wanted the puritanical alcohol ban repealed, Madden vouched for Chin, suggesting that his friend was worthy of their support as a hardworking immigrant who had contributed to Wellesley. And though Chin may have been leveraging his personal relationship with Madden, Madden, in turn, leveraged his personal networks and helped to end temperance in town. The effects ripple out.

In other instances, micro-level interactions in the context of local politics were not so positive; sometimes members of new groups were explicitly targeted. In 1976, town meeting approved the building of a swimming pool at the high school, as they had the prior two years, but given the significant cost, the proposal had to be put to a debt exclusion vote by the entire town. Every district voted against the pool, but "in Precinct B," wrote *Wellesley Townsman* editor-in-chief Max Marple, explicitly calling out the town's Italian American residents, who primarily lived in Precinct B, "the no vote was especially resounding—741 no and 207 yes, for a smashing 3½ to 1 ratio."[60]

Anger followed the publication of Marple's piece, with complaints to the newspaper and letters to the editor, including one from Wellesley resident Bruno Mortarelli: "It is true that we are a large sector of Wellesley's Italian-American population," he wrote, then pointed out that "we are also very proud of our heritage."[61] He also stated that the Italian community made up less than one-quarter of Precinct B. Another letter, by resident Robert DiSchino, stated, "I never knew that we United States citizens of Italian descent constituted such a large proportion of Precinct B. Apparently being of the correct ethnic background gives one the advantage of always being on the side of the majority, although it seems that I heard somewhere that the major proponent of the pool facility was of the same ethnic background."[62] DiSchino, like Mortarelli, refused to let the Italian community be blamed for the defeat and refused to accept the historic discrimination. The response from Marple, who was from the established community, was a letter of apology: "To my friends (and ex-friends) of Italian descent, I can only say that I am sorry."[63]

This exchange over the debt exclusion vote, which may not seem like a major issue, should not be dismissed. In an illustration of the processes of both racialization and assimilation, the vote elicited a response that targeted the Italian community based on their ethnicity. The Italian community responded to this racialization by launching a letter-writing campaign—a long-standing means of civic engagement—in which they made a claim to their Americanness ("We United States citizens of Italian descent"). The outcome of that campaign was an apology from an established individual with a large megaphone (the *Wellesley Townsman*), who most likely wrote differently from then on about new groups in Wellesley.

The interviews also revealed some of the political influence of members of new groups on the established community. Henry, the still-active nonagenarian, explained that while running for townwide positions, he had one-on-one interactions with people from varied backgrounds that compelled him to recognize their different experiences and needs.

Established residents James and Nick felt like they had become more educated human beings, with a more global view, as a result of their diverse relationships. Although they did not explicitly say that their political views had changed, that is, in essence, what happened. James said that his friendships with people from around the world had helped him to better understand US foreign policy and its implications, beyond what he had learned from a textbook. He was also able to see how complicated it was for his closest friends from China, India, and South Korea to travel back to visit family. Nick said he had "candid conversations" with his Iranian friend about what it was like to be Iranian in the post-9/11 era. These conversations were possible only because of the footpaths that had developed between new and established groups in Wellesley. Nick said that these conversations were "insightful and a little eye-opening," even while insisting that his friend's ethnic identity did not come into play in their relationship and that he did not notice it.

Members of new groups who were interviewed spoke to their feelings of individual political efficacy in local politics. For example, Anjali discussed the expansion of the holiday calendar: "I am thrilled Wellesley High School, come 2024–25, is going to have Chinese New Year, is going to have Eid and Diwali. . . . So, two people voted against it, and I'm going to be giving them a few speeches on school committee. Two people who voted against are going to hear from me." Anjali was speaking as an individual rather than as a member of either a formal or informal group. Mainstream political interactions reflect her civic assimilation.

A Greater Global Toolbox

Multiple established residents discussed other ways in which they had been impacted through their individual interactions with members of new groups. They mentioned language, diverse activities, cultural practices and norms, and greater global knowledge as just some of the ways in which brushing up against newer members of the community had influenced their lives.

Of the five established residents married to foreign-born individuals among the interviewees, two spoke their partner's language in the household and had passed it on to their children, who were bilingual. The workplace was another area where individual relationships translated into the acquisition of a second or even third language. Lucas, the Italian American small-business owner, learned Italian from his grandmother. With many of his employees hailing from Portugal, Brazil, or another part of Latin America, he spoke what he referred to as an "Italian-Portuguese-Spanish mash-up."

Joyce, a woman in her seventies, had become highly involved with capoeira, an Afro-Latino activity that is part dance, part sport. She had even learned some Portuguese as a result of her participation in capoeira and regularly attended social events with Brazilian friends she had made through this activity in Wellesley. Her participation in capoeira had expanded her cultural knowledge beyond the activity itself.

Established residents also discussed the knowledge they had gained from their more diverse contacts. Tammy had learned much more about the Middle East through a friend of hers from Egypt, including the fact that not all Egyptians were Muslim. Nick, in talking about his Iranian friend, explained that "sometimes he makes me aware of interesting experiences, or, you know, he has to go to Iran when his dad died, and just kind of the customs around dealing with a death or something in another country was all interesting."

For a few established residents, their contact with other groups had enriched their lives both personally and professionally. Theresa, a proud Irish American resident who worked in real estate, talked about what she had learned culturally in her job and from her increasingly diverse clientele:

> It's so diverse now, which is wonderful, and culturally you learn things. And each culture is different. And objections are real cultural objections. Indian culture doesn't want to have any houses facing south because that's where death comes from. And it doesn't matter if it's in their price point in a location they want. If it's south-facing, they won't do it.

Of her Chinese clients, Theresa said, "When you're negotiating . . . they'll often say, 'Can we make the number $450,888?' 'Sure. Why's that? Is that positive or is it a good luck number?'"

Theresa connected her career as a realtor with the need to be much more attuned to cultural differences—what mattered to a family because of their ethnicity, the impact of a multigenerational household on a family's needs, respect for the taboos in a particular tradition. Theresa was able to experience such impacts because her clients had opted for residential assimilation in moving to Wellesley rather than looking for property in an ethnic enclave, like Chinatown, or a Boston-area ethnoburb, like Quincy.[64] Their structural integration was her variegated assimilation.

Lucy, who worked in consulting, thought that her contact with those from different groups had improved her professionally: "I have a different perspective on my job and my community and my purpose." Lily, a teacher, also felt that she had benefited from contact with more diverse students and parents. She explained that, to her, the idea of "culturally responsive teaching" meant "having a clue what your culture is [and] that other people's culture is different." These impacts on established residents are made possible only when new groups integrate into mainstream neighborhoods, workplaces, and educational systems.

Identity

Established residents also spoke powerfully about how their identity had been shaped by the entrance into Wellesley of new groups and the unending process of becoming for both the town and the larger society. A number of Jewish residents talked about their experiences growing up as Jewish kids in Wellesley and about what they thought had changed for the better. Their views reflected not only the altered composition of the town's established residents but also how the larger society had diversified. Noah said:

> Today, I mean, everything is celebrated. And I think I noticed that with high school, right. I mean, when there's a holiday for any ethnic group, I know that there's a celebration, because I know my daughter has gone to a few things, and I can't be specific on which ones, but she's like, "I went to Mina's," or "Mina and I got together today." And it was her friends, and they celebrated whatever it was. And it was kind of cool, you know? And so it's nice to see that everything stood out there now, and I've also noticed, too, with kids now that people aren't as uncomfortable to express who they are and where they're from. I think growing up, you know, growing up Jewish, yes, it was uncomfortable. Yeah, it was uncomfortable. It wasn't easy. My friends made it easy for me.

Noah's statement that "everything is celebrated" will be examined in chapters 5 and 6, which look at issues around identity and recognition moving out of private households and one-on-one friendships and into public realms. Leah, a slightly younger Jewish resident, shared feelings similar to Noah's:

> I had, probably in my friend group, there was one Jewish person, but most of my friends were not Jewish. Being Jewish felt very different. I don't think for them [my children], I think it was a different feel for them. But I also think it's just a different time. So, for me, I felt being Jewish and I'm not sure they felt being Jewish. Does that make sense? You know, some of it's internalized for me, how I always felt like an outsider. I don't think that if I were to talk to them [my children], they did not feel that way at all, I don't think. So I think they loved growing up in Wellesley, let's put it that way. And I did not. . . . They definitely just felt very connected to the town, they felt part of the town.

Abby, another Jewish resident of similar age, said, "I didn't want to move here specifically because of that. But that part is different here now."

Jewish lifelong residents were not the only ones whose sense of identity and belonging had changed for the better over time. Gianni, an Italian American resident, described his experiences:

> I went over to my friend Matt's house, so we were on the same team, and I walked into his house, and they lived in the estates area. His dad was a banker, which was really popular. . . . So, totally rich family. And the mother looks at me, and she looks at me, she goes, "Oh my God, Gianni Franconi, I thought you were gonna look so much more ethnic."

Another friend's father gave Gianni a nickname, based on his Italian ethnicity and Italian-sounding name. A college roommate in the 1980s commented on his complexion. Gianni went on to talk about the changes he had experienced:

> You know, just on the name thing, you know, now my name is kind of intriguing to people, right? Because Italian culture has changed. Italian culture is now popular. People realize how important Italian culture has been to art, to food, to science, to everything, engineering, you know, you name it, accounting. A lot of it started there. So now when I say "Gianni" to people, they're like, "Ooh, that's . . . that's like a royal Italian name." So I get a very different reaction now than I did when I was a kid. . . . So the diversity that's grown around me has actually helped me. You know what I mean? We were sort of stand-alones, you know, because everybody here who was Italian were basically the people that built the houses and did the stonework. We were some of the first Italians that came in that the dad or mom actually did not work in the trades. You know, and then the diversity that came around us helped us become more normal.

Gianni talked about how his child's experience had differed: "My daughter's name is Giovanna. . . . But when Giovanna went to school, we called her 'Joanna.' By the time she graduated Wellesley High School, every one of her friends and her teachers was calling her Giovanna. So, Joanna looked at it as a way to differentiate herself." As American society has become increasingly diverse and multiculturalism has been embraced, Gianni saw the effect on his children—an example of the global touching on the local to influence individual experiences. The ability of new groups to retain their ethnic identities at lower cost today than in the past has implications for old new groups.

In a similar vein, Phil, a second-generation Chinese American college student, used to speak only English with his parents, in part because the local elementary school encouraged them to speak English at home. Other Chinese residents told similar stories. As he entered high school, Phil decided that he wanted to retain his Mandarin; now he spoke only Mandarin at home with his parents. In a less explicit way, Theresa's contact with a more diverse real estate clientele caused her to rethink her own history. She saw her clients' immigration histories as all connecting back to her own family's immigrant past, and she was able to identify similarities between individuals and groups that are essential for improving minority-majority relationships.[65] These are all illustrations of retaining and reconnecting with one's ethnic past, even as individuals are increasingly assimilating into the mainstream—but a mainstream that is increasingly diverse.[66]

At the same time, Frank, an Italian American resident in his eighties who stressed the latter identity, discussed the impact of the changing demographics and climate on his ethnic attachment. While Gianni attributed his greater acceptance in the community and his children's desire to be known for their Italian heritage—a result of their more global outlook and more positive view of Italian culture—Frank attributed his increased connection with his Italian background to feeling under siege. Wellesley, like many towns across the country, has in recent years had significant public debates over the removal or renaming of Columbus Day, a topic discussed at length in chapter 6. These public debates and one-on-one interactions had impacted Frank's identity:

> I am third generation. I don't think of myself as an immigrant. I didn't face the obstacles my grandfather faced. I don't know if you've been following this or not, but there was a recent vote in the town. The Italian Americans in Wellesley were trying to save Columbus Day, and people think I just got off the boat. Well, I didn't. How am I supposed to react to this, you know? But these people were so persistent about changing, replacing Columbus Day and not taking a day that has been set aside for them anyway, the day after Thanksgiving.... Yeah, well, this is something I got swept up in that I didn't think I would have any role to play. I was born here and I'm a native.

Frank had very recently been doing a lot of research into his family background, both in Italy and in Wellesley. When asked what prompted this recent interest, he replied, "As time goes on, you realize that you know, the roots that we thought we had settled are kind of tenuous, you know? So it's multiple questions. I'm always interested in history, and now that we have been swept up in the Indigenous/Italian American [debate], I had been collecting, for no reason, stories and articles from the *Townsman*." Such ethnic reactivity is not unusual, nor has ethnicity become fully irrelevant to most Americans.[67]

It is important to note that while Gianni discussed the positive factors that have influenced how he and his children identify ethnically, the discussions around removing Columbus Day from the calendar have also made him feel under assault. Christopher, while not connecting his feelings of "otherness" to the Columbus Day debate, talked about feeling like an outsider growing up. He had observed a form of racialization experienced by Italian residents throughout much of the twentieth century in Wellesley. "I think when you're young," he explained, "... then ... you really ... it's important to fit in to your peer groups. Like, we always felt we were the Italians, you know. We're a little different than everybody else."

Some established residents of Jewish or Italian ethnicity who had struggled with their identities throughout their lives found greater acceptance today than they had as children. Meanwhile, other lifelong residents were seeking greater ethnic identification. Among some of those who had long been accepted, today's more permitted, and even celebrated, cultural diversity had translated into a greater desire for an ethnic identity of their own. This seemingly ironic influence of new members on established residents' sense of identity has been recognized in prior research by Jiménez.[68]

Courtney, introduced earlier as the product of a Jewish father and a Christian mother of western European descent, desired something she thought was more interesting than her own background:

> White people often want to, in some ways, distance themselves from their Whiteness, and I think as a young person that was sort of done for me and I did it for myself. And so, I'm a White woman, but because I had Portuguese ancestry and a Jewish last name—and because I think other people—I have a friend of mine, we grew up in Wellesley together. Her mom's Puerto Rican and her dad's White, but we would joke, like, we're the most ethnic girls that Wellesley's got in our grade. And I think part of it is like, literally, also just because I happened to be dark-haired. The first time I met someone, before I moved [back] to Wellesley, I met someone, and he said to me, "You can't be from Wellesley, you don't have blond hair," and we laughed. But I do think some of that—in that time there was so much homogeneity in the community that I was identified a little bit as an "other," and I think I sort of enjoyed that. And ran with it.

Growing attachment to an ethnic identity is a trend seen in an increasingly multiracial and multiethnic society, and darker skin tones, both relatively and objectively, are viewed as more "authentic."[69]

The aversion to whiteness showed up in an interview with Maria, a highly educated Latina immigrant in town. Her daughter had come home from elementary school years earlier, she told me, asking if the family was White. Both Maria and her daughter were light-skinned, but Maria rejected a White identity, firmly stating that she was Latina. This stance was in marked contrast to how prior generations of immigrants sought to position themselves in closer proximity to those deemed White, as evidenced by the numerous books and articles invariably titled *How the [Name of Ethnic Group] Became White*.[70] These changing trends also speak to the ways in which national and even international sociohistorical trends influence individual identities.[71]

Other lifelong residents also discussed a desire for greater ethnicity. Lily, of WASP descent, sought an identity she thought more interesting than her own.

> So occasionally in school, somebody would say, "What's your ethnic background?" And I'd be like, well, maybe like, there's something interesting,

but mostly, it's really boring. And other people had really cool ethnic backgrounds and spoke cool languages. And you know, [the name] Smith is not really great. My mother's last name is Wadsworth, right? Like, pretty darn English. You know, if you look [it] up, it's like Longfellow and Johnson and you know, like, just . . . nothing. So I mean, at the time, you know, I was awash in White privilege, but did not recognize that for what it was. And I felt, you know, kind of left out of the cool stuff. Because I had no color and no interesting ethnic traditions, no interesting clothing, right? Like English, English was kind of boring.

Joyce's Irish Catholic background was not emphasized by her family when she was growing up, in contrast to the families of many others with an Irish Catholic heritage. She had longed for an ethnic identity: "I used to pretend I was Jewish. I'd always be like, 'Baruch atah Adonai Eloheinu [reciting a Hebrew prayer]. . . . It's like I did everything. I tried to fit in. My sister actually converted to Judaism." Joyce said that the various backgrounds of her contacts and friends "makes them more interesting to me, I think, you know, [they] bring more from their backgrounds, and it's just more fun. And actually, I find that immigrants are way friendlier and more fun than Americans in many ways." She preferred to socialize with friends she had made through ethnic-specific activities, in contrast to the trend occasionally identified by prior research of established White Americans emphasizing their general European background and their whiteness.[72]

Conclusion

Chapter 3 explored the various settings that allowed interfaith, interracial, and interethnic friendships and intimate partnerships to develop across Wellesley over time. This chapter has examined what actually happened "on the ground," presenting extensive evidence of the footpaths that developed between members of the established and new groups. These footpaths exposed established residents to religious traditions new to them, unfamiliar ethnic-specific foods, altered political views, and practices and artifacts from different cultures, including languages, leisure activities, and norms.

The generally positive micro-level interactions identified in these data—in contrast to findings from other case studies on immigrant-established relations—points to a number of differences within this setting.[73] With Wellesley's high socioeconomic bar for entry, most new residents are from the top 1 or 2 percent of the population. Ethnoracial differences may matter somewhat less in a context of uniformly high socioeconomic status. As we will see in the upcoming chapter, conflicts certainly occur in Wellesley, but in contrast to other towns that have been examined, conflicts tend not to fall out along ethnic lines. Although

Wellesley has become significantly more diverse than it once was, White Christian residents are still the majority. Other towns studied present more extreme cases; with foreign-born and non-White residents making up a significantly larger percentage of their population, established residents in these towns are likely to feel a greater sense of threat. Perhaps over time, with shifts in demographics, the debates and tensions in Wellesley will take on a racialized nature. We can only hope that will not be the case.

Wellesley's changing nature has also inspired established individuals to consider, or reconsider, their own ethnic identity. Some established residents from old new groups, such as Jewish Wellesleyites, have felt a greater sense of inclusion, while others, such as Italian residents, feel that their identity has been under threat. Still other members of the established community have been prompted by the town's increasing diversity to seek a greater ethnic identity in their own lives.

The influence of new groups on established groups can only be understood by examining *both* groups, as they exist in relationship to one other. Individuals from newer groups may work to retain aspects of their cultural heritage, for both themselves and their children, but having opted to live in a community such as Wellesley rather than an ethnic enclave or ethnoburb, they necessarily brush up against and have an influence on established residents, even when they do not intend to. Alternatively, newer residents may seek to become integrated into the community by establishing new relationships or celebrating "American" holidays while still maintaining aspects of their own cultural background. Many individuals from newer groups practice both cultural retention and assimilation at the same time. But it is not only the actions of newer group members that matter. How the established community responds to newer residents, particularly if it reacts with racialization and discrimination, can set off its own chain reaction and reformation. All these paths lead to variegated assimilation for established residents. The glocal nature of assimilation can be seen when stirrings of change locally, nationally, or internationally influence attitudes and reactivate long-dormant ethnic identities.

The influences of new members on established residents and their respective responses also speak to inequalities between individuals and groups.[74] Micro-level interactions between individuals take place in private spheres, but they also occur within a larger context that may prioritize the practices, needs, or desires of one group over another's. Ethnic-specific, hybrid and mainstream formal organizations play important roles in the transformation of a community, especially when tensions rise as groups brush up against each other in public settings. In chapter 5, we turn to an examination of these community organizations.

= Chapter 5 =

Community Organizations as Cause and Consequence of Change

Phil, the young American-born Chinese resident who insisted on speaking only Mandarin at home when he was in high school, told me that he always wanted his mother to volunteer with PTO because that was what the other moms did. Phil's mom, like many other immigrant parents, shied away from such participation. Chinese residents were unfamiliar with school volunteerism, since Chinese schools were the sole domain of educators. Chinese residents also explained that their language skills made them hesitant to participate, and their full-time jobs added another barrier. Nevertheless, both new and established residents discussed how some immigrant and ethnic members of the community participated in PTO and other school-related organizations, teaching about Lunar New Year, Diwali, or Hanukkah, for instance, or providing skill-based assistance with STEM activities. Such instances of engagement illustrated the civic and social assimilation of new residents, who brought their ethnic, religious, and cultural backgrounds to interactions with the larger established community.

Jing, a Chinese resident with several children who attended Wellesley public schools, put great value on her Chinese language and culture, which she wanted to pass on to the next generation. This commitment to retaining her cultural background led her to participate extensively in the Wellesley Chinese Language School (WCLS), where she filled various administrative and academic roles. Through her WCLS involvement, Jing planned community-wide Chinese New Year events attended by those of other backgrounds, worked with the Wellesley school district to have Mandarin courses offered in the high school, and engaged with established residents to do everything from leasing space for the WCLS to working with town officials when Asian hate crimes began to spike during the COVID pandemic. Jing's attempts at cultural retention translated into contact with and impact on the established community.

Lakshmi and Sherry, as well as many other new and established residents, discussed World of Wellesley, an organization, established over thirty years earlier, that described itself as "anti-racist and anti-biased." Events sponsored by the organization included an annual community-wide Martin Luther King Jr. breakfast, which was often held at one of the town's three colleges; Eid celebrations cosponsored with Muslims of Wellesley; and multicultural festivals and book clubs. The nonprofit was founded after a Black professional athlete was stopped by Wellesley police and accused of robbing a bank. While this organization was formed in reaction to this explicitly racist incident, it had expanded to address various forms of racial and ethnic discrimination and to create a sense of belonging for all residents by increasing knowledge about and appreciation of a variety of cultures. This reaction to a racist incident in the community translated into an organization that impacted much of Wellesley, reformulating mainstream institutions and practices. Some established residents, however, view the organization as politicized and divisive.

One of Tocqueville's major observations about the early United States generally and New England in particular was the extensiveness of its civil society.[1] He argued that this characteristic was critical for a healthy democracy. Émile Durkheim, writing in Tocqueville's own language and land more than fifty years later, also addressed the importance of civil society and the intermediary bodies that functioned between the unbridled desires and sovereignty of the individual and larger governmental institutions, particularly during periods of rapid change.[2] These *"corps intermédiaires,"* Durkheim wrote, could integrate individuals and groups, creating a sense of social solidarity; establish a moral framework; and provide advocacy and serve as a counter to the state.

Civil society remains vibrant in Wellesley, which has a long and rich tradition of citizen engagement. Formal organizations in town include PTOs, scouts, Rotary, Kiwanis, Elks, women's clubs, the library, the local newspaper, and various other private social, political, civic, and business organizations.[3] These mainstream organizations provide information and services, government accountability, and advocacy. Further, they provide settings for the assimilation of new groups, as well as stages for interaction between members of new and established groups. Sometimes an organization's inclusion, interaction, or transformation efforts are intentional, recognized, and accepted by established groups. At other times, its work toward inclusion of new groups and transformation of a community go unrecognized, even when there is evidence that change has occurred. In still other cases, such changes are recognized but considered unwelcome.

Immigrant and ethnic-specific organizations also serve a vital role in both cultural retention and assimilation. Immigrant-serving organizations

Community Organizations as Cause and Consequence of Change 99

play critical roles for new residents, even while they may lack the resources of the mainstream.[4] In addition to providing services to help the newest immigrants assimilate—such as language classes, housing, job postings, and citizenship information—today's immigrant-serving organizations tend to take a strength-based approach, recognizing the various forms of cultural capital that groups bring with them. Such organizations are no longer simply about Americanization, along the lines of the old-school settlement houses of the late nineteenth and early twentieth centuries, but also serve to make claims around cultural recognition, functioning as powerful forces of incorporation and neo-assimilation.

Ethnic organizations are often distinct from immigrant-serving organizations, as their constituents may be second-, third-, or even fourth-generation Americans. Herbert Gans identifies four distinct roles that these organizations may play in a community for later-generation ethnic Americans: promotional, commercial, performing, and preserving, with some serving multiple functions.[5] Promotional organizations keep an ethnic identity alive in part by just existing; commercial organizations produce or distribute ethnic goods and services; performing organizations enact or reenact ethnic traditions for both coethnics and other groups; and preserving organizations pass down traditions by providing language and other cultural heritage classes. Both immigrant- and ethnic-serving organizations illustrate and even facilitate aspects of mainstream assimilation and cultural retention, often at the same time. They may also serve as vehicles for responses to racialization and discrimination.

Finally, there is the formation and transformation of hybrid organizations that intentionally straddle both old and new groups. These include interfaith, intercultural, and civic groups focused on including newer residents, increasing everyone's sense of belonging, and making Wellesley a more welcoming place. These groups and others like them often explicitly build footpaths between individuals of different backgrounds and bridges between groups.

Just as the micro-level interactions and influences examined in the last chapter speak to a process of variegated assimilation for the established, similar processes are found at the organizational level. New residents participating in established institutions are practicing a form of civic assimilation, and in turn the backgrounds they bring with them influence established residents. Members of immigrant and ethnic groups may band together to establish an ethnic-specific organization in an effort to retain their cultural identity, but inevitably they come into contact with established residents, be it to rent space, request language assistance, or sponsor community-wide cultural events. Finally, members of new groups may work to reform established institutions, or they may start new ones in reaction to their experiences with racialization and discrimination, either within the organization or outside of it, with far-ranging implications.

The Remaking of Established Organizations

Interviews with organizational leaders and lifelong residents, participant observations, and archival data point to varied degrees of inclusion, transformation, and recognition of change within mainstream organizations in Wellesley. From the perspective of new group members, such inclusion and activity signal forms of structural integration and civic assimilation. But because new members in any of these mainstream organizations remain small in number and the organizational focus is not on specific ethnic, racial, or religious groups, recognition of the organization's increasing diversification and the effect of that diversification often goes unnoticed.

Pam, a former president of a social club, followed up after the initial interview to say that she had since realized that there were women of varied ethnic backgrounds in her club whom she had not recognized as such owing to their high levels of education and income. She said, in regard to immigration, "I think of like Dreamers and DACA [Deferred Action for Childhood Arrivals] and immigration at the border, and certain things come to mind, and I don't think of women who came over to do graduate school and then stay and have a family and live in Wellesley or these various other people that, like, they're technically immigrants, and I just didn't . . . that's not how I think of them." This statement is an explicit recognition of how difference is, or is not, constructed. Pam may have been unable to see diversity within her group because she felt no pressure or threat from the foreign-born members. She discussed the backgrounds of club members born in Europe, Latin America, and Asia and then explained a proposed antipoverty initiative to be undertaken in one woman's country of origin. Although its community-focused charter prevented the organization from taking it on, even the discussion of the initiative spoke to the new member's influence.

Similarly, Liam, a former president of another civic organization, when asked whether his club had changed in terms of ethnicity or race, responded that there was "one African American" member. Liam's and Pam's limited view of diversity—that one must be Black and/or lower-income to be diverse in Wellesley—recalls many of the conversations discussed in the prior chapter. Liam did, however, go on to talk about a Latina woman in the organization, and the organization's funding of a program in adolescent wellness in that member's country of origin. A member who hailed from Africa had initiated a program to tackle local food insecurity. Such organizational boundary expansion results in diversified programming and initiatives that reach out into the broader community, touching even those who are not members of the organization.

The one-on-one footpaths discussed in the prior chapter are often the starting point for new members participating in mainstream organizations—an established resident inviting a new neighbor to attend a meeting, a parent speaking to another parent at school pickup. These individual relationships transform into ladders, leading up to organizations. The influence of members from new groups touches other individuals within the organization. Additionally, programming and organizational initiatives can serve as bridges reaching outside of the organization and across the town to impact both new and established residents.

The Evolution of Holiday Celebrations

Interviews with both past and present leaders of mainstream organizations revealed clear evidence of the impact of new groups on the established community, even though it was not always recognized. Pam said that her organization, which largely reflected the demographics of the town, had struggled to diversify. She also noted that the club's reliance on personal networks to recruit often reinforced the club's homogeneity. She said that "we really rely on our members to recruit other members," rather than coming up with a strategy to diversify their ranks. She reminisced about how the club had changed over the decades:

> I think like any modern-day organization, we don't really touch religion. So it's not like we do one thing around the holidays. We do a Yankee swap, and I guess technically that could be more related to Christmas than anything else, although we're careful or thoughtful in not making it a Christmas party. We have an event that would occur during the holiday season, but it's a community celebration. It's not a religious one, and it's not affiliated with a religious holiday. If I had to guess, I know that there are many women who are Jewish in the club.... I do know that there used to be a big event in the Christmas season where I think Santa was there, if I'm remembering correctly, and it was really for members and their kids and it was very Christmas-oriented, and we don't do that anymore.

Santa appeared annually at the club until about 2010. This is clearly a change in the organization, and one most likely felt by both members who were part of the old established community (White and Christian) and members of newer groups (Jews, Muslims, Hindus, Buddhists, and other members of non-Christian groups). Their efforts to retain their religious and cultural identities ended up transforming this established organization. In recent years, some of the organization's leaders had even come from these new groups—Jewish, Muslim, Asian—in a power redistribution that reflected greater relational equality and integration.[6] The assimilation of women from new groups into the organization eventually led to organizational change.

It is also important to note that Pam described the community-wide event taking place around the holidays as a "community event," not a "religious event." Making this distinction was intentional, and the event was explicitly planned as nonreligious and open to people of all backgrounds. Expanding the historically Protestant hierarchy to one more Judeo-Christian in nature—and perhaps even further to include other religious traditions—is another illustration of the organization's greater relational integration and extension of bridges beyond its boundaries. This event was planned as a townwide celebration in which everyone in town could participate without feeling like they needed to repress some part of their core identity.

Knowledge of new holidays spread to other far-reaching organizations in town, such as the PTOs. These institutions not only expanded their boundaries to include members of new groups but also reformulated programming, initiatives, and practices that touched established residents in the broader community. Interviews with lifelong residents provided further evidence of this spreading influence, both in their own lives and in the lives of their children. Anna talked about her children's greater exposure to other cultures through non-academic programming featuring parent school volunteers: "You know, my kids had someone come in, and they talked about Diwali, and my kids got this little beautiful, from India, a little incense holder. You know, that's kind of more of a meaningful, real experience, because it's firsthand. But I didn't have anything firsthand."

Kate, whose children were active in both a dance troupe and scouts, discussed how her children's participation in mainstream organizations had increased their exposure to other cultures:

> Both my girls have always been dancers. And so, you know, they've been part of a small dance studio . . . since they were three. And in that group, we've had a couple of Chinese families. And one of the women is involved in the local Chinese school in the annual Chinese New Year program. And so our girls have gone and been part of the performance.

Kate's example illustrates how established residents are impacted by the diversification of mainstream organizations. Kate's children felt the impact of group diversification when they had the opportunity to dance in the Chinese New Year's program, but it resulted from new residents' participating in established organizations. Her words also revealed the impact of ethnic-specific organizations' practices to preserve and promote an ethnic group's cultural heritage and the cross-pollination with mainstream groups that occurs.

Interviews with Chinese and Indian residents underscore the stories told by established residents. A number of the former discussed going into their children's schools to teach about Lunar New Year, Diwali, and

Holi. Some individuals participated through a PTO, others volunteered independently, and still others said that a teacher reached out to them. These various forms of participation align with the micro-level footpaths that people developed with neighbors, fellow parents, and teachers and that sometimes transitioned to ladders drawing individuals from new groups up and into community organizations. Mei, Jing, and Anh organized events in both the public school system and the Chinese Language School, making both events open to everyone. These interviewees, within the context of this organization, were working to practice, preserve, and promote Chinese culture, along the lines previously identified by Gans.[7] Priya and Lakshmi participated in Hindu celebrations in the schools, both despite and because of feelings of marginalization and experiences of racialization; their experience illustrated the interactive process of racialization, reaction, and reformation of the established. As these parents worked to retain their cultural identities and pass them on to their children, they were also influencing established residents, such as Kate's and Anna's children. Such unintentional impact on the mainstream by those engaged in cultural retention has been identified in prior research.[8] New residents take multiple paths in pursuit of cultural retention, resulting in variegated assimilation for the established community.

A Changing Culinary Landscape

Food as a form of cultural exchange was discussed in the prior chapter's examination of individual relationships, but new foods can also be spread more broadly through mainstream organizations, altering the culinary landscape.

One of the main functions of the *Wellesley Townsman* has long been keeping its readers apprised of community events, ranging from church services to lectures to social events. Starting as early as the 1930s, Chinese food began appearing in the *Townsman* as a regular culinary option, a trend taking place across the country.[9] From the 1940s through the 1980s, organizations such as the Wellesley Hills Congregational Church, the Wellesley Hills Junior Women's Club, and the Republican Club, as well as numerous other mainstream organizations, either regularly served Chinese dinners at their events or held their events at Chinese restaurants in the area.[10] Chinese restaurants are examples of commercial cultural ventures.[11] Established residents may have viewed Chinese dinners as an "exotic" cuisine, giving diners a feel of sophistication and cosmopolitanism. Their adoption of Chinese food is an early example of cultural omnivorism—a theory that the elite develop broader palates than those of lower socioeconomic standing.[12] Their taste for Chinese food was yet another marker of distinction and difference. Ironically, the expansion of palates and cultural boundaries maintained other borders around class and status.

Mainstream grocery stores, including A&P, Star Market, and First National, began advertising Chinese foods—or American versions of them—in their advertising circulars in the 1930s.[13] Fuji Foods was highlighted in these advertisements, which listed chop suey, chow mein, bean sprouts, and imported soy sauce. In 1940, these same grocery stores began to advertise "Jewish bread by Kasanof's Model Bakery," later renamed "Kasanof's Jewish Breads."[14] Kosher pickles also appeared in circulars.[15] A March 1960 A&P circular advertised "Chinese-Italian-Kosher foods . . . imported and domestic specialty foods to please particular tastes."[16] Although the pitch may have been directed at those originally from China, Italy, and eastern Europe, the presence of these food items on the shelves of mainstream grocery stores reflected the expansion of American foodways. Bagels also began to appear in ads in the 1960s; the Wellesley Supermarket advertised them as "delicious when toasted."[17] Starting in 1973, Lender's Bagels were regularly advertised in grocery store circulars.[18] The bagel had gone mainstream.

Ethnic foods also appeared on the menus of mainstream restaurants, in keeping with the macro-trends identified in prior research.[19] A 1932 article on the Chinese Liichee Grove Restaurant in Wellesley discussed the popularity of the restaurant's chop suey and noted its appearance on menus at other restaurants that had never heard of it before.[20] An advertisement from 1939 in the *Wellesley Townsman* for Fred Kennedy's Grill in Natick introduced "our homemade Chinese chicken chow mein."[21] These local examples are emblematic of what was going on nationally.[22] The Beaconsfield Hotel began to advertise its kosher options in 1959, and in 1960 its ads regularly publicized "Halls for Rent—Catering for Kosher, Chinese, and Italian food."[23]

The diversifying population and the accompanying demand for ethnic foods had several implications for the established community. Although it was unlikely that someone who did not keep kosher would choose to have a kosher wedding at the Beaconsfield Hotel, the fact that hotels and mainstream grocery stores had adjusted their offerings was an important change. As new groups moved to the suburbs and advanced economically, mainstream organizations probably did the economic calculations and decided it was worth the cost to offer such options.

A different calculation may have been behind the Chinese and Italian offerings on "American" menus and in mainstream grocery stores as early as the 1940s and '50s. Aware that the established community saw these offerings as "exotic" options for consumption, mainstream restaurants and grocery stores adopted ethnic foods as a form of appropriative assimilation.[24] When aspects of the immigrant or ethnic culture are acquired by the established culture and become a part of it, the established culture is reshaped in a never-ending process of becoming.

This integration of ethnic food into the Wellesley mainstream continued through other channels. Chinese and Italian food became part of the regular rotation on school lunch menus, as well as at the senior center, beginning in the 1970s. A letter to the editor of the *Townsman* in 1983 from the president of an elementary PTO cited the school year as an "an unqualified success. . . . Parents of varied cultural heritage involved the children in preparing Japanese sushi, Greek pastry, and Jewish potato pancakes."[25] Sophia, a woman of Greek descent, said that she learned about Hanukkah and the foods associated with it through a PTO initiative during her time in the Wellesley Public School System. As a parent who went in and did just such a lesson, Sadie echoed this experience.

Chinese cooking classes were also marketed to the established community, first by Chinese immigrants and then by established residents themselves.[26] The "Everyday Gourmet," a local woman, ran weekly ads, starting in the 1970s, for her Chinese, Japanese, French, and Italian cooking classes—a clear illustration of appropriative assimilation.[27] And in a sign of old new groups gaining hold of the microphone, a Jewish guest writer for the *Wellesley Townsman* provided recipes around the Jewish holidays throughout the 1980s.[28]

New Language Opportunities

Italian language classes offered by the YWCA were advertised in the *Wellesley Townsman* as early as 1933, most likely aimed at those established residents who viewed a knowledge of Italian as critical to understanding high art and music. It is of note that Italian ceased to be taught at the high school in 1939, and in 1940 the evening classes in Italian were not offered owing to low enrollment. The international scene, specifically the war and Italy's alignment with Germany, may have played a role in these local shifts, speaking to the larger context in which local decision-making takes place.

In contrast, a 1964 classified ad offered tutoring in Yiddish, and in 1971 Boston University advertised classes in "exotic" languages, including Yiddish.[29] The BU ad made an explicit appeal to older generations, who were likely to have assimilated to the point of losing their knowledge of this Judeo-German dialect. These various linguistic initiatives were attempts to preserve heritage languages like Yiddish.[30]

Wellesley Continuing Education began to offer Mandarin in 1964 with "Mrs. Wang" teaching these classes.[31] Ruth Tung, an elderly resident living in a nursing home in Wellesley, began advertising her services as a Mandarin tutor in 1971.[32] Language schools saw a shift starting in the 1970s, when more of their teachers were now established residents. One advertisement offered "Chinese lessons, Mandarin pronunciation,

Wade-Giles, Harvard, or Yale Romanization."[33] An article in 1977 about Mandarin classes through Wellesley Continuing Education provided the credentials of the teacher, James Lanigan, who had a degree in Chinese studies and learned Chinese while serving in the US military.[34] Mrs. Wang and Mrs. Tung had been replaced—or at least supplemented—by Mr. Lanigan.

These language schools were a significant indication that established residents were opting to acquire another language rather than passively encountering it in the public realm. This new interest in languages reflected the growing role of multiculturalism, globalization, and cultural omnivorism among the upper tiers of both Wellesley and American society.[35] The rising interest in Mandarin in particular reflected America's growing interest in China as President Richard Nixon moved to encourage the country to open up. The data also illustrate a certain amount of appropriative assimilation as classes came to be taught by established residents.[36]

Changes in the Local Vernacular

Among immigration scholars, language is often looked upon as both indicator and predictor of assimilation. Speaking English influences the extent to which members of new groups can succeed academically, integrate into the mainstream economy, gain information, and participate in the larger conversation in the host society. The effect extends beyond an individual's ability to speak the language to *how* they speak it—their accent and vocabulary as well as their confidence.[37] Language reflects and reinforces power dynamics. As such, the transformation of English, from the inclusion of new words to the modification of old phrases, speaks to the growing influence of new groups.

The *Wellesley Townsman* introduced in small ways the transformation of the English language. As early as 1951, articles about Jewish holidays, while often still written by established journalists, at times used Hebrew words, such as the Jewish months of the year. In the same year, announcements about upcoming services at a local synagogue used the word "shabbat" rather than "sabbath," although that usage alternated for decades.[38] The newspaper's move to incorporate Hebrew words at this particular time reflected the changing international climate—namely, the founding of Israel in 1948. Once again, the local reflected the global. The Yiddish words and phrases that occasionally appeared in the *Townsman*'s articles were part of the wave of new words incorporated into the English language over the course of the twentieth century. A 1970 article on a local election was entitled "Counters (and Kibitzers!)" and a 1972 ad for a home goods store in town referred to a *"balaboosta,"* a Yiddish term that means a "perfect homemaker."[39]

Like many local newspapers, religious services and events appeared weekly in the *Wellesley Townsman*, in a section entitled "Church Services." Since the wording of this heading remained unchanged long after Temple Beth Elohim was founded in 1960, synagogue services were listed under this banner of Christianity. In 1976, the *Wellesley Townsman* changed the heading to "Religious Services," and then to "Worship Services." These seemingly small changes were in fact symbolically important. Although there were periodic reversions to using "church" as an umbrella term for all religious institutions, there was clearly a trend toward changed language. Similarly, ads as early as 1942 advertised "non-sectarian" funeral services, and the John Doherty Colonial Funeral Home promised that "our staff are equipped to serve every family of every religious belief and are familiar with the rites of every religious ceremony."[40] Starting in 1948, the wording was changed to "serving all religions."[41]

The *Wellesley Townsman* also showed evidence of a transitioning voice—that is, who it chose to speak for a group. Established residents had firmly held the microphone in the early years, but in the latter half of the twentieth century members of new groups began to take control and write their own stories, both figuratively and literally, thus altering the newspaper's language (recall the article title "Counters [and Kibitzers!]"). In the interest of showing readers what life was like in mental health facilities, an article from 1979 described a fictitious patient at Charles River Hospital, who was given the option of attending Friday night services at a local temple.[42] Other articles also exhibited greater inclusivity in language, such as an article from 1981 that discussed the many roles played by teachers, including "mother, father, priest, or rabbi."[43] Judaism was becoming mainstream.

The impact of new groups on the English language is further evidenced in an interview with a local journalist. When asked how changes in the composition of the community had influenced him and his organization, he cited some contemporary linguistic considerations: "I would say, even recently, writing about Lunar New Year. We've referred to it in the past as Chinese New Year. And so, I didn't know enough about whether, should I be calling it Chinese New Year or should I be calling it Lunar New Year?" As he continued, another view of how members of new groups in town had influenced the established community came into focus:

> We actually reached out to a student I know who has a Chinese background.... I've talked to her before about various things, and I bounced it off her. So, you know, that is the kind of thing where I think people from different backgrounds in town are maybe a little more visible than they used to be. Like, a student is actually telling me... I felt comfortable reaching out to her to ask her about this. And, you know, she was happy

to respond to me. So we did refer to it as Lunar New Year this year, even though I know it's a little more nuanced than that, because she said Lunar New Year is kind of more acceptable now, because Lunar New Year is celebrated in more Asian communities than just China.

Multilingual Resources

The library is another setting in which new groups—whether Italian, Chinese, or Jewish—influence the mainstream in regard to language. Over the course of the twentieth century and into the twenty-first, the library bought books to assist new residents who were not native English speakers. The Wellesley Free Library acquired books in the early 1920s to assist those taking Italian classes (with students who were probably both Italian and established residents), and in July 1925 it promoted books explicitly for use by Italian residents to help them learn about the United States and US citizenship.[44] In the early 1970s, the library advertised books on tape for the blind. These books were recorded in various languages, including Italian and Chinese, and the library was looking for Italian and Chinese speakers to record additional publications.[45] The early 1970s also saw announcements about large-print books in Mandarin for those who had difficulty seeing, the *New Encyclopaedia Judaica*, and newly added magazines related to Judaism and Israel.[46]

Interviews with both lifelong residents and community leaders revealed other ways in which new groups had transformed the library in regard to language. Bethany, a longtime volunteer and leader within the library, said, "We've had a lot more requests for materials in different languages. This year there was a specific request organized by the Chinese Language School here to have more materials in Mandarin." Those requests were made by a new group actively reaching out for what its members needed and wanted. Such requests also reflected, once again, the simultaneous process of cultural retention and cultural assimilation: new residents were utilizing and impacting established organizations to maintain their ethnic identity.

Grace discussed the children's story hours held at the library in Mandarin and Spanish: "I know that a couple of Chinese friends were asked to lead Chinese story hour. I think they had Spanish story hour. So I definitely appreciated those efforts by the library." The Friends of the Wellesley Free Library now supported a monthly Mandarin story time. Courtney discussed the English for Speakers of Other Languages (ESOL) program that had been in place for some years: "They've had the ELL [English Language Learner] program at the library for a long time. There's a director of English language learner services at the library. . . . Sometimes when my kids were little, I [would] take them to the Hills branch, and my mom actually used to volunteer in this organization, but there would be Asian—it would be an ELL class meeting at the library." This program now had a full-time director, employed approximately twenty volunteers, and served over sixty adult students from various countries of origin.

PTOs had also responded to changing demographics, as evidenced by their altered communication strategies. Courtney thought there had been some real progress in regard to diversity in town, but also felt that "the PTOs are still really White, for example. I think a lot of organizations in town have done the work of making space or saying they want to be inclusive without realizing how active inclusion has to be." She explained: "I know a couple of years ago some PTOs were like, 'We would love to have translators who could translate our stuff into those languages or any other language that's spoken at our school. Vietnamese, Korean . . . what have you.' And so I think, again, that's something that's bubbling up."

Some PTOs have in fact been translating their emails and fliers into Spanish and Mandarin for close to ten years, a critical step in increasing access for all members. Because PTOs are not a formal part of the Wellesley Public School System, and because each public school has its own PTO, there is wide variation in how communication is sent out. Even so, these piecemeal changes evidence the impact of new groups on the established community, both through expanding membership and changing policies and practices to reach those who are not part of the organization.

At the other end of the age spectrum, the signs in Spanish, Mandarin, and Portuguese seen during a visit to the Council on Aging immediately revealed the influence of new groups.

The spread of languages other than English sometimes unveiled tensions in the town. Mike, a man in his sixties, spoke honestly when he said:

> But sometimes I fear that there is less uniform desire for assimilation from all ethnicities entering the US. And I think that it's good to have a common language. And again, I don't think it's necessarily a good thing to admit, but there's sometimes when it's like, "Press one for English, two for Spanish." Well, wait a minute. Why do I have to do that? And then I say, "Okay, chill out."

Mike gave voice to the tension he felt, the feelings of tribalism whispering against the louder voice of inclusion and expansion. In this instance we see the effects of multidirectional assimilation beyond the private sphere on individuals who, without having opted into the interaction, feel the effects of brushing up against members of other groups. At the federal level, President Trump signed an Executive Order in March 2025 to make English the official language. It is not yet clear how that policy will impact local decisions.

Additional Cultural Influences Across Organizations

Other aspects of new groups also spread throughout mainstream organizations. Theresa, the realtor from the last chapter who was actively involved in the town, noted that various quasi-public organizations had changed. At the Council on Aging, for example, "we have all sorts of speakers," she said, "and they have really reached out to a variety of cultures, whether it's paper making dolls [origami], or whatever they're doing, and they're doing a lot of diversity, and exercises [Tai Chi]. It's been well received." Activities listed on the council's website also included mah-jongg. The Italian American Frank, who was a regular at the senior center, had observed an increase in the number of Chinese residents who used the services, and he hoped that they would become more involved in the leadership of the organization. Clare, the executive and uber-volunteer, discussed this issue as well. She told me that because a lot of the elderly Chinese residents had limited English skills, it had been hard to get them to take on leadership roles. She had been able to get a second-generation Chinese American man to participate; although he was on the younger side and did not yet use the services of the senior center, his parents were avid users.

The Recreation Center also now offered more varied classes, including capoeira, Tai Chi, various language options, and cooking classes featuring ethnic foods such as Chinese buns and bao. These influences on leisure did not suddenly arise in the twenty-first century; mah-jongg was discussed nearly one hundred years ago in the *Townsman*. A 1939 article explained an American version, with tiles picturing state capitals rather than Chinese characters.[47] Another article from the same time period discussed children playing bocce at Sprague, the elementary school that served the Italian enclave at the time.[48] A bocce league offered by the Italo-American Educational Club remains active in town to this day.

The Formation and Influence of Ethnic and Hybrid Organizations

Mainstream organizations, such as PTOs, the Council on Aging, civic clubs, the local newspaper, and even restaurants and grocery stores, interact with members of new groups and, as demonstrated, are influenced by them, wittingly or unwittingly. However, the purposes and goals of mainstream organizations are not specifically focused on the concerns of racial, ethnic, or religious minority groups. In contrast, ethnic-specific organizations, as their stated goal, serve the interests of a particular group. Somewhat counterintuitively, ethnic-specific groups often have a far greater impact on the community as a whole than do mainstream organizations, driving some of the largest and most durable changes. Prior research has identified the influence of immigrant and ethnic-specific groups on the mainstream.[49] The development of such organizations, even those focused on cultural retention, impact the established community, ranging from ethnic festivals open to everyone to initiatives that affect the community writ large.[50]

Initially, such organizations may focus on housing, job opportunities, English language classes, and citizenship acquisition to move individuals and groups toward traditional assimilation, along the lines of the settlement movement of a century ago. Ethnic rather than exclusively immigrant-serving organizations may play additional roles, including preserving and promoting ethnic culture. Further, new groups often establish commercial enterprises such as restaurants and businesses that provide services.[51] Some start these businesses to meet the needs of coethnics; others do so because they are shut out of the mainstream economy.[52] These various ethnic organizations also serve as settings for the development of micro-level footpaths and bridges between mainstream and ethnic-specific groups, and they lobby decision-making bodies on behalf of their membership, as will be discussed in the next chapter.

Each of the new immigrant-turned-ethnic groups in Wellesley has followed this path of institution-building. For Italian immigrants and their children, it started with the formation of the Reliance Club in 1925. A decade later, in 1936, the Italian Educational Civic League and the Wellesley Italian Civic League joined forces to become the Italo-American Educational Club, an organization that still exists (figure 5.1). Other Italian organizations included the myriad Italian women's groups (Stalla Italia, Italian Emilian Women's Sewing Club), the Ferioli and Roma Dramatic Club, an Italian-specific scouting troop, and various Italian political organizations. These groups offered English language and citizenship classes, but they also worked to promote the interests of the Italian and Italian American community and continue to do so today. Further, many of the early Italian residents established their own small businesses in landscaping, construction, and other trades, as well as restaurants and hair salons, and all of these enterprises touched the established community.

Jewish residents of Wellesley engaged in extensive institution building over the course of the twentieth century, as they did across the country.[53] Jewish residents, most of whom entered the community as second- or third-generation Americans, were less concerned with English language ability or citizenship acquisition, as they were both English speakers and American citizens. Jews in Wellesley built institutions largely around practicing Judaism and maintaining cultural traditions. The Wellesley Hebrew Community Club, first documented in the *Wellesley Townsman* in 1935, was followed by the Jewish Community Group of Wellesley in

Figure 5.1   The Italo-American Educational Club, Wellesley, Massachusetts, 2024

Source: Author's photo.

1949.[54] The group was started by twenty-two women and initially focused on developing social activities for the small number of Jewish families and Jewish educational activities for the children in order to maintain their ethnic and religious heritage and provide social support to the community. These organizations were clearly focused on preservation and practice.[55] The Jewish Community Group began to include men in 1950 and then went on to become the core of Temple Beth Elohim, founded in 1960 and today one of the largest reform congregations in the country.

Other organizations that developed included Hadassah (a Jewish women's social service group) and the Mayflower chapter of the Anti-Defamation League of B'nai B'rith (ADL). A branch of Jewish War Veterans also opened in the area in the post–World War II era. In addition to aiding Jewish veterans, this group enabled Jews to demonstrate their Americanness and loyalty by having served the country. The veterans' group also annually provided an award to a Wellesley High School graduate, who frequently was not Jewish. Additionally, Jewish hospitals and even a Jewish university were established within range of Wellesley.

Community Organizations as Cause and Consequence of Change   113

These organizations met the needs of Jewish residents, including fighting against anti-Semitism, but they also had various impacts on established residents outside of the Jewish community.

Institution building by Chinese and Chinese American residents has been undertaken far more recently. The Wellesley Chinese Language School was founded in 2009, the same year the Asian Culture Club started at Wellesley High School. In 2016, the Wellesley Chinese Action Network, known as WeCAN, was founded. These organizations have had multiple goals—to maintain Chinese language and tradition for Chinese residents and their children, to protect the civil rights of group members as anti-Asian sentiment has increased, to serve as an organized lobby for the community, and to build bridges with members of the established community.

Hybrid organizations intentionally straddle multiple worlds, bringing together members from diverse groups, established and new. Such institutions may have the explicit goal of including new groups so as to make Wellesley a more welcoming place where everyone feels they belong. Such Wellesley organizations include the Interfaith Council, which has been operating in various forms since the mid-twentieth century; the Fair Housing Committee, also established in the mid-twentieth century; and the Human Rights Commission and World of Wellesley, both founded in the early 1990s. The last two groups were formed in response to the police actions against Celtics player Dee Brown and anti-Semitic graffiti at the high school during the Jewish High Holidays in the fall of 1991.[56] Although members of these organizations are self-selecting, they serve as an important engine of change. Hybrid organizations' advantage is having both institutional knowledge from and connections with the established community and the drive for change from new groups.

Through individual-level footpaths between new and established individuals, new residents sometimes are able to climb up ladders to join these hybrid organizations. Mei, Courtney, and Anjali all told such stories. From there, intentional bridges are built within the organization, with multidirectional influences on members. The influence does not stop there, however: bridges are built to other organizations in town, as happened with the dance studio of Kate's children's and the Chinese Language School. Ladders are also built to decision-making institutions within the town. For example, World of Wellesley has served as a launching pad for numerous individuals who are now active participants in townwide institutions.

It is critical to note the tensions that sometimes develop within, between, and in response to ethnic-specific organizations and hybrid groups. Although some hostilities appear as ethnic and hybrid groups are gaining strength and building bridges, greater fractures appear as ladders are built and these groups attempt to restructure larger institutions in

114   Beyond White Picket Fences

the town. Conflicts arise between ethnic groups and members of the established community as the new groups make claims within the public realm and as various resources are redistributed. Tensions also arise within ethnic organizations and more broadly within ethnic groups, as they are not monolithic in their thinking and worldviews.

Political Party (Re)Alignment

Mike was a man in his sixties who identified as an American and a Bostonian. He began by telling me how Wellesley had changed over the course of his lifetime:

> So it has become significantly more progressive. It was an incredibly conservative town. By way of example, if children, certainly elementary children, tend to mirror their parents' views, I was in the only class at Kingsbury Elementary School that voted for John Kennedy when I was in third grade. So it was rock-ribbed Republican. And I think that it was . . . not just conservative, small "c," but I think it was . . . bigoted. It is a bit of a strong word, but I don't think it was a very enlightened town. We did not have very many Jewish people. Certainly, very few African Americans, equally small numbers of Asian Americans. It was a, you know, pretty much a WASPY—although, you know, if you differentiate WASP from Irish, you know, we had a good number of Irish as well. And it was an interesting town in that it did have a . . . a core section of working-class Italian immigrants over in the Sprague school district. And that was really a heavy ethnic enclave.

Although Mike was not drawing an explicit connection between the demographics and political affiliations of the 1960s and the changes in both today, there is evidence to suggest a connection.

The Italian community in Wellesley gained a foothold in the local political scene relatively quickly, in part because the Italian-specific organizations provided candidates with an obvious audience and a potential body of voters to mobilize. By 1938, the estimated five hundred to six hundred voters of Italian descent in Wellesley had become a force in local politics.[57] At the local level, the Wellesley Italian Educational League hosted politicians from both the Democratic and Republican Parties, who were targeting Italian and Italian American residents throughout the 1930s.

Early on, tensions arose within the Italian community about which party they should collectively support; this conflict spoke to the heterogeneity within a community often assumed to be monolithic. Letters to the editor of the *Townsman* from 1936, written by individuals identifying as Italian American, pushed for support of the local Republican Party.[58] One letter encouraging Italians to vote for Republicans mentioned that the Democratic governor James Michael Curley, had vetoed the Columbus Day bill, which became law only because of state-level Republicans.

On the other side, political signs posted around town in Italian pushed residents to support the Democratic Party.

Nascent political engagement within the Italian American community continued and grew through ethnic organizations. The Italo-American Voters League cosponsored a Republican voter drive in the fall of 1938. A full-page ad in support of Republican candidates and placed in the *Wellesley Townsman* was signed by Felix Juliani as a representative of that same organization.[59] An editorial from November 1938 applauded the high level of voter turnout and explicitly thanked the Italian community for its role in the impressive level of engagement.[60] A ladder had clearly been built between the Italian immigrant-turned-ethnic community and the local Republican Party. Throughout the twentieth century, the Italo-American Educational Club would host speaker forums for candidates. Juliani would become a pillar of the community and remain active in local politics until his death in 2006.

The town remained solidly Republican into the 1970s, with Congresswoman Margaret Heckler serving as one of the town's representatives. (Wellesley has long been divided between two congressional districts.) It was during this era that profound political and demographic changes began in both the Democratic and Republican Parties. Historically, the Republican Party was more progressive, particularly on civil rights issues, and more libertarian on social, economic, and immigration issues. The first Black senator in the post-Reconstruction era was Ed Brookes, a Republican from Massachusetts. The Republican Party was also consistently the party of the Boston WASP elite, while the Democrats tended to be associated with ethnic workers.[61]

An ad in the *Wellesley Townsman* from 1977 demonstrated the Republican Party's recognition of the town's changing demographics. Republican state committee chair Gordon Nelson stated, "We're trying to appeal to the everyday person. . . . I'm the first Jewish Chairman of the Republican State Committee and I'm not rich." He went on to tout that the first Black senator, the first female congresswoman, and the first Italian congressman were all Republicans.[62] In 1978, the Republican candidate for state treasurer did a meet-and-greet at the home of a Wellesley resident to engage representatives of the Jewish community. The Republican Party was seeking to gain inroads with groups that had traditionally identified with labor.

Congresswoman Heckler, the longtime Republican representative of Wellesley, had received support for many years from at least some segment of the Jewish community in town. In addition to speaking at Temple Beth Elohim, she received the Histadrut Award from Hadassah for her support of Israel. When she was challenged by a Democrat for her seat in 1980, the fissures within the Wellesley Jewish community came into relief. As Jews had increasingly aged into the established population, their political opinions had become more diverse. Quoted in a *Townsman* article from August 1980, her Democratic challenger said that Wellesley "is no longer a WASP town. Newer people have moved in from Newton, West Roxbury and Brookline. This is as much a Catholic and Jewish town now."[63] As new groups had become established, they had variably assimilated into the political system, altering it for everyone.

By 1980, Congressman Barney Frank represented Wellesley. His identity as a Jewish gay Democrat spoke to the demographic sea change taking place in Wellesley, with political implications for the whole community. This change was further evidenced by an October 1988 *Townsman* article covering a heated debate at the Jewish Community Center in Newton in which two Wellesley residents, Republican Ruth Kleinfeld and Democrat David Roberts (director of the Jewish Federation in Portland, Oregon, for eighteen years), discussed the qualifications of Vice President George H. W. Bush. They both extolled the public records of their candidates on issues of concern to the American Jewish community.[64] Just as Italian-specific organizations in an earlier era had participated in political parties at the local, state, and even national levels, the same could now be seen among Jewish organizations.

Immigration Policies

Immigration is an issue with real implications for new groups in a community. With the overturning of the Chinese Exclusion Act in 1943, Dr. Tehyi Hsieh, representing the Chinese Service Bureau, wrote to the *Wellesley Townsman* to thank the paper for its support in overturning the exclusionary law.[65] Noting that he had attended the many meetings and hearings held on the act, he wrote that he appreciated the numerous resolutions sent by churches and interfaith organizations working in support of the Chinese people. A similar article related to immigration appeared in the *Wellesley Townsman* in 1952.[66] Abraham Alper, a Wellesley resident and president of the New England American Jewish Congress, urged President Harry Truman to veto the McCarran-Walter Immigration Bill, describing it as racist and "deplorable" because it discriminated against people from southern and eastern Europe. The local Jewish community, as represented by the New England American Jewish Congress, had been actively engaged in campaigning against the bill. Truman did veto the McCarran-Walter Immigration Bill, but Congress overrode his veto.

The Jewish community, as represented by various Jewish organizations, including Temple Beth Elohim, was engaged in the topic of immigration throughout the twentieth century. By the 1960s, the American Jewish community had shifted its focus to anti-Semitism in Russia. Temple Beth Elohim began hosting speakers on Russian Jewry in the late 1960s; as a mainstay of the temple's agenda through the 1980s, the issue spoke to the connections between the international and the local. Republican Congresswoman Heckler became actively involved in this issue: she spoke at the temple in the 1970s and in Congress pushed for sanctions against the Soviet Union and for funding Israel. Congressman Frank, who continued to work on issues related to immigration and Soviet Jewry, spoke at the temple in 1985. One of the topics of the October 1988 political panel with Republican Ruth Kleinfeld and Democrat David Roberts was the situation of Soviet Jewish refuseniks, among whom were the Fuchs-Rabinovitch family, who had emigrated to Wellesley through assistance from Temple Beth Elohim.[67] The temple's Committee on Soviet Jewry participated in a hunger strike and protest outside of Lieutenant Governor Evelyn Murphy's Boston office.[68]

Temple Beth Elohim continues to engage in issues of immigration to this day. The focus is no longer on Jews from eastern Europe, as it was during the early twentieth century, or Jewish refugees after World War II, or Soviet Jewry in the 1970s. The temple now advocates for those from Syria, Afghanistan, Venezuela, and other parts of the world and has helped to resettle refugees of various racial, ethnic, and religious backgrounds in town.

Civil Rights and Housing

One of the early instances of ethnic and hybrid organizations seeking to have a political impact was in regard to housing. Housing discrimination arose as one of the primary issues in the 1950s as Jewish and Black Americans seeking to move out of cities and into suburbs often encountered resistance. In 1958, Robert Segal of the Jewish Community Council was hosted by the Universalist Women to discuss the topic.[69] By October 1959, Wellesley's selectmen had endorsed fair housing practices, following an informal conference with members of the Wellesley Fair Housing Practices Committee, the Jewish Community Council, and the Anti-Defamation League of B'nai B'rith.[70] The Fair Housing Practices Committee hosted a panel entitled "Integration and Our Suburbs."[71] By 1963, an estimated six hundred to eight hundred Jewish families lived in Wellesley, comprising approximately 3 percent of the town.[72] Highly educated and no longer working exclusively in small businesses, they had harnessed the institutional infrastructures in place in both Wellesley and the broader Jewish community. Such groups also lay claim to their rights through newly passed federal civil rights legislation.[73]

The Fair Housing Practices Committee, whose members included both Christian and Jewish clergy, continued its work throughout the 1960s, holding forums, hearing testimony around the anti-Semitic experiences of residents, and taking out full-page ads in the *Wellesley Townsman*. Mike, the Bostonian who talked about the community's political realignment, also spoke of his father's involvement with the NAACP in the 1960s to ferret out racial discrimination in housing. In 1967, the agenda of a meeting held among realtors, clergy, and members of Wellesley's Fair Housing and

Equal Rights Committee was to ensure that Black Americans had equal access to housing in Wellesley.[74] In recent years it came to light that racially restrictive housing covenants had been in place in parts of town until at least 1970. The archival data suggest that public discussions around housing segregation, both ethnic and racial, had lessened by the late 1960s. At the same time, the interview data suggest ongoing anti-Semitism in housing practices until the late 1970s or even later, and discrimination against the exceedingly small number of Black Americans in Wellesley through today. This reality is a reminder of the voices we do not hear in this case study—those who could not or chose not to live in town.

In more recent years, as real estate prices have exploded, there has been a growing focus on affordable housing in town. Although national research shows that Black Americans are still disproportionately denied housing on no basis other than race, a comparable challenge today is affordability, particularly in a town such as Wellesley. Individuals and groups are cognizant that greater racial diversity requires the removal of economic barriers. Temple Beth Elohim is in partnership with the Interfaith Housing Justice Campaign, a hybrid group, to improve access to housing in Wellesley and beyond. Ronnie, an elderly Black resident in town, discussed her engagement with Temple Beth Elohim members involved with the Greater Boston Interfaith Organization, especially the organization's housing initiatives.

Heritage Language Lessons

As discussed earlier in this chapter, Italian, Yiddish, and Mandarin lessons became available to the established community as early as the 1930s, often offered by mainstream groups and advertised through mainstream mechanisms. Ethnic organizations have also played important roles in the diffusion of heritage languages to the established community.

Starting in 1934, the Italian Education Civic League opened up its classes to the general public, sensing the interest of established residents.[75] In 1936, the Italian language evening classes taught at the high school—sponsored by Mr. V. S. Martino, a local resident and businessman—were billed as being of interest to music lovers, "as most music terms are Italian."[76] After the Italian classes offered at the high school were discontinued in 1940, the Italo-American Educational Club began to offer them.[77] Such initiatives may start with a focus on preservation but develop an element of promotion.[78]

The Wellesley Chinese Language School reflects these dual goals in the twenty-first century:

> The Wellesley Chinese Language School was founded on the premise that everyone can learn Chinese, whether coming from a bilingual, "heritage" background or beginning Chinese as a monolingual adult.

Community Organizations as Cause and Consequence of Change 119

> While this is still holding true, we keep asking why should a Chinese descendant study Chinese? One of the most popular answers would be for the inheritance of Chinese culture. We have read much about what should be inherited, who should spread, and how to spread the culture. Yet, we seldom talked about the question why should the descendants of Chinese parents shoulder the task of inheritance. We are in the United States. Most communities do not rely on Chinese for their daily life, including study and work. There is no need in reality, thus no motivation, for the kids to study Chinese.
>
> Hence forth, **_the new mission requires Chinese schools to reach beyond the Chinese communities, or even Asian communities_**. When more and more communities joined Chinese study, the need in reality could be created for social life, for jobs, and for the pride in Chinese language. By collaborating with local public and private schools, Chinese language will no longer be the obsession of parents. The term "Asian Parents" will no longer be the most powerful weapon for Chinese teenagers to refute their parents. (formatting in the original)

Aware of their reputation as "Tiger parents," this organization is not seeking to assimilate to the English-dominant, monolingual way of life, but rather to make Mandarin mainstream and part of the dominant culture. This initiative is consistent with other findings on the growing educational competition between new and established residents as members of new groups try to reshape academic practices of the established, rather than simply assimilate to those expectations.[79] These data also reflect the process of normative inversion, whereby patterns of behavior that have been racialized and deemed undesirable are utilized by the stigmatized group and incorporated into the mainstream.[80]

Health and Well-Being

Many of the Jewish American residents who moved to Wellesley in the 1950s and 1960s worked in medical professions, many of them at Beth Israel Hospital. These health care professionals focused on both physical health and mental well-being. In 1947, the Institute of Psychiatry and Religion held a conference at Temple Israel's meetinghouse in Boston under the direction of Rabbi Joshua Loth Liebman. The speakers included Dr. Erich Lindemann, a Wellesley resident, Dr. Lydia Dawes, Dr. Harry Solomon, and Albert Deutsch. The pastor of the Community Universalist Church of Wellesley attended.[81] Wellesley-based Jewish organizations also took up this focus on mental health. In 1952, the Jewish Community Group of Wellesley hosted Dr. Lindemann, the director of the Wellesley Human Relations Service (HRS), the first community mental health facility in the country.[82] In 1958, HRS and the Wellesley public schools teamed up to establish a mental health institute that was run by Dr. Norman Klein and other doctors from Beth Israel.[83] The early

120   Beyond White Picket Fences

1960s saw Morton Darman, president of Temple Beth Elohim at the time, elevated to run HRS.

The Jewish Family and Children's Services, established in Wellesley in 1977, provided extensive support groups, interventions, and other forms of mental health care. Although some of the programming was specific to the Jewish community—for example, support for Holocaust survivors and their children—much of it was not.[84] The organization offered support groups on a range of topics, such as single parenthood, single adults, aging adults, parenting adolescents, caring for elderly relatives, family issues, divorce, bereavement, parenting gay children, and widowers.[85] The doors were open to all.

The health of Wellesley residents was shaped by new groups in other ways. Acupuncture was introduced to Boston in the early 1970s and soon appeared in Wellesley as well. Dr. Bernard Huang, who was born and raised in China and immigrated to the United States in 1950, discussed the technique in an address to the Charles River District Medical Society in 1972.[86] But acupuncture really took off after Secretary of State Henry Kissinger's visit to China in 1972. One of the reporters covering Kissinger found great relief from the treatment while on the visit, speaking to the glocal nature of assimilation. A year later, in July 1973, a clinic opened in Boston with six Chinese acupuncturists, overseen by an American-born doctor. Boston was considered the center of early acupuncture in the United States, owing to its "progressive laws."[87]

By 1974, the *Wellesley Townsman* was running ads for acupuncturists, including an advertisement stating that "ACUPUNCTURE is coming to Wellesley" (capitalization in the original). The New England Center for Acupuncture advertised on that same page; in that ad, the Chinese acupuncturist listed his extensive education at several Chinese institutions, under the supervision of a licensed doctor who was part of the established community.[88] Later that year, Acupuncture & Pain Therapy Associates of Wellesley opened its doors, offering a "live demonstration by a Chinese acupuncturist."[89] A local automotive shop even advertised "automotive acupuncture is preventive medicine," describing acupuncture as "the increasingly popular Chinese medical treatment."[90] Acupuncture also began to be more broadly explored in traditional Western medical settings; for instance, Dr. Lennig Chang, a Newton-Wellesley Hospital internist, ran a study in 1975 on acupuncture as a form of pain management.[91] Additional centers advertised in the *Wellesley Townsman* throughout the 1970s and 1980s, including the Acupuncture Center, the Acupuncture Pain Control Center, and Acupuncture Associates of Natick. These commercial enterprises helped to spread Chinese cultural practices, just as an ethnic grocery store would.

While these organizations all explicitly described their acupuncturists as "Chinese," "Asian," or "Oriental" and sometimes included Chinese symbols in their ads in a show of authenticity, the therapy began to flow into the mainstream in terms of both who sought it out and who provided it, suggesting multidirectional assimilation. A 1980 nutritional educational lecture series hosted at the Church of Christ listed a talk on acupuncture given by Norman Smith and John Myerson.[92] And in a sign of multidirectional influences between groups, the Wellesley Knights of Columbus hosted James Paisner, an acupuncturist, to speak at St. James the Great Church about the technique.[93] By 1984, both of the acupuncturists in a photo in an ad for the Wellesley Acupuncture Group appeared to be White. Other acupuncture centers opened in Wellesley, with doctors from established groups.

Further, by the 1980s, the ads began to emphasize acupuncture as a cure for sports injuries, stress, anxiety, and depression, whereas the focus had previously been on pain management.[94] The technique was being adapted to respond to the maladies of the established population and began to be offered in clinics and doctor's offices that offered counseling, meditation, and "body work." By 1985, a classified ad that ran weekly offered acupuncture for dogs and cats.[95] As new groups came onto this stage and both assimilated and retained their cultural backgrounds through organizations that worked to preserve and promote traditions, often concomitantly, the script was renegotiated and the fabric of the entire community changed.

In more recent years, the Wellesley Chinese Language School and WeCAN played a critical role during the COVID pandemic. Far more aware of what was to come than the average established resident of Wellesley, WeCAN scheduled a meeting for early March 2020 to discuss the impending pandemic, entitled "Protect Ourselves and Communities from COVID-19." The group switched the meeting from in person to online for safety. The organizations' leaders said that they were somewhat better equipped than others in the United States because they had been following events in Wuhan closely and helping medical workers there. By mid-May 2020, the two Wellesley organizations had distributed more than fourteen thousand masks locally, accessed through contacts in China, and raised more than $12,000 from the Wellesley Chinese community for local hospitals.[96]

"Public" Education

Ethnic organizations in Wellesley influenced the established community through various forms of "public" education relevant to these groups. In the first two decades of the twentieth century, there were frequent lectures on China, with topics ranging from education to religion to trade. Initially, the lectures were exclusively given by members of the WASP class, including Charles Tenney, Reverend George Hinman, Marshall Perrin, Charles Gammon, and others. These individuals had worked as missionaries, on behalf of the US government, or for US business interests. The mid-1930s began to see the small number of Chinese residents speaking on behalf of various Chinese organizations as both internal and external pressures rose in China and the Chinese government sought support. Dr. T. Z. Koo, a statesman, writer, student leader, and head of the World Student Christian Federation, gave a lecture in 1936, as part of a public lecture series at Wellesley College, in which he discussed Chinese politics, economics, and Japan.[97] As the situation in China deteriorated, Dr. Tehyi Hsieh, head of the Chinese Service Bureau, gave regular lectures locally and served as an important cultural liaison to the established community.

The Mayling Soong Foundation, started by Madame Chiang Kai-shek in 1942 at Wellesley College, also served to educate the general public through lectures, exhibits, and movies related to China. Of note is that the featured academics, artists, and speakers were most often Chinese immigrants or of Chinese descent and the events were open to the public. A lecture by Professor Chi-Chen Wang of Columbia University was advertised to the public in 1943.[98] Later that year, Professor Yuen Ren Chaoc of Harvard gave a talk on Chinese music. Numerous other Chinese faculty from around the Northeast also gave public lectures.[99] In 1950, the Mayling Soong Foundation held symposia on topics such as "Problems of East and Southeast Asia." That same year Madame Chiang Kai-shek directly addressed the foundation on the threat of communism.[100] In 1976, the foundation underwrote Wellesley College's "Asian Month," which is held to this day.

The Jewish community, via Temple Beth Elohim, cracked open the town's seeming aversion to discussing the Holocaust, at least within the context of the local newspaper, which covered all manner of other international events. One such example of this avoidance of the Holocaust appears in an article from February 3, 1955, about Henri Aubert, a Jewish violinist who was performing at Dana Hall.[101] His religious affiliation was not mentioned, but the story noted that "his career was interrupted in 1941 when he was deported to the notorious Buchenwald Camp, where he remained for four years." There was no mention of the Holocaust, Nazis, or anything more informative than the "notorious Buchenwald Camp." Later in the article was a mention of his invitation to play in Israel in 1948. Similarly, when the Wellesley Players staged the play *Anne Frank* in 1959, the review made minimal mention of concentration camps, never mentioned the Holocaust, and largely focused on the goodness and bravery of the Christian family who hid the Franks.[102] When the same play was put on again in 1964, the *Wellesley Townsman* remained similarly evasive.[103]

It was not until December 1970 that any public discussion began, with a showing of a film about Elie Wiesel, a Holocaust survivor, at Temple Beth Elohim. This was the first time this language was used in the *Wellesley Townsman*.[104] Holocaust Remembrance Day began to be commemorated the following year. Although these events were situated within the temple, a community-wide discussion had begun. In 1974, Wellesley College began to hold events to educate students and the community about the Holocaust.[105] This appears to have been the first large-scale, mainstream discussion of this historic event—the first time the murder of six million Jews was publicly mentioned in Wellesley. Another first was the showing in 1969 of a French film, entitled *The Two of Us*, about a French grandfather who ends up sheltering and becoming very close to a young Jewish boy during the war. The *Wellesley Townsman* notes that "Gramp" "fulfills the part of a lovable grandfather in most respects, [but] has one failing— his blustery anti-Semitism."[106] This description presents anti-Semitism as just one "failing," like any other. By 1974, the discussion of the film had changed.

In 1976, a town librarian, Angela Mays, organized a four-week educational series on the Holocaust at the Wellesley Free Library.[107] Children at the Schofield Elementary School, the school in the Jewish enclave, ran a car wash to support the effort, raising $114.[108] The Friends of the Wellesley Free Library also provided financial support for the series. Mays received a commendation from Temple Israel in Boston, and the *Wellesley Townsman* received twenty-five letters thanking the librarian for the work she had done.[109] In 1977, a synagogue in Newton provided the Wellesley Free Library with over one hundred books on Israel, anti-Semitism, and the Holocaust.

But the higher profile of Jews in Wellesley and the discussion of the Holocaust also raised some tensions in the town. In 1978, after the film *Holocaust* was shown, the outdoor bulletin board at Temple Beth Elohim was set afire.[110] A decade later, another local temple was burned down.[111]

Facing History, an organization begun in Brookline in 1976 by a Jewish teacher, focused initially on teaching the Holocaust, a topic that had been almost entirely neglected in American education. In the early 1980s, Temple Beth Elohim and the Wellesley Hills Congregational Church joined together to offer an interfaith Facing History course under the auspices of the Wellesley Interfaith Alliance.[112] Marie, a woman in her late forties of Irish and German background, discussed the Facing History curriculum she encountered in her private middle school. Although the discussion of the Holocaust began within Jewish organizations and initially focused on their members, these ethnic-specific groups built bridges to mainstream organizations, thus shaping the experiences of others.

Conclusion

Community organizations have played a critical role in the reshaping of Wellesley and communities like it. These organizations reflect macro-level shifts such as changes in immigration policies and micro-level footpaths leading to interfaith marriages. At times, these formal groups are prerequisites for change. In Wellesley, hybrid and ethnic-specific groups, including the ADL, brought anti-Semitism in the housing market to light, a critical first step to diversify the town. This history demonstrates the ability of community organizations to speak out on behalf of the individual and hold government more accountable, particularly on behalf of new Americans.[113]

Over time established organizations may expand their boundaries, incorporating members of new groups and providing a setting for contact between new and established residents. These individuals may also influence a group's programming and initiatives, thus extending their influence beyond the boundaries of the organization. These are additional forms of bridge building that allow influence to flow in multiple directions.

Ironically, however, the presence of ethnic-specific and hybrid groups has a greater impact in the community. Formal ethnic organizations may be formed out of a desire to promote ethnic identity, perform cultural practices, preserve language, or fill an ethnic niche in the local economy.[114] In forming, however, they also transform the larger landscape. These are the groups that build ladders up to decision-making bodies and push for structural changes as individuals come to feel they have a right to buy homes in any part of the town, be represented in school curricula, and see their holidays on the calendar. Prior research has found ethnic-specific institutions disadvantaged in terms of financial support and political attention, with suburban communities free-riding on the immigrant and ethnic-specific institutions that are usually located in urban areas.[115] These forms of relational inequality are less extreme in Wellesley, however, perhaps because of the high levels of income and education among members of new groups in town. With the growth of formal groups and advocacy in Wellesley, the result has been greater distributional equality.[116]

At the same time, self-advocacy and claims-making by formal immigrant and ethnic groups expose the tensions that arise when members of the established see and feel changes in their town that they cannot avoid. The redistribution of resources requires groups share what they previously controlled exclusively, in what comes to feel at times like a zero-sum game. Chapter 6 examines the larger-scale changes in Wellesley as new groups built ladders up to decision-making bodies, and the fractures that appeared as a result.

= Chapter 6 =

Durable Institutional Changes Across the Community

Elizabeth had served for decades on various town committees, both appointed and elected. She came from what one would describe as a WASP background, and she knew few Jewish students during the 1960s and 1970s, when she was in school. She recalled the election of the first Jewish select board member in the early twenty-first century and that individual's push to remove Christmas decorations from the literal public square. Her insistence on religious neutrality in public spaces reflected a Jewish community that had grown in numbers and confidence over the prior forty years and held an increased level of relational equality with the established. The engagement of the Jewish community in the public square reflected the duality of civic integration alongside cultural retention, or variegated assimilation.

Andrew, a teacher and administrator, talked about the increasing push by Chinese American students and parents to have Lunar New Year included on the school calendar. Articles on the topic appeared in the high school newspaper and *The Swellesley Report*, a community publication, throughout 2022 and 2023. Residents also attended school committee meetings and made public comments during the period known as "Citizen Speak" before the start of meetings. As a result of these attempts at cultural retention, utilizing various forms of mainstream civic engagement, Lunar New Year, as well as Diwali and Eid, were added to the school calendar.

Cleo had lived in town for years. She felt "a great sense of belonging in my neighborhood.... I love it!" Still, at PTO meetings other Wellesley residents had assumed that she was a nanny and a resident of "the projects." In response to these sorts of racist experiences, Cleo had made the decision to get involved in the town in various ways. "I really started delving into different specific committees that I felt were lacking a chair for a Black person at the table," she said. Her response to racialization was institutional reformation.

Research on the city of Marseille, France, has found that leaders of ethnic-specific groups are essential players on the local political scene.[1] The local elected officials view them as indispensable partners, but they also advocate for their groups, insisting on various forms of honor and recognition. Tocqueville argued that, "in the long run, the political society cannot fail to become the expression and the image of civil society," and to some extent this rings true not only in present-day Marseille but also in Wellesley.[2] This chapter explores how new groups have remade and continue to remake Wellesley in regard to the town's school curricula and policies, official holidays, and religious and cultural representation. The chapter also looks at the historic and continuous challenges around transformation in the town as even newer groups enter and the old new groups become established.

Claims-Making

Ethnic-specific organizations serve as important lobbying bodies and political launching pads for members, as has been the case for centuries across varied groups.[3] In the 1930s, Felix Juliani was a leader of various Italian-specific organizations in Wellesley as well as in the local Republican Party. He went on to hold numerous elected and appointed positions across town, and the largest meeting room in town hall is named for him.

Juliani was born in Italy, but many other members of immigrant groups did not become significantly engaged in the town politically for a generation or two. Jewish residents became involved in town government affairs in the early 1960s, largely as second- and third-generation Americans. The year 1964 saw Arnold Waldman and Morton Darman run for town meeting and Ruth Segel run for library trustee.[4] All three held significant leadership positions at Temple Beth Elohim: Waldman and Darman each served as president, and Segel served as chair of the Temple Library Committee.

By the early 2000s, Chinese American residents began to engage in townwide politics, holding positions on town meeting, the school committee, and other elected boards. More recently, Wellesley residents born in China have engaged politically. A board member of the Chinese Language School is also an elected town meeting member, and one of the library trustees is a Chinese immigrant who has twice won townwide election. This individual built footpaths to members of the established community who encouraged her to run and then helped her campaign, American-style, all of which was new to her. She was unfamiliar with "pulling papers" and shied away from putting up yard signs with her photo on them.

It is at this townwide level that some of the largest changes take place; here we see the most visible forms of relational inequality and unequal integration, as well as attempts at redistribution and recognition.[5]

Such claims-making by new groups at a town, state, or national level is often the point at which underlying tensions fully break out into the open, for it is on these most public of stages that debates over resource (re-)allocation take place. New groups may be viewed as too aggressive or unappreciative for smaller concessions that have already been made.[6] In more resource-deprived communities, tensions may appear earlier, such as at a food pantry where members of new groups are getting more than they are perceived to deserve, in a public school system where large parts of the school budget are going toward ESOL classes, or in a local labor market where immigrants are viewed as undercutting wages. Such is not the case in Wellesley, owing to its privileged economic position. It is not simply established residents who are wealthy and well educated but also immigrants and members of recent ethnic groups. Unlike immigrants in suburban areas with less infrastructure to serve new Americans, these newest Wellesley residents depend on neither the charity of the local community nor the assistance of far-off immigrant-serving organizations in Boston or other urban areas.[7] Consequently, it is relatively easy for the town to welcome new individuals and groups when little is asked of it in the way of resource distribution.

Relationships between new groups also factor into townwide dynamics as groups both learn from and compete with one another around the distribution of honor when it comes to holiday recognition on the calendar, school curricula, and representation on the town green.

School Redistricting

Wellesley has long prided itself on its walkable elementary school districts. Nevertheless, the town has often had to contend with population change and redistricting. For many in local and city politics, school redistricting is the "third rail" to be avoided if at all possible, and Wellesley is no different.

The 1930s saw an early case of redistricting in the town. In August 1936, the *Wellesley Townsman* published a new map indicating which elementary school Wellesley children would attend, based on their street address.[8] The unusual aspect of this redistricting plan was that those living in the area of the Isaac Sprague Elementary School, the Italian enclave, could opt to attend the Hardy, Brown, or Hunnewell Elementary School rather than Sprague (figure 6.1). The school committee had argued that it would benefit the children of the Sprague neighborhood to be split up. By the fall, however, it was clear that the option open to all had been utilized exclusively by established residents, sixteen of whose children had been

128   Beyond White Picket Fences

Figure 6.1   Isaac Sprague Elementary School, Wellesley, Massachusetts, 2024

Source: Author's photo.

moved out of the Sprague school and placed in one of the three other schools. The incoming kindergarten class totaled only nine students.

On November 20, 1936, Isaac Sprague, the chairman of the school committee, published an open letter to "The People of Wellesley" in which he explained that the committee had identified ways to improve the educational opportunities for *all* of the town's children, without increasing costs to the taxpayers.[9] The fight over scarce resources had clearly begun. This plan included the "doubling" of classes—in other words, mixed-grade classrooms where enrollments were low. This plan had specific implications for Sprague, given the school's declining enrollment. A week later, scathing letters to the editor regarding the redistricting plans were published in the *Wellesley Townsman*. The signers of one letter—James Bresnahan, chair of the Sprague PTO, Mrs. Le Forest Gardner, Mrs. D. G. Dischino, and Mr. L. S. Campana—noted that the out-migration of students from Sprague to Hardy had shrunk the population of the former.[10] In a separate letter written weeks later, Mr. Campana noted that Isaac Sprague lived a quarter-mile from his namesake school but sent his children to a school two miles away.[11] Other residents also took issue with Sprague being designated the "helping center" for the entire town. Another letter writer stated:

> The Sprague School is one of the best in Wellesley. The teaching staff is as good, if not better, than other schools. May I ask again—what is the reason? There is only one answer to this question, and here it is. There are too many children of Italian extraction for the so-called Americans to have their children attend the Sprague School. Did this make any difference in the front-line trenches in 1917 and 1918?[12]

The ethnic composition of the Sprague neighborhood appeared to have factored into the redistricting decision, or at least was perceived that way by those opposing it.

A raucous meeting took place between parents and the school committee, and a subsequent student strike was covered not only by Boston papers but also in the international press. In another editorial published the week of December 4, the *Townsman*'s editor squarely sided with the superintendent" "We realize that two of the most active members of the committee are comparative newcomers to our town."[13] Another writer, Helen Shaw, stated that "the Sprague parents want what they can get for their own children. . . . I am not new in this community. I have sent four children to the Wellesley Public Schools in the last fifteen years."[14] She strongly supported the school committee. This language of who was "new" and who was "not new," by attempting to mark the Italian residents as newcomers and outsiders and to minimize their voices, suggested that their positions on the issue were less worthy than the positions of those who had been in town longer. Joseph Touhey, playing on this idea in a letter to the editor, began his correspondence by describing himself as "another newcomer"; he ended his letter by stating:

> I understand the Sprague School student body draws a great proportion of its total number from Italian homes. These youths then are the daughters and sons of honest hardworking parents who are doing all within their power to give their offspring a good American school education, a majority of this percentage gets little or no help at home because unfortunately through no fault of their own their parents have had no American school education. . . . In view of this fact, does it not seem reasonable that this should be the last school to have double grading?[15]

By June the school committee had made the decision to eliminate "optional zones," but also to close Sprague and send its students to Hardy.

Although there were other redistricting fights across the twentieth century and into the twenty-first, the most recent one also raised the issue of ethnic composition. This time, however, both the dialogue and

Figure 6.2   John D. Hardy Elementary School, Wellesley, Massachusetts, 2024

Source: Author's photo.

the outcome suggest a process of relational integration more than one of traditional assimilation. This more recent controversy also reflected the changing migration flows in the post-1965 era. Whereas the redistricting fights in the early twentieth century had been about the consumption—and perhaps a perceived overconsumption—of resources by children and families deemed unworthy (recall Sprague's argument that the school committee had identified a plan that would benefit all, at no additional cost), the early twenty-first-century redistricting battle reflected a growing celebration of multiculturalism, both locally and nationally.

In 2015, the school committee made the decision to close the Hardy Elementary School (figure 6.2) given its declining student population, and to renovate two other existing elementary schools. As one of the older elementary schools in town, Hardy had needed renovation so extensive that the project would have been cost-prohibitive. The response to the school board's decision to close the school was swift and fierce: a formal organization called Save Wellesley Neighborhood Schools (SWNS) was almost immediately formed to counter the decision. This hybrid organization included parents from a range of backgrounds, both new and established. Later organizations were also formed, including Put Wellesley Students First and Parents for HHU. Over the next five years, members of the Hardy community, as represented by these various organizations, held meetings, wrote letters, displayed lawn signs, circulated petitions, and waged an intensive battle. They worked to build ladders to the school committee and the select board. In 2020, the town decided to close another school and to rebuild Hardy, keeping the Hardy community intact.

Both of these redistricting cases focused, intentionally or unintentionally, on schools that were more diverse than the town as a whole. The Sprague school nearly one hundred years ago was overwhelmingly Italian. Hardy in the twenty-first century had a large Asian population, overall minority enrollment was 52 percent, and children came from households where eleven different languages were spoken. Hardy had also been ranked as one of the top 25 elementary schools in Massachusetts and was designated a national Blue Ribbon School in 2021, one of 325 across the United States.

Eleanor, an octogenarian with both children and grandchildren in town, said, "I think that what Hardy has done over the last ten to twelve years to make their reputation so wonderful are the teachers and their commitment really. Hardy has done such an exceptional job. It's probably the worst building in town. And all the others, they can't match it. They really can't match it." She went on to talk about the demographics of the school: "They had a lot of Asians in their classroom. I think that they have Indian. I have seen some of their classrooms, especially Hardy, especially the kids at Hardy. You know, to them, it's no big deal." Eleanor did not make the explicit link between school performance and the school demographics, but she noted both. As far back as September 2012, others had noted these two characteristics. An online review read:

> The Hardy School Community is the most diverse of all the elementary schools in Wellesley. This provides a wonderful learning experience on the elementary level. The TEST SCORES are the HIGHEST of all the elementary schools in Wellesley—a testimony to the excellent staff. Additionally, having had children in one other elementary school in Wellesley in addition to Hardy I can say that Hardy is certainly the most welcoming school community in town. (capitalization in the original)[16]

The diversity of the community became a rallying cry when the school was slated to be closed in 2015 and was also incorporated into the platform of the parent group pushing to save Hardy. One talking point sent out in a March 2020 email by SWNS read: "Closure decreases our goal of diversity by building two large schools in the most affluent areas of town." Throughout 2020, advocates became even more focused on maintaining the diverse Hardy community rather than scattering it across the district, most likely influenced in part by national events, including the Black Lives Matter movement and the rise in Asian hate crimes during the pandemic. The local organization focused on "saving" Hardy harnessed larger societal winds of change and directed them toward its goal.

A number of factors were responsible for SWNS's success, including the ethnic, racial, and religious diversity of the parents involved. They represented old and new, immigrant and native-born. While diverse in ethnicity, they quite uniformly possessed high levels of education, income, and feelings of efficacy, assets that translated into high levels of organization and mobilization. They presented a sharp contrast to the Sprague Elementary School PTO that sought to save Sprague nearly one hundred years before; that group was largely comprised of Italian immigrants with lower levels of income and education. The performance of the schools was also a factor in the differences between the two initiatives. The children at Sprague were viewed as in need of remedial learning, and Italian students were often tracked toward shop classes. Eleanor and Christopher both recalled this view of Italian children as less capable. In contrast, the argument went, how could the town close Hardy, an elementary school that was one of the best in the country? Although arguments were made about the quality of the education and, separately, the school's diversity, the two trends were likely connected, as has been illustrated abundantly in prior research.[17] Such arguments often morph into dangerous stereotypes about the "model minority"; nevertheless, the data show a pattern of consistent academic success that probably played a role in "saving" Hardy, an outcome that had implications for the entire town.

School Performance and Curricula

As mentioned in the previous section, the most diverse public elementary school in the community, as measured by the percentage of students who identify as non-White, is also the highest scoring on standardized tests and has been for several years. In a town like Wellesley, test scores and rankings matter. In fact, established and new residents alike cited "strong schools" as a feature of the community. The new immigrant families described the schools as their primary motivation to move to Wellesley. One Chinese resident interviewed specifically spoke of Wellesley as a "top ten" school district when she moved in, though, to her dismay, the school rankings had slid since then. In 2023, a Chinese American Wellesley High senior was named a Presidential Scholar, an honor given to only 161 graduating seniors across the United States.

Under certain circumstances, members of new groups may not be viewed as liabilities, burdens, or challenges, but rather as assets to the town. The educational performance of the second generation, benefiting from what is known as the "second-generation advantage," has been documented in both large-scale quantitative research and in case studies.[18] Thus, there is little room for criticism around the disproportionate consumption of public resources to fund programs like ESOL classes. This trend toward hyperselectivity and superior academic performance has been particularly pronounced among Asian immigrants and their children in the post-1965 era.[19]

Instead, the reproach comes from the opposite end of the spectrum: some new Americans are perceived as "too good," as competing with wealthy, White young people for coveted spots at the country's elite exam schools, colleges, and universities.[20] This is the same criticism leveled at the children of Jewish immigrants in the early twentieth century. However, there was limited mention of these concerns in interviews, in contrast to prior research.[21] One lifelong resident described her children as not having any of the "essential hooks" that elite colleges were looking for and then proceeded to tick off the list, which included being a recruited athlete or a member of a minority group. A teacher interviewed discussed the extreme pressure that his Chinese students felt, particularly the girls, to be "better than perfect." Two lifelong residents discussed their perceptions of the historic impact of Jewish residents on schooling. The elder resident discussed the integration of her neighborhood and the resulting perception of her neighborhood elementary school as being more academic; the younger woman reported a heavy concentration of Jewish students in her honors classes. Although they were expressing "positive" views of the Jewish community, their comments suggest stereotyping and racialization of certain behavior patterns as intrinsically "Jewish" or, later, "Asian." More often, however, parents discussed the general pressure their children felt without explicitly connecting it to the changing demographics—or at least they chose not to discuss it in the interviews.

What is at play and of great concern for some Wellesley residents is the declining ranking of Wellesley High School. Concerns about the rigor, the limited number of AP classes, the declining MCAS scores in the wake of COVID, and a move to standards-based grading have caused angst in the community. At a meeting the district held on the grading system in March 2023, parents of varied racial and ethnic backgrounds voiced their concerns about grading, school rankings, and college acceptances. Some communities have seen such concerns divide squarely along racial lines.[22] This is not the case in Wellesley, where parents of varied backgrounds—viewing access to elite education as the key to both attaining and maintaining status in the face of growing income inequality—want the town to return to being a "top 10" district.

Curriculum is often discussed along with school rankings, rigor, and college acceptances. A formal parents' group with a large and vocal presence online and in public meetings frequently addresses these topics, with a heavy focus on college acceptances. White, Asian, and mixed-race families dominate the group, which otherwise has no clear racial trend. Indian and Chinese residents with whom I spoke told me they would like to see more rigor, particularly in regard to STEM classes. Avi, Anjali, Anh, and Jing all supplemented their children's math education through programs like Russian Math, the Center for Talented Youth, and the Chinese Language School, which offered a rich array of programming. A few of these parents also volunteered to support STEM initiatives in the schools, benefiting everyone.

In Wellesley there was convergence along racial lines, rather than divisions, in regard to schooling. An important difference between new and established parents, however, was that, while parents from newer groups seemed focused on content, established parents often tied their disappointment with the curriculum to broader social and cultural issues. The discussion of STEM at times became tied to critiques of social and emotional learning and diversity, equity, and inclusion initiatives. Newer groups, in contrast, focused almost exclusively on STEM.

A school administrator talked about changes in school curriculum and grading:

> There are different perspectives that come in, right, and I think, different ways of approaching school, different ways of approaching anything, athletics, whatever. So, you know, there have been growing pains.... And, you know, well, it's a very successful district. And why change anything here? That's an old meme, right, that you don't change anything in Wellesley, because this works. That's why people move here, right? Because they want the product that they've read about. So, if you start changing, I'm gonna get really nervous about that. I think, even for some of our Chinese families, when we change, they don't understand the change necessarily. They're like, "Okay, well, no, we wanted this then, so don't change that." And, you know, when I say this, I guess I'd be referring to sort of the traditional three R's and AP classes. You know, the rigor down the line, and trying to get high AP scores, and SAT scores and admission to the most prestigious colleges that people normally think of. So I think that there's some times when there's been different kinds of competition that's come in as a result and challenge some people's thinking.

This administrator did not see parents' concerns about AP classes, SAT scores, and college admittances as exclusively the concerns of any one ethnic or racial group, even stating, "You don't change anything in Wellesley, because it works," as well as saying that "even some of our Chinese families" didn't want to see change.

Established residents were more likely than new residents to discuss and critique the humanities. The latter told me they didn't know what should be taught in these areas. Like Marie recalling the Facing History curriculum to which she was exposed in her private middle school, others discussed the incorporation of related topics in the public school arena. Part of the Wellesley Middle School experience is a world religions curriculum that a long-term administrator estimated had been in place for fifteen to twenty years. He explained the academic program:

> World religions is taught in sixth grade . . . that includes field trips, they go to a mosque and they go to a temple. Those are the two experiences that they have, and then they learned in the classroom about different religions, forms of Christianity, etc. We had a panel of Christian leaders who came in to speak of their experiences, everything from Unitarian to Catholic, you know, all the different [traditions]. And so, you know, I think the idea is to give sort of a well-rounded sense for students, it's not to preach any one religion is better, which I think would be obvious to us in the public schools that we would not do that. And yet, I have to admit that, you know, we did get a couple of responses from parents who were concerned about what we were saying to kids about religion. So, you know, I think there's still question in the community by some people, even though we would never do something like that in the school. We're not here to tell kids what to think, just how to think about things.

A clergy member discussed the impact of the temple on the school system, referencing this world religions curriculum: "Yes, they have a synagogue visit now, and they incorporated Hanukkah music, and we work closely with the schools on the curricula." Clare also discussed the clergy's involvement with the middle school's world religions curriculum. Her son came home after visiting the synagogue during a field trip, she said, having decided he wanted to be Jewish. Although Clare said that jokingly, others see such a curriculum as a threat.

As the administrator mentioned, religious institutions as a stage for greater knowledge of and contact between and among groups has occasionally raised concerns. In the spring of 2010, as part of the standard curriculum, students visited a synagogue and a mosque. A parent chaperone recorded five White boys who seemed to be praying at the mosque and shortly thereafter contacted the district as well as various news outlets. The district was sued by a small group of parents, a harbinger of the fights that would only grow around school curriculum and its intersection with increasing diversity and politics. The district apologized and, in the wake of this incident, did not include the field trip in the curriculum the following year.

The teaching of American history had also recently raised tensions in the Wellesley school community, as it has around the United States.[23]

For example, the middle school humanities curriculum on exploration and colonialism had students do a project in which Columbus was put on trial. Gianni said, "Now we get in a fight over whether Columbus was a rapist and a murderer, or perhaps somebody that helped us discover the New World. It's a tough one. I mean, what's the answer to that one? He maybe was both." He felt that the teaching of American history had become too politicized and "woke." He also criticized the teaching of critical race theory, although it was not clear whether Wellesley did in fact teach it.

Sadie, a community member who had taken on numerous leadership roles in schools and in social and civic organizations, also discussed changes in the school curriculum. Interestingly, Sadie, as a Jewish woman, did not like the recent direction of the schools.

> You ever notice they'll talk about the vernal equinox? Talk more about the things that are the season, from a weather perspective, than pieces of one's religion or what they observe? That's much less the conversation. So they're cutting snowflakes and they're not making menorahs. Even Christmas trees, you don't see that anymore either. It's equal, but I think those things are important. How do we learn about each other if we don't understand?

Sadie criticized the move toward a "colorblind" community, which she saw as neither genuine nor helpful. Gianni saw a rigid, black-and-white interpretation of history. What both of these residents were saying, from their different religious, ethnic, and political perspectives, was that the absence of nuance in a town and country that have become increasingly diverse is a problem. These local conversations reflect larger sociopolitical fights across the United States.

In less contested areas, the school curriculum in Wellesley had expanded to include new languages, including Italian throughout periods of the twentieth century and Mandarin in the twenty-first century. These languages were added to the curriculum apparently as a result of both the demands of new groups as they gained power in the community and the desires of established groups. For example, the periodic addition of Italian classes—first in 1936, the same year as the founding of the Italo-American Educational Club—may have spoken to the rising clout of the Italian community across the town, as well as established residents' ongoing love affair with high Italian culture. The classes stopped being offered in the late 1930s, possibly in response to global events, including the formalized pact between Italy and Germany in 1939. The introduction of Mandarin classes at the high school, the founding of the Asian Culture Club, and the opening of the Chinese Language School similarly occurred during the same period, all starting in 2009. Many Chinese American students enrolled in the classes, often to acquire written skills they might not have been exposed to at home, even though they were fully bilingual speakers. All of these additions may have spoken to the growing power of new groups.

A school administrator discussed the implementation of a Chinese AP exam at the high school level:

> So there was a Zoom school committee meeting [attended by] I would say twelve or so people in the community, some students, some parents, some community members.... We had an interaction with the Chinese Language School in town. We only really give AP tests at Wellesley High School for classes that we teach, for students that go here. And there are kids who take AP Chinese at the Chinese Language School, need a testing center, and wanted to be able to take it at Wellesley High. And so they were appealing to us to do that. So we do now. Not for kids who live outside of town, but for Wellesley residents.

Jing spoke proudly about her role in convincing Wellesley High to provide testing space for the Chinese students enrolled in the Chinese Language School and on behalf of town residents generally:

> It's very fortunate we have that option for our school kids, or our residents, whoever wants to take that, you know, to have an opportunity to take it at Wellesley High. Whether you want it or not, it's up to the student, but now we have the opportunity. Initially, they didn't even give that opportunity to the kids, but how is it fair, right, that you have Spanish, but you cannot have the preceptor for supervising the exam for me? It is just not right. So our school [Chinese Language School] did lead that discussion.

Jing was working to retain her cultural heritage and pass it down to her children, but her engagement with the school system also spoke to her assimilation. In claiming that Mandarin students had as much right to be tested at Wellesley High as students learning other languages ("How is it fair, right, that you have Spanish?"), Jing was working to expand opportunity for everyone, including established residents who may have had an academic or cultural interest in Mandarin or saw future professional or economic benefits.

School Events

There have also been significant changes within the schools outside of the classrooms. *Fiddler on the Roof*, the musical about Russian Jewish immigration to the United States at the end of the nineteenth century, was first performed at Wellesley High School in 1967. The musical, which had recently been performed on Broadway, told a story that Jewish Americans, now maturing into their third generation, recognized as their own. The impact of the Wellesley production spoke to how local ethnic organizations can channel the zeitgeist. For example, when the Wellesley

Middle School staged the play in 1980, a teacher reached out to the rabbi at Temple Beth Elohim and asked him to meet with students involved in the play to help them better understand the history of Jewish migration to the United States. The *Wellesley Townsman* article, headlined "'Fiddler' Cast Gets a History Lesson," described this interaction: "The rabbi discussed with the young thespians the history of the Jewish people during the late 19th century in Russia. Included in his most informative talk were topics such as the role of the mother and father in the Jewish family, the importance of Sabbath, and the meaning of various terms e.g. including 'maseltov.'"[24] *Fiddler on the Roof* was performed again in 1985, but this time by a St. John's Evangelist Catholic Church group, with another local rabbi cast in the play.[25] As these cultural initiatives by Jewish residents of Wellesley demonstrate, attempts at ethnic retention can translate into larger cultural transformation.

School clubs in Wellesley have grown to include the Chinese Culture Club and the Translation Club, a high school group that assists individuals and community organizations when they need to have documents translated from English into another language with which some students are familiar. An inaugural "Color Dash" event was held at one of the public elementary schools in May 2022, and it was replicated in 2023. "The Color Dash," according to the website, "is an untimed, non-competitive, all-inclusive event—no winners, no medals, no prizes . . . all fun! Originally inspired by the Hindu festival of Holi, color runs have become wildly popular globally. This event embraces the core values of our school by bringing the community together for a fun, active celebration." The language used here—becoming "popular globally," representing "core values"—seeks to create a common understanding by using the same language used for other such events. The website photos show children of a range of races and ethnicities, as do the names of the volunteers. In collaboration with PTOs and other groups in town, schools have also recently held "international nights" that showcase food, dance, music, and other cultural artifacts from various countries. These events reflect simultaneous cultural retention and assimilation, with ancillary impacts on the established community.[26]

School Policies

Unlike changes to optional activities like performing in plays or joining clubs, other school system changes are mandated and widespread. The annual public school "Christmas Concerts" were so named until 1986, but as the community became more diverse, questions about the name arose.[27] In 1987, the superintendent, working to remove obvious religious celebrations in the Wellesley Public School System, passed a policy that disallowed Christmas decorations and the singing of blatantly religious songs in the holiday concert, provoking a backlash by some residents.[28]

Durable Institutional Changes Across the Community   139

As established groups experience claims-making by new groups seeking greater relational equality in the integration process, they may fear that their status is being downgraded along with their traditional celebrations.

Anna, in her late forties at the time of the interview, was Jewish and had graduated from Wellesley High School in the late 1980s. "Back in the day," she recalled, "we had Christmas concerts and we were singing about Santa and Holy Night, one 'Dreidel, Dreidel' at the end. You know, just throw it in there for those couple of Jews." Hannah, a Jewish woman in her late fifties, and Lily, a woman in her late forties who was raised Episcopalian but identified as atheist, both recalled their mothers going to the schools to talk about the blatantly religious Christmas songs at the annual Christmas concert. Speaking of her children's experiences, Abby, a Jewish woman in her late forties, said that "my son calls them 'Jesus songs.' They are still sung in the high school and the choir, and that's why my son won't do it." At the same time, others discussed a broader musical representation in today's concerts, which are now called "winter" or "holiday" concerts. Lily said that the schools now even perform songs that are neither Jewish nor Christian.

Relatedly, there are policies around holidays, both those officially recognized on the school calendar and those only now beginning to receive recognition. Clare discussed the policies in place around the Jewish High Holidays before they were formally incorporated into the school calendar— no homework on those nights, no new material covered in class, no tests given. Lunar New Year, Diwali, and Eid received the same treatment before they were incorporated into the school calendar for the 2024–2025 school year. Leah, a Jewish woman in her early fifties, discussed sports policies in regard to religious holidays.

> They wanted to do a boys and girls varsity thing . . . and they were trying to figure out a day, and they're like, "How about on Yom Kippur?" And they're all like, "Oh, my God, that's a great idea." And I'm just standing there, like, "Oh, this is gonna be a disaster." I didn't say anything. I'm like, "This is gonna be a disaster, because [my daughter]'s gonna have to go to temple. She was the only Jewish kid on the team. . . . And so then someone says, "Do you think we can do it on Yom Kippur?" And then they turned, everyone turns to me.

Leah neither gave her okay for practice to go forward nor even responded to the group's question. She was pleased to learn that the head of the athletics department informed parents that they could not hold the practice that day. She remarked that this was "a huge change. Like back when I was young, we didn't have the holidays off, and it really didn't matter."

Sadie talked about another policy change reflecting changing demographics—the scheduling of the Massachusetts Comprehensive

Assessment System (MCAS) exams, the multiday, multisubject, state-mandated tests whose results have implications for school funding and rankings. Some years ago, one of the MCAS exams was scheduled on the first day of Passover, an important weeklong Jewish holiday in the spring. A school committee member recalled a conversation about this scheduling: "They were trying to figure out why certain kids need to be rescheduled for MCAS." She explained to the school committee that it was the morning after the first seder, an important festival meal that often went late into the night. Multiple Muslim parents and students cited as an issue the scheduling of classwork, AP tests, and MCAS exams during the monthlong holiday of Ramadan. Going forward, the school committee was looking at the calendar and the range of holidays before scheduling work, but they pointed out that MCAS and AP exams were largely beyond the control of a local school committee.

The Wellesley Public School System established an Office of Diversity, Equity, and Inclusion in 2019 and also launched a series of affinity groups in 2021 as part of the district's five-year Diversity, Equity, and Inclusion (DEI) plan, itself a sign of a changed and changing community. These programs were developed partially in response to the Black Lives Matter movement and the rise in Asian hate crimes during the COVID pandemic to create spaces where students of color could speak freely, without risk of offending someone from another group. This became a particularly contentious initiative following the murder of Asian and Asian American women in Atlanta in March 2021, when the district sent out an email explicitly providing support for students of color. Parents Defending Education, a national organization seeking to develop local roots across the country, quickly filed a lawsuit claiming that establishing racial affinity groups and explicitly supporting students of color were racially discriminatory acts against White students. The district settled the lawsuit in 2022; in retaining the right to have such groups in the system, the district made them open to anyone interested in joining, regardless of race or ethnicity. This back-and-forth illustrates the ongoing fluidity of intergroup relations and the ways in which national events take on local significance—in this case with national media outlets spotlighting Wellesley. These national conversations have only grown more strident in President Trump's second administration, with the threat and actual removal of federal funding from academic institutions with diversity, equity, and inclusion initiatives of any kind.

A school administrator also explained that communications are now distributed in multiple languages. As discussed in chapter 5, PTOs have done this going back more than a decade, but in piecemeal fashion. The school system more recently undertook the policy of distributing information in a range of languages when the need became obvious during the COVID pandemic. Signs within the schools are also posted in English,

Figure 6.3 Multilingual Signs Posted in Wellesley High School, Wellesley, Massachusetts, 2024

Source: Author's photo.

Spanish, and Mandarin (figure 6.3). An executive order signed by President Trump in 2025 declaring English as the official language of the country raises questions about what this will mean at the local level.

Finally, the Wellesley High School graduation ceremony is always held on the first Friday in June. A rabbi interviewed commented on this practice:

> We have asked them not to do it on Friday night, and their response was usually "It's before sundown." Now, in truth, we start services every week at six o'clock. So one could say it's not sensitive to our practice, even though

philosophically they're saying it's allowed for a Jew to come, but they've never changed it off a Friday night.

What is less well known is that the graduation time was changed in 1982, in response to requests from the temple and members of the Jewish community in town. A *Wellesley Townsman* article discussed a school committee meeting in which future graduation times were moved from 6:00 p.m. to 5:00 p.m. for the explicit purpose of making the timing of graduation more accommodating to members of the Jewish community who were celebrating both Shabbat and high school graduation.[29]

Changing Holidays

One of the clearest illustrations of the impact of new groups on the established community is a changed holiday landscape. The ability to incorporate new holidays into the American canon speaks to a group's civic and social assimilation combined with cultural retention.[30] It also speaks to an ethnic group's organizational and political power.[31]

Groups utilize multiple strategies to this end, including tying holidays to "traditional" American values to make them more palatable and accepted.[32] Depending on the flexibility of the holiday and the rules governing it, another possibility is expanding its observance to those outside of traditional celebrants.[33] Groups may also make claims, insisting that they have a right to the honor and deference accorded other groups.

These strategies are illustrated in the archival documents, interviews, and participant observation data, as well as across ethnic groups throughout the twentieth and twenty-first centuries. For example, Grossman's Lumber Yard placed this ad in the *Wellesley Townsman* in fall 1955:

> In Observance of Jewish Holy Days, all Divisions of Grossman's will be closed. In the same way the Grossman Company closes its main office and all twenty New England Branches on the most solemn Christian holy days during the year, so does this traditional closing encompass the entire organization on these highest Jewish holy days. In this way the Grossmans show their sincere regard for the spiritual values in this age of materialism.[34]

Although this was not the first year that the company had closed for the holidays, it was the first time the closure had been explained this way. It is not clear whether the ad was attempting to justify the closing or to connect through commonly shared values, or perhaps both. As time passed, Grossman's would drop this phrasing, then stop advertising its store closings, and then stop closing for the holidays altogether. Both the religious observance of the holidays and Grossman's response illustrate Jewish residents' cultural retention and assimilation, as well as the resulting variegated assimilation.

In a slightly different way, Asian residents also attempted to make common cause with other residents through holidays such as Lunar New Year, Diwali, and Holi. Stanley and Paul Chin, owners of Chin's Village, a Chinese restaurant that operated from the 1940s until the 1980s, worked to broaden these connections. An October 1971 *Wellesley Townsman* article cited the participation of Chin's Village in the annual Veterans Day parade with a Chinese dragon to celebrate Chinese New Year.[35] Although Chinese New Year would not take place for months, the Chins' participation in this November event spoke to the malleability of the holiday.[36] It also connected Chinese New Year with the most American of events—a small-town Veterans Day parade.

In more recent years, Wellesley High School, in anticipation of Diwali, sent out an email explaining it as a festival that "celebrates good over evil and the triumph of inner light over ignorance." A widely distributed Holi invitation highlighted the celebration's "delicious food," "Bollywood music," and "crafts for kids." In an event similar to the Color Dash held at one of the local elementary schools, the local temple now sponsors a "Dreidel Dash" 5k race to celebrate Hanukkah. The race attracts temple members, Jewish nonmembers, and even those from other religious and nonreligious backgrounds. In each of these examples, a new group intentionally Americanized its holidays and cultural traditions, even while working to retain them.

Tensions develop when new groups move from requesting acceptance of their ethnic holidays and offering participation in them to insisting on formal recognition. The three greatest such changes over the past thirty years were the addition of the Jewish High Holidays to the school calendar in 1996, the removal of Columbus Day from both the school and town calendars in 2021, and the addition of Lunar New Year, Diwali, and Eid in 2024.

The particular holidays discussed by interviewees appeared to be generational, suggesting that the context in which individuals came of age mattered.[37] Older participants were more likely to discuss the observance—or lack of observance—of the Jewish holidays. Mike, a man in his mid-sixties who identified as Episcopalian, said sarcastically, "By the way, no acknowledgment or time off for any of the Jewish holidays, because why would you? There's no one who's Jewish here," referring to when he was a public school student. Clare mentioned the tension she felt each year around the Jewish holidays because school was not closed: "It was always frictional, being closed or not, having to make up work, and it was tough on the Jewish kids. It was a problem." Articles in the *Wellesley Townsman* reveal these tensions. One piece entitled "School Start Date Irks Jewish Parents" was followed a week later by a letter to the editor taking issue with not only the town's refusal to close the schools but also the paper's characterization of the Jewish parents as "irked."[38] It was not until the 1996–1997 school year that the Jewish High Holidays were officially incorporated. A school committee member explained that the decision came down to a numbers issue—there were too many students and teachers absent during the Jewish High Holidays. Moreover, the district policy was to disallow giving tests or covering new material on a religious holiday, even with the schools open. It no longer made sense to have school on those days, the school committee decided, given the changing demographics.

Siobhan did not view it as a problem for students to take the day off for religious reasons and would have preferred maintaining the old policy. As a single working parent, she was impacted by the changing demographics in the community and resulting changes in the school calendar. "When are they in school? At the beginning, you know, from September to December, if you're a working parent, it's hard all the time. And I guess I just, I don't see it as a big deal if your kid doesn't go to school, they're not penalized. I guess that's different from when we were kids." Siobhan had no issue per se with new holidays being added, but she did object to the burden placed on parents when schools were closed on holidays that were not more widely recognized in the workplace.

The Jewish participants remembered having to explain why they were not in school. Anna recalled that, "growing up, we didn't have the High Holidays off. So, you know, that was something that I had to, you know, do different, which is like 'Why didn't you come to school those two days?' 'Oh, you know, it's Rosh Hashanah.' It was just hard to explain." Leah had a similar experience in school: "We didn't have the holidays off, and it didn't really matter. And you had to raise your hand, 'Who's not going to be here on Rosh Hashanah?'" Today's holiday policy was a "huge change," Leah said, from when she was in school in Wellesley. Hannah, a Jewish woman in her late fifties, said, "I remember calling my brother, being like, 'You are not going to believe this.' I remember it was huge. I was shocked when Wellesley started giving Yom Kippur off."

Starting in 2021, discussions began around putting Lunar New Year and Diwali on the school calendar. Speaking to the ongoing demographic shifts in the town, a student wrote a November 2022 article for the high school newspaper, the *Bradford*, entitled "The Wellesley Public Schools' New Strategic Plan: Is It an Opportunity to Add Religious and Cultural Holidays to the Academic Calendar?"[39] The author was a second-generation Asian American.

The subject of the school calendar arose in an interview with Andrew, a teacher and administrator. He stated, "There was a request from some students. And actually, there was a school committee meeting earlier this year (2022–2023) where some community members joined to try to get Lunar New Year on our calendar." A January 2023 article in *The Swellesley Report* on the meeting in which residents advocated for the inclusion of Lunar New Year reported: "During Citizen Speak ... members of Wellesley's Asian community—including parents, the Wellesley Chinese Language School's principal, and students—lined up online to make their case for Lunar New Year's importance."[40]

The multiyear push by the Chinese community to have Lunar New Year added to the academic calendar had an unintended consequence: members of the significantly smaller Muslim community were mobilized to speak out and request that Eid be added to the calendar as well. Five Muslim community members spoke passionately at Citizen Speak about the importance of Eid's inclusion. A Chinese American Muslim man explained that not all observances were equally flexible: he could celebrate Lunar New Year with his children on a weekend but Eid required attendance at the mosque. The Muslim community, which lacked the formal organizational structure in town of other new groups, had been following the Chinese community's push for Lunar New Year and followed its lead. At the December 2023 school committee meeting, the five-member board voted three-to-two to add Lunar New Year, Diwali, and Eid to the calendar.

The push to add new holidays also revealed tensions between groups. One new resident said of the addition of new holidays: "We have way too many holidays just for Catholics and Jews." Another new resident explained the additional holidays in stating, "You have a lot of Jewish festivals, right? So [the schools] wanted to diversify that."

There was significant outcry in Wellesley over the addition of these holidays. Parents complained that the school year would extend too late into June, impact the ability of students to attend summer programs that had already started, and be particularly challenging to manage for households with two working parents. Forty of the more than seventy emails received by the school committee after the vote were from individuals who did not want to see any changes, twenty-five were from those who wanted an expansion (thirteen for Lunar New Year, Eid, and Diwali; seven for Lunar New Year; five for Lunar New Year and Eid), and six requested the removal of the Jewish holidays and Good Friday—in other words, reverting to federal holidays only. For some established community members, the calendar change represented "wokeness" and multiculturalism run amok. One parent writing on a website in response to the changes said, "It almost seems like DEI is totally opposite to democracy. The less people support anything, the higher priority DEI will get." Complaints about the new school calendar and the process by which it had been decided led to the formation of a holiday task force.

Somewhat surprisingly, concerns around adding holidays to the school calendar were echoed by a few Chinese immigrants interviewed. Although they liked the idea of Chinese New Year being a holiday, they recognized that the inclusion of Lunar New Year also meant the inclusion of other holidays they did not celebrate. Mei and Anh viewed these extra holidays as unnecessary days off from school when kids were already not in school enough (even though the state mandate that the academic year would have 180 school days did not change), and they were also concerned about the challenges for households with two working parents. Anh said, "There are people like me who think we should remove all those religious holidays from the school calendar, but the kids can be excused from the school if they want to celebrate the day." A clear majority of Chinese residents, she said, wanted to see only Chinese New Year added.

Mei reported that a young, second-generation Chinese American approached her about speaking out in favor of adding the holiday to the calendar, but she declined. Similarly, the Muslim residents who spoke were uniformly second-generation (or later) Americans. These trends may speak to their assimilation to difference in twenty-first-century American society and their feeling of having a right as Americans to make such demands.[41] Mei and Anh, both first-generation immigrants, were more focused on supporting their children's education and getting themselves to work.

In contrast, Jing who was very active in the Chinese Language School, was pleased with the addition of the holiday. The process by which the school calendar was reformed displayed the particularly critical role played by ethnic organizations through engaging with local government, an indicator of civic assimilation.[42] Interestingly, the interviewees who showed the greatest level of support for the calendar changes did not celebrate any of the new holidays. But they viewed the changes as a sign of greater inclusivity within the town, as well as a signal to those outside of the community of how much Wellesley had changed.

The holiday debates also illustrated the extent to which settling such issues comes to be viewed as a zero-sum game—in contrast to the non-zero-sum assimilation model posited by Alba.[43] Sadie, an active volunteer and elected official, said, "It's not an accident that it's called winter break. It's not called Christmas break, it's called winter break." She saw this as an attempt to protect the Christian holidays by removing the religious component from the term in a sort of "whitewashing." Such changes in nomenclature are similar to what was seen around the renaming of holiday concerts. Sadie cited a recent discussion about the calendar:

> There's Rosh Hashanah and Yom Kippur that are given off. We have a much higher than typical New England town percentage of Jewish students in our town. I don't even know how the conversation started, but it was, well, "If we are giving these two, we're giving Jewish holidays, should we be giving Diwali? Should we be giving blah, blah, blah, blah?" And is it okay to say, "You know what, we're not going to give Good Friday? But if we don't do that, are we then taking away Rosh Hashana?" So there was almost like, there has to be this tit-for-tat kind of situation if we're going

to do away with anything. Well, of course, these conversations, when they get going like this, they get going. And so, one of the rabbis came to school committee. The rabbi came, and he sent a letter or something and ... everyone found that, they felt it was very important that these remain the same, but it was a couple of weeks–long conversation about what we're going to do with these calendars.

The Jewish holidays remain on the calendar for now, with supporters having utilized their ethnic-specific organizations. Newer groups, utilizing their own ethnic organizations, have now made their own mark on the school calendar.

Another sign of changing demographics is the removal of Columbus Day from both the school and town government calendars. An acrimonious campaign was waged for over a year before a nonbinding town-wide referendum was held in 2020: 49 percent of voters voted in favor of the change and 43 percent against it (8 percent abstained). In 2021, the five-person elected select board then took a vote: four members voted to change the name of the holiday and one voted to keep it as Columbus Day. The holiday was changed.

This local issue reflects larger national and even global conversations around colonization. As American society has diversified, history is being reconsidered and collective memory questioned.[44] Research on Columbus Day conducted by Arianne Eason and her colleagues finds that American identity is an important predictor of who wants to maintain it.[45] Gianni connected Columbus's journey with the journey taken by his grandfather: "It's like going to the United States. He did the same journey, right?" Columbus Day lost its place on the town calendar, even while its defense was largely based on its Americanness. Simultaneously, the discussion about this very American holiday reactivated ethnic identity. Clearly angry and hurt, Gianni said:

> I think we only celebrate anti-ethnic activities. I think we protest more about the potential of activities, like Columbus Day. And you name it today. You know, no one's allowed to do anything anymore. I think there's a push towards anti-religion in our communities, and I think there's a push towards anti-ethnicity, unless you're, unless you're from an ethnic group that is being oppressed. And it's really sad to see this. . . . Is there a way we can celebrate Indigenous People's Day and celebrate the best that Columbus brought to the United States, to Italian culture? Can't we do that? Can you see my side of it? You know, but you can't, because if you like Columbus, you're racist.

Not all Italian Americans took this position, however, and tensions arose within the Italian American community in interviews. The coalition to change Columbus Day to Indigenous People's Day comprised people of different racial, ethnic, and religious backgrounds. One Italian

American resident interviewed referred to the person of Italian descent involved in the campaign as a "former friend." Another Italian American resident questioned whether that person was really Italian. He had not known them from the "neighborhood" and thus did not believe they were really of the same background. Another Italian American interviewed, someone highly engaged in the community but of a younger generation, did not see Columbus Day in the same way as older Italian Americans.

The removal of Columbus Day highlights a difference from how the other holiday debates played out. The synagogue in town had come out to "protect" the Jewish High Holidays and had thus far been successful. The Chinese Language School succeeded in having Lunar New Year added to the calendar. Both were instances of ethnic organizations engaging with mainstream institutions in an effort at cultural retention.

In contrast, the Italian organizations in the community had appeared to decline in influence, most likely because of Italian Americans' position in the cycle of immigration and assimilation. An obituary from 1983 for ninety-one-year old Peter Amalfi, an Italian immigrant and the first president of the Italo-American Educational Club, illustrates the progress of the immigrant-turned-ethnic Italian community over the course of the twentieth century.[46] By the end of Amalfi's life, the community of third and later generation Italian Americans had blended into the established community as rates of intermarriage rose and the group's ethnic salience declined. Eleanor, an elderly woman who was not Italian but knew the community well, discussed the formal removal of Columbus Day: "I always thought precinct B would come out and fight for it. And interestingly, they didn't, because they lost Precinct B." Precinct B is historically the Italian enclave where the Italo-American Educational Club is located, but after decades of segregation, the Italian community has now spread out beyond the boundaries of this neighborhood. She continued: "It could be that the Italian group which was all fired up last fall just sort of frittered away. They didn't have the energy, and they didn't have the organization." Eleanor understood the critical role of ethnic organizations.

At the same time, the removal of Columbus Day from the calendar should not be interpreted as the end of Italian ethnic identity in the community. While some have argued that Italian Americans are in the "twilight of ethnicity," that idea has been reconsidered.[47] For some with Italian backgrounds, the removal of the holiday activated dormant cultural connections. In a much less publicized decision taken shortly after the formal change, the select board renamed October "Italian Heritage Month." While much of the Italian community's ethnic solidarity and mobilizing power had declined, the ladders the community built upward were not entirely gone.

Public Religious Representation

Until 2005, the only holiday with any religious affiliation recognized on town property was Christmas. Originally, the holiday was celebrated with a creche, but the creche was swapped out for a Christmas tree in front of town hall. After a local Jewish group threatened to bring a lawsuit seeking equal representation, a menorah also appeared in front of town hall, and a few years later a crescent moon (a representation of Islam, not any particular Islamic holiday) was added. These new additions were discussed by numerous residents, Jewish and non-Jewish alike, including Elizabeth, who began this chapter:

> When I was on the board of selectmen, we had our first Jewish selectperson, who was so completely opposed to the town's focus on Christmas as a holiday. So they brought—I think there was a council of clergy that met monthly. So she brought them all together and said, "We can't have wreaths everywhere, we can't have a Christmas tree in the town hall. We can't do this. We can't do that. We have to be more open, and we need to recognize that there are other groups here in the town for whom Christmas is not their holiday. And what do we do about it?" And honestly, honestly, this went on as a debate, you know, this isn't that long ago. Well, it had to have been like 2007 or 2008, hardly any time at all. And this debate went on, and on and on. And I think the Council of . . . Clergy people are more advanced and thoughtful about this than our little board of selectmen. So finally, as you know, we get input from everybody and oh gosh, it was tough, and only ended up with—I don't even know if you've noticed at holiday time, what's up on the hill, at town hall?

Elizabeth was referring to the three symbols on display—the Christmas tree, the menorah, and the crescent moon—which she described as required to be of the same height and equidistant from each other (figure 6.4). In her reference to the Council of Clergy, an interfaith group in town, we see the influence of another hybrid organization on townwide decisions. In April 2020, an obituary commemorating a Muslim doctor and fifty-year resident of the town appeared in *The Swellesley Report*. He lobbied to have both the menorah and the crescent moon added to the public space.[48] The subtitle of the article, "A Reminder of How We Got Here," speaks volumes about individuals and groups in the community building ladders up to townwide institutions.

The push for this form of public representation was not welcomed by all members of the Jewish community, which, like any seemingly monolithic group, held a diversity of opinions. A rabbi explained:

> See, the [other] rabbi really takes a very active presence while I'm here. . . . I'm very friendly with him, but whereas [our synagogue] was in a cul-de-sac

Figure 6.4   Town Hall in December, Wellesley, Massachusetts

Source: Author's photo.

with no Jewish symbols, he has a giant menorah on, and he starts to become very vocal in the *Townsman* and at town meeting, wanting to put a Hanukkah menorah on town property. So I definitely get called in for that one. . . . So he pushes the envelope in ways of Judaism in the public square that [our] members did not invite or welcome.

Interestingly, Gianni, an Italian Catholic and lifelong resident, raised the issue of the menorah on the town green when asked about changes in the town. Although he was critical about changes in school curricula and the removal of Columbus Day, he had this to say about changes from when he was a child: "More stuff gets done because more people of diversity came positioned in town to make that kind of stuff happen. I think if you don't make it happen, whatever your thing is, it won't happen."

Public Celebrations

Evidence of a changing community is also found in public celebrations. For decades the main community-wide event has been the Veterans Day

Parade. Traditionally held in November, the parade has in recent decades been made a part of "Wellesley's Wonderful Weekend," a community-wide celebration that takes place in May. As previously cited, Paul Chin, owner of Chin's Village, became a sponsor of the event in 1971, when it was still a fall parade for veterans. The restaurant's float was a Chinese dragon, representative of Chinese New Year. In more recent years, the Chinese Language School has cosponsored the now-springtime event and runs a booth at the Sunday night fireworks. Other sponsors include a variety of other immigrant-owned businesses, such as the Russian School of Math and Kumon, reflecting changes that other research has identified in similar suburban communities.[49]

Other public celebrations have also undergone changes. The Interfaith Thanksgiving Celebration has often been held at the temple as well as at local churches in town. Various rabbis through the years, going back to the 1950s, have been commencement speakers at high school and college graduation ceremonies. It has not been unusual to hear a rabbi giving the invocation at public events, such as a townwide Memorial Day service, a Veterans Day event, or the opening of town meeting. Historically, community involvement like this has been a relatively easy and low-cost way to expand the boundaries of the Jewish community. What has also changed can be seen in what no longer takes place—such as the church service once held before the big Thanksgiving football game each year. That change came the year a rabbi received a phone call from a temple member. The member's son was the high school team's quarterback and did not want to attend the church service before the big game. After the temple reached out to the Wellesley Public School System, the traditional service was discontinued.

Town Meeting Resolutions and Responses

In recent years, the town has also passed a series of what are largely symbolic resolutions. One could argue, however, that the symbolism itself matters, particularly given the town's history. In 1963, a town resident and the president of B'nai B'rith Wellesley approached the board of selectmen for a proclamation honoring the 120th anniversary of the Jewish civil rights and social service organization. The governor of Massachusetts and the mayor of Boston had both signed such proclamations, but the town of Wellesley refused.

In April 2023, a town meeting member evoked the town's recalcitrance in the past when arguing in favor of supporting funding for an equity audit and passing a resolution stating, "As a Town, we will respond to stop intolerance or hate based on race, skin color, religion, national origin, ethnicity, sex, gender, gender identity/expression, class, socio-economic status, sexual orientation, disability, or any other like characteristic." This member spoke at the meeting about recently learning that racially restrictive covenants had been in place in her neighborhood until 1970.

In prior years, the town has passed resolutions speaking to both local and national issues. A 2021 resolution stating the town's anti-bias and anti-racist position was a response to both the Black Lives Matter movement and the rise in anti-Asian violence during the pandemic. A resolution against anti-Semitism passed in 2022 specifically repudiated the "Mapping Project," which identified the names and addresses of Jewish nonprofits and businesses that were being targeted for their support of Israel. In 2023, town meeting passed a diversity, equity, and inclusion statement for Wellesley.

Such initiatives would seem to be relatively straightforward, but they are not. One resident, speaking against Article 17, the 2023 resolution to "stop intolerance," felt that it "wrongfully condemns the town." She argued that Wellesley "has a pattern of accepting people (such as Italians) after some initial bias."[50] Further, town meeting coupled the resolution with $100,000 for an equity audit, an initiative to assess the town's strengths and weaknesses in regard to diversity, equity, and inclusion. The proponent of the article was a refugee who came to town as a child, and it received widespread support both from established residents and residents of formerly new groups who had been folded into the established community. The passage of the article, its proponents, and the money allocated for it all speak to a town very different from the one where Schofield Elementary School students had to raise $114 in 1974 for a Holocaust exhibit held at the Wellesley Free Library.

In addition to these resolutions, the town government has responded in other ways to the changing community. Jing, who had been active in the Chinese Language School from its inception, discussed the racism experienced by Asian members of the community, particularly following the COVID pandemic. She told me that residents were yelled at, spit on, and, in a meeting she was running for the Chinese Language School, Zoom-bombed. National and global events were having clear impacts locally.[51] The racialization of COVID and its implications for Chinese immigrants and Chinese Americans is also reminiscent of the mainstream contestation over Jewish American incorporation during the Red Scare of the 1950s and 1960s and the focus on organized crime in discussion of the incorporation of Italian Americans.[52]

The experience of this racism during the pandemic motivated the Chinese Language School to organize an educational listening forum for the entire Wellesley community. Both Asian and non-Asian residents attended the Zoom forum, including the chief of police. In addition, the group organized—with assistance from the multiethnic group World of Wellesley and the larger New England Chinese American Alliance—

a "Stop Asian Hate" rally at the town hall in March 2021. Local and statewide representatives attended and spoke out in a show of support. The news article reporting on the event also provided a Mandarin translation just below the English article.[53] The racialization of the Chinese community was not met with silence but rather with an organized response from the established community.

Conclusion

New groups can reshape the larger structures within a community, but it takes time, often generations, as well as resources. A critical mass of members of a new group needs to amass prior to the formation of organizations. As these organizations assist their coethnic members in adjusting, "assimilating," and retaining aspects of their cultural background, they also serve to build bridges to other organizations and ladders up to decision-making bodies. Equally as important, these groups act as training grounds and launch pads for their members to become part of the mainstream institutions in the community. It is only through this form of engagement that a group can begin to gain relational equality and have a say in the public institutions that affect them as a group.

The data in this chapter illustrate the many ways in which new groups have impacted Wellesley. Through changes in school curriculum, the holiday calendar, and representation on the town green, various forms of relational integration are no longer optional for established residents but the current reality. While residents are not required to attend a lecture on the politics of China or join an intentionally multicultural club, they cannot send their children to school on the Jewish High Holidays, nor can they (legally) remove the crescent moon from the town green. A private business may still post a sign that states "Closed for Columbus Day," as some local businesses do, but the town calendar says otherwise.

None of this is to suggest that the change is complete, but rather to illustrate the process of change as continuous. Changes are made manifest in a community owing to a range of factors, including the existence of relevant organizations in the community and whether they have the energy to engage their base and their allies and the power to exert sway at higher levels. These organizational characteristics are influenced in turn by a host of other factors, such as group size, socioeconomics, and tenure.

Immigrant groups may not immediately have the organizational resources to achieve their desired goals, whether it is introducing a new language into the school curriculum or having a holiday added to the school calendar. Members of a new group may be less likely to participate in the public sphere if they are less comfortable with English or are unfamiliar with the American system of government. The town meeting structure, unique to New England, adds another layer of learning. Clare described her experiences with her Chinese neighbors and friends:

> Most of my road is Chinese. And some of them are very friendly. I've gotten to know them. They realized I was an elected official. I became their personal elected official. The first time I ran, they came down to ask me what it would be that I would be doing and then they stayed—When would I know I won? They went to the polls and waited for the results. And now they check with me. I'm their gatekeeper of information, because they've never known someone in the government. I talked to the Chinese Language School when we were doing the town government study thing. They were afraid of the government. They didn't know the government was friendly. The government's friendly.

Although the government may have felt friendly to Clare, a member of the established population, it might have felt quite unfriendly to those with limited language skills and knowledge of the government. She was a critical player in the incorporation of these new residents, as was the Chinese Language School. Local elected officials and leaders of local ethnic-specific organizations work hand in hand.[54]

For Jewish residents who are native-born citizens and native English speakers, public engagement has taken time for a different reason—a wish to maintain a low profile. The rabbi interviewed spoke of a desire to not stand out in the community, as reflected in the location of the main synagogue: it is largely hidden from street view and has no discernible signage or religious representation on the outside. Elizabeth, discussing the Wellesley of her earlier years, said, "So it was a very White community while I was growing up. A very White Protestant/Catholic community when I was growing up. The Jewish population was limited, and I think very cautious about their involvement in town." This was in the 1960s and 1970s. Although Jewish residents are now heavily involved in town governance, and there were nascent signs of such engagement as early as the 1960s, it took many more decades for Jewish residents to participate more fully. Today Jewish residents in Wellesley are overwhelmingly third-, fourth-and even fifth-generation Americans whose ancestors immigrated between 1880 and 1924; thus, they are officially part of the established community. Even with their longer tenure in the town and the societal expansion of group boundaries from a Protestant society to a Judeo-Christian one, Jews' religious practices, periodic upticks in anti-Semitism, national and international attitudes toward Israel, and their numerically small numbers continue to mark this group as distinct. As a result, Jewish residents of Wellesley have an ethnic identity that continues to maintain a sense of separation.

Longer tenure in Wellesley had different implications for the Italian Americans in town. While more time in the country and in Wellesley raised the participation rates of Jewish residents and strengthened their feeling of having the right to make claims, longtime tenure in the town made ethnicity optional for Italian Americans.[55] This group has now become part of the established community, as have Jewish residents, but with fewer qualifications. With their ethnic identity no longer a mobilizing force, some Italian Americans in Wellesley have responded to this change by becoming less engaged.

Events like the removal of Columbus Day from the calendar, however, may reinvigorate Italian identity and political engagement for some in a form of bumpy line or reactive ethnicity.[56] People's ethnic background can be revitalized when ethnic-related issues arise. Such was the case for Frank and Christopher, the oldest Italian Americans interviewed. Gianni said that he felt defensive about his religion and his ethnicity: "When that starts happening, I'm gonna start pushing back a little bit, you know what I mean?"

Racial identity may also emerge and make some Italian Americans feel that their status in the community is more liminal, their position questionable. As discussed in chapter 4, others raised Gianni's skin tone and ethnicity repeatedly in both high school and college. His college roommate commented, "Dude, I thought you were gonna be some like short Puerto Rican guy." Lucas, also Italian American, was asked by a Black acquaintance if he was Black. Lucas explained that he was complaining about White people, adding that "it was summertime, I had a tan." Taking no offense, he said "no." A woman in her seventies of southern European descent said, "When I was probably eight or nine, in the summer I would get really tanned, and I remember kids, some kids at the playground calling me the N-word." All of these experiences demonstrate how the darker complexion of some Americans of southern European descent is sometimes perceived and how that perception influences interactions, politics, and worldviews.[57]

Socioeconomic status may also factor into feelings of difference. Many Italian Americans in Wellesley have become highly successful as small-business owners and professionals in a range of fields. Some also have significant real estate holdings, their fathers and grandfathers having long ago bought the buildings in which those early businesses were housed. Although some industries in Wellesley continue to be viewed as ethnically concentrated, Italian American business owners in Wellesley today play a role far different from the role played by their grandparents' generation.[58] Still, feelings of being slightly lower status may persist. Lucas, a successful owner of a construction company, told me that he had never been invited to join the town's business organization, and he was not sure why. Gianni said that his father was one of the first Italian American residents to have a college degree and a job that was not in the trades.

Established groups in Wellesley are continuously changed by new groups as the latter develop their own ethnic-specific organizations and build bridges and ladders to make claims on mainstream institutions. The claims of new groups may be honored, in whole or in part, and integrated into the core. At least for now.

Who comprises the established will also change, as the new will eventually become the old. For some new groups, being swept into the established community corresponds with a decline in ethnic identity and only an occasional look back. For other groups, some elements of difference remain, and they may insist on maintaining these variations as part of the mainstream. At least for now.

Chapter 7

A Variegated Process: Three Paths to Change and the Road Ahead

Over the past one hundred years, Wellesley has moved from being an overwhelmingly White, Protestant, and restricted town to one with significant percentages of Italian, Jewish, and Asian residents. A town that had only a creche on the town green until the early twenty-first century is now a community that includes the Jewish High Holidays, Eid, Diwali, and Lunar New Year on the school calendar. Neighborhoods, workplaces, and even households have a range of races, religions, and ethnicities, in keeping with larger demographic trends.[1] Foodways are increasingly varied, and signs and emails appear in multiple languages.[2]

Prior research has largely focused on either the ways in which immigrant and ethnic groups influence the established community to remake society[3] or the ways in which the established community racializes new groups.[4] This case study has identified both neo-assimilation and racialization. This is a story of "both/and" rather than "either/or."[5] Further, prior research has tended to focus on only one level—either the micro-level processes of daily one-on-one interactions or the macro-level changes that can be identified only after decades of incremental change.[6]

The findings from Wellesley illustrate the need to incorporate micro-level interactions into theories of neo-assimilation, but within a larger local, national, and even international framework. Without considering the many levels of society and how they interact, any theory will be incomplete. The changes in Wellesley became possible only after various macro-level policies—economic, educational, civil rights, immigration—were changed. Richard Alba and Herbert Gans have both argued that social and economic policies played a critical role in the inclusion of second- and third-generation ethnics in the post–World War II period, a time of unprecedented educational opportunities and expanded economic growth. This non-zero-sum form of assimilation allowed racial and religious boundaries to be lowered so that *some* new groups, such as Italian and Jewish Americans, could become part of the mainstream. Jews would also come to rely heavily on the civil rights legislation of the 1960s to further break down barriers arising from housing discrimination. Similarly, Chinese and Indian immigrants are now Wellesley residents as the result of macro-level policies, specifically the 1965 Immigration Act, which prioritized immigrants' skills and opened the gates to people from a wider range of previously barred countries.

While these various macro-level policies set the stage for what *could* happen in Wellesley and beyond, they do not tell us what actually happened or how. Community change, such as what we have seen in Wellesley, results from the micro- and meso-level interactions and negotiations that take place on the ground but are only made possible through the larger macro-level conditions. Concomitantly, these macro-level changes are the result of micro- and meso-level processes. Consider the role that Madame Chiang Kai-shek's presence in Wellesley may have played in encouraging established residents to push their representatives, through the medium of the *Wellesley Townsman*, to overturn the Chinese Exclusion Act in 1943. In a much lighter vein, Madame Chiang Kai-shek's choice to wear slacks on her return visit in 1943 reverberated across Wellesley College and led to discussions about the dress code.

The smaller-scale actions that influence and reshape the mainstream sometimes arise from individuals and groups assimilating, sometimes from individuals and groups retaining their ethnic identities, and sometimes from reactions to racialization. These behaviors are interactive and take place across both sides of the equation. In traditional assimilation, an individual both moves toward the established community and is accepted by that community. But the cross-border interaction is not a simple story of invitation given, invitation accepted. The newest resident inevitably brings her own background to her new relationships with established residents, with impacts on the latter. Footpaths allow for multidirectional traffic. Cross-border interactions may also be the outcome of efforts by individuals and groups to maintain their cultural heritage, but again, such interactions do not remain on one side of the equation. Space must be rented, calendars negotiated, and particular food items purchased; all of these activities require interactions with the mainstream.

Finally, individuals and groups from a range of backgrounds may experience racialization and discrimination in the form of housing segregation or blatantly racist or anti-Semitic actions. Although this case study suggests that life in Wellesley is relatively harmonious, this characterization of the town should not be exaggerated. As discussed in various places throughout the book, ugly, racist, and anti-Semitic incidents have and continue to take place periodically in Wellesley. The high school valedictorian on his way to an elite university told his story of being accused of shoplifting. Chinese residents reported being spit on and harassed at a local grocery store during the COVID pandemic. Swastikas occasionally appear as graffiti in the school bathrooms, and Jewish residents recalled pennies being thrown at them or their children. But none of these examples represent the end of the story. As agentic beings, individuals react and push back against such behaviors, thus crossing over boundaries and shaping the mainstream.

These various pathways of assimilation, ethnic retention, and racialization, outlined in figure 1.2, continuously reshape the mainstream in a form of variegated assimilation. Keeping in mind that more than one of these processes may be taking place at a given time, it is also important to recognize that one pathway may be more dominant during a certain period or in a certain sector of the community. For example, the concomitant processes of assimilation and ethnic retention may be the main drivers behind changes in foodways or other nonthreatening cultural practices. In contrast, racialization and reactions to racialization drive larger structural changes, such as those related to housing.

Community organizations, most often ethnic-specific or hybrid groups, play critical roles in the reshaping of a community. Individuals from new groups coalesce for various purposes, including maintaining an identity, passing down traditions, and gaining a political voice, among many other reasons. In so doing, they are both assimilating to aspects of mainstream society, by utilizing mainstream tools, and retaining cultural identity. These actions, again, do not remain on one side of the equation but have impacts across borders, resulting in a process of variegated assimilation for the established community. This process of change only continues as mediating bodies build ladders up to decision-makers in a position to reshape the entire community.

As argued throughout this book, all of these interactions take place in a larger sociohistorical framework. The micro- and meso-level interactions in Wellesley, as well as in thousands of communities across the country, both reflect and reinforce the zeitgeist of the time. Fights over DEI are not a Wellesley issue but rather a larger battle across the country around who gets to tell the story of America and who receives status and honor. Further, conversations around what is going on in our schools arguably reflect and grow out of something still larger—the growing political polarization within the United States, which is tied to globalization, the automation of jobs, and increasing income inequality.

Such macro-level concerns may seem far afield from a case study on the impact of new residents on an established community of thirty thousand people, but this is the larger stage on which new groups are meeting the established across the country. Second- and third-generation Italian and Jewish Americans came of age in the post–World War II era, when they encountered unprecedented economic opportunities, a declining acceptance of anti-Semitism in the awake of the Holocaust, and expansion of civil rights. The climate of the time allowed the mainstream to expand, both racially and religiously.[7] New groups could be allowed in without old groups being made to feel they were being pushed out.

Two interconnected questions arise, questions that have been contemplated for decades. First, how do visually distinct groups become folded into the mainstream? Scholars have made notable contributions by providing new frameworks for thinking about the changing racial hierarchy in American society.[8] A movement from the White/Black dichotomy of the twentieth century to the Black/non-Black dichotomy of the twenty-first century has allowed education, socioeconomic status, skin tone, marriage partner, and myriad other factors to be considered in determining both how individuals see themselves and how others see them. This is the framework we have seen playing out in Wellesley. Chinese and Indian immigrants with consistently high levels of education and income comprise close to 15 percent of the town, and closer to 20 percent in the schools. Increasingly diverse friendship networks are helping the second generation fold into the mainstream, and there is every reason to believe that they and their children will see rising rates of exogamy.

I do not mean to suggest that race is irrelevant, but to argue that the role it plays is mediated by factors beyond racial categorization and varies depending on the larger national and international climate as well as various "weather events." The children of wealthy, well-educated Chinese and Indian residents may well fold into and become part of the American mainstream, but their visual differences are also likely to come to the fore when national or international events are racialized. The most recent such "weather" events include the blaming of Chinese people for the COVID pandemic and the ongoing demonization of China and the Chinese people by Donald Trump. While China is thousands of miles away, the effects of such racialization are felt in communities across the United States, as racial projects are transnational.[9] Such effects have been felt both in Wellesley and in towns and cities across the country. This observation should not, however, be interpreted as dismissal of the impact of Asian immigrants and their children on established communities, but rather as recognition that historic racial boundaries, while softening and lowering, continue to exist and become "brighter" during unsettled social, economic, and political times.[10]

The American climate continues to be highly racialized, and generations of Black Americans in particular remain consistently disadvantaged, be it in regard to employment, education, housing, or the criminal justice system. This racialization can be seen in Wellesley, both statistically and experientially. Black residents of Wellesley continue to be small in number and are disproportionately concentrated in public housing; their experiences are still marked by prejudice and discrimination in the form of low educational expectations and geographic misplacement.[11] "Weather events," such as George Floyd's murder and the racial reckoning of 2020, have pushed the town to grapple with many of these long-standing issues. Rectifying racial inequity requires a serious commitment to more affordable housing in town, beyond public housing, and the community has very recently begun to make this commitment. Only time will tell if the town's efforts will succeed in creating a truly multiracial community.

The second question is tied to the first: How do new groups fold into the established community during a period of growing income inequality and levels of polarization not seen since the Civil War? The early days of President Trump's second administration saw the political demonization of immigrants, immigration raids, and the further militarization of the southern border. Today's climate is vastly different from that of the post–World War II period. Individuals' anxiety over macro-level conditions shapes the micro-level interactions that play out on school committees, in town government, and in the workplace. While the post–World War II period of economic expansion created feelings of opportunity for all, this era most certainly feels like a zero-sum game in which the gain of one individual or group is another's loss.

In a town like Wellesley, populated by highly educated and compensated residents, the fights are not about having wages undercut by undocumented immigrants—as in communities with different demographics—but about maintaining a privileged position and ensuring that the next generation inherits it. The lawsuit *Students for Fair Admission v. Harvard*, which overturned affirmative action, was brought by a group of Asian students who felt they had been denied admission because of their race, while Black and Latino students with lower scores had been accepted. One group's gain is viewed as another group's loss.

The issue of access to elite education has been studied in prior research on immigrant and established groups, finding that new groups are racialized as overly ambitious and competitive.[12] That trend is not nearly as pronounced in Wellesley. While there is concern over Wellesley children being able to go to top colleges, the concern is voiced by both White and Asian parents, creating a cross-racial and cross-ethnic coalition concerned about Wellesley public school rankings.

Although some Americans' tremendous anxiety about their children's ability to attend elite colleges is unlikely to subside within a climate of such income inequality, the significant decline in birth rates, first because of the 2008 market crash and then because of the COVID pandemic, will result in fewer college applications. Certainly, the most elite schools will continue to accept only a very small percentage of applicants, but colleges even one notch lower may become significantly more accessible, thus alleviating some of these concerns. Alba argues that the mass retirements of the overwhelmingly White baby boomers may open up the economy for the newest Americans across the board in a non-zero-sum form of assimilation in the twenty-first century.[13] The declining birth rate may have a particularly important effect on the incorporation of young second- and third-generation Chinese and Indian Americans whose parents and grandparents entered the United States as immigrant outsiders but with the skill set to advance them into the mainstream.

Anxiety around income inequality and polarization also manifests in feelings about honor and belonging, particularly in communities like Wellesley where highly educated, upper-middle-class new groups come into contact with one another and with established residents. Alba argues that "moral elevation" has long been a critical factor in the assimilation of new groups.[14]

The concepts of honor, belonging, and moral worth have been evident in Wellesley in regard to holidays. The inclusion of a new group's holiday on the calendar may not only reflect group destigmatization but also result in moral elevation. With the holiday calendar increasingly viewed as a zero-sum game, the presence or absence of a holiday pits groups against each other. Wellesley's Jewish residents, and Jewish Americans across the United States, have largely been folded into the mainstream economically, educationally, residentially, and racially. However, they continue to occupy a somewhat distinct space. While America is now commonly viewed as a Judeo-Christian society, distinctions still remain, and there are boundaries within boundaries. The threat of having the Jewish High Holidays taken off the calendar because too many new holidays have been added raises tensions between groups and the Jewish community's fear of losing their place.

The idea of removing all holidays from the calendar that are not federal gained support in Wellesley when three new holidays were added in 2024. Sherry, a Black resident, said that this suggestion reminded her of the communities that filled swimming pools with cement rather than racially integrate them in the 1960s. Adding up the necessary days off for the Jewish High Holidays, Diwali, Lunar New Year, and Eid annually from 2024 to 2029 shows as few as two additional days off in some years, depending on what days of the week the holidays land. However, the addition of new holidays to the school calendar presents an extra challenge for working parents that needs to be acknowledged. From a policy perspective, assisting parents might include offering subsidized childcare for children under a certain age on days that are not federal holidays. Such a solution would not only allow the recognition of holidays important to new groups but relieve some of the burden such recognition places on those who do not have time off. All sides have valid claims.

Relatedly, the increasing focus on diversity, multiculturalism, and the history of racism in American society has accelerated a move toward "color-blind" rhetoric and policies. Interviewees told me that they didn't see race, while others suggested that they were afraid to talk about race and didn't know what language to use.[15] Removing all holidays except federal ones (Christmas is a federal holiday and thus would remain) and thereby refusing to acknowledge racial and ethnic identification will not translate into a more equal, welcoming community but rather a more isolated and divided one. Removing Columbus Day from the calendar was painful for many Italian Americans in the community who remembered a time when they were segregated in town, funneled into "shop" classes, and generally treated with derision. The debate over removing Columbus Day hardly acknowledged that pain. That Christopher, Frank, and Gianni reasserted their identity during these conversations strongly suggests that ethnicity is not yet fully in the twilight.[16] Their response to the debate demonstrated that identity can reemerge as new groups appear on the stage and highlight their own cultural backgrounds. As Noah, a lifelong resident of Wellesley, said, "Everything should be celebrated so that person feels like they're seen and heard and welcomed, you know?" Noah was advocating for moral elevation. As Gianni said about the discussions around Columbus, "We get in a fight over whether Columbus was a rapist and a murderer, or, you know, perhaps somebody that helped us discover the New World.... I mean, what's the answer to that one? He maybe was both." Public discussions and school curricula must be approached with greater nuance. Public officials, ranging from town meeting members to administrators to teachers, need to dig more deeply into all sides of issues like this one when they arise.

Further, those who supported keeping Columbus Day on the calendar were sometimes vilified as racists, a reaction that only further chilled the conversation. A small number of Wellesley residents have engaged in civil discourse training, a set of practices that teach people how to civilly discuss difficult topics and deeply listen to one another. Both town government and the schools should require civil discourse training for elected officials, teachers, administrators, and students. Such a policy is not about mandating ideas but rather about creating frameworks in which to discuss those ideas.

Global events like the COVID pandemic and the Israel-Gaza war further complicate the picture given that large diasporas are tied geographically, religiously, and emotionally to China, Israel, and Palestine. Such "weather events" within an increasingly unequal and politically fraught climate add further challenges. In a community like Wellesley with relatively large Chinese and Jewish populations—compared to both the state and the country—these international issues have reverberated very close to home. Although the pandemic and the Israel-Gaza war have sometimes prompted racialization and discrimination, there have been bright spots of coordination and an understanding of each other's point of view. For example, the backlash to adding three new holidays to the 2024–2025 academic year inspired the formation of a school calendar committee in Wellesley. One young Jewish woman with children in the school system told me that she was very worried that the Jewish holidays would be removed from the calendar and the menorah taken off the town green. She told me that she would move if these things happened. Although she was a well-established American whose family had been in this country for generations, her religious identity held firm and may have been further strengthened in recent months. At the same time, her participation in the holiday discussions had connected her with Muslim families in town who also felt isolated, and this new connection had been important to her, and a bit of a bright spot.

World War II gave Americans something beyond the largest economic expansion in the history of the world: it forced Americans across ethnic and religious lines to share army barracks, foxholes, and mess halls.[17] Military personnel met other Americans from outside of their own ethnic enclaves, churches, and synagogues. Shamefully, the military remained segregated until 1948, but the institution did create cross-ethnic contact between second and later generation Americans. Additionally, the war created a sense of linked fate, a sense that everyone was in it together and everyone's futures were interconnected. Further, it gave members of new groups the opportunity to "prove" their Americanness as they fought in US uniforms, sometimes in lands from which their parents and grandparents had emigrated.

Unquestionably, no one wishes to see such an "opportunity" again, but the connections made during World War II do raise the question of whether a common experience for Americans could be created that allows individuals from new and established groups to meet. Required national public service, a bipartisan issue but a costly one, could go a very long way in this regard. Within Wellesley, the focus should be on creating as many opportunities for small-scale interactions and shared spaces as possible. In a town as wealthy as Wellesley, substantial portions of the population send their children to private schools, attend private country clubs, and spend summers away, making cross-group contact more challenging. Creating new ways in which to engage people across racial, ethnic, and religious lines could play an important role in increasing footpaths and enabling residents to really see each other.

Wellesley, like communities across the country, is constantly in flux. We must acknowledge this flux as a matter of course, a fact to lean into rather than shy away from, as we all continuously co-create what it means to be American.

Appendix A

Methodology

Data collection began in March 2021, after I received approval from Emmanuel College's institutional review board. The project relied on five forms of data: (1) semistructured in-depth interviews with lifelong residents; (2) semistructured in-depth interviews with diverse residents; (3) semistructured interviews with organizational leaders; (4) items appearing in the *Wellesley Townsman*; and (5) participant observations at public events, as well as in the daily lives of residents.

From March 2021 through September 2023, I conducted forty-seven interviews with lifelong residents of Wellesley who were ages eighteen through ninety-five. The average age of participants was fifty-three, and with one exception, all identified as White. Twenty-nine participants identified as female and eighteen as male. Six identified as Jewish, twenty as Catholic, and five as Protestant. The remainder identified as being lapsed (two Catholic and one Protestant), having no affiliation, or being atheist. The sample of diverse voices, collected between March and May 2024, comprised seventeen residents, of whom four identified as Black or African American, five as Southeast Asian, seven as Chinese, and one as Latina. The average age of these diverse interviewees was fifty-two. Fourteen of them identified as female and three as male. Six identified as Christian, four as Hindu, and seven as atheist. With the exception of four interviews, all were conducted over Zoom and recorded with the permission of the participant. Of the four that were not conducted using Zoom, three were in-person interviews and one was conducted as a recorded phone interview. Interviews ranged in length from thirty minutes to nearly three hours. On average, interviews lasted approximately one hour.

I conducted twenty-one interviews with community leaders from local government, town agencies, schools, and nonprofits in the educational, civic, and social service sectors. That fourteen of these interviewees identified as women was unsurprising given the volunteer nature of these positions. These interviews were also conducted over Zoom and lasted approximately forty-five minutes.

All interviews were uploaded and transcribed using Otter.ai. Student researchers then reviewed the transcripts to correct mistakes. Interviews were coded inductively and a codebook created based on the data and then organized under larger themes.

I also talked with individuals who had important insights into the town but did not qualify as lifelong residents or community leaders because they had moved into town after age eighteen, they no longer lived in the town, or they did not meet the criteria in some other respect.

Three datasets—one for the Chinese immigrant/ethnic community, one for the Jewish immigrant/ethnic community, and one for the Italian immigrant/ethnic community—were created from the 1906 to 1989 issues of the *Wellesley Townsman*. The following terms were used to create the dataset on the Chinese community ($n = 5,592$): "Chinese," "Chin's Village," "Chuck Wong's Laundry," "Mandarin," and "Cantonese." To create the dataset for the Jewish community ($n = 5,584$), the following terms were used: "Jewish," "synagogue," "rabbi," "Shabbat," "sabbath," "B'Nai," "Anti-Defamation," "mitzvah," "Israel," "Holocaust," "Hebrew," "bagel," and "Kosher." The dataset for the Italian community ($n = 12,528$) was created using the search terms "Italy," "Italian," "Italo-American," "Dante Alighieri," "Columbus," and "Reliance." Each item was included in an Excel spreadsheet with the date, main topic of the item, and what type of item it was (ad, letter to the editor, obituary, content, wedding announcement, and so on). The archival data cited within the project are illustrative of larger trends and are not exhaustive. I chose the most relevant items, but there were often dozens of others that would have illustrated the same point equally well.

The quality of the digitized material varies. Some fonts are more easily read by the search engine than are other fonts. In other instances, words that are similar to, but not the same as, the search terms used here are incorrectly identified by the search tool (for example, "Jewels" rather than "Jewish"). In still other instances, cutting and scanning each item was done with varying quality, and certain parts of ads that would have identified them as relevant were cut off (for example, the "Chinese" description of a restaurant at the top or bottom of an ad not being included). My researchers and I have made every attempt to rectify these errors, but it is important to know that these limitations exist. All of the items are publicly available through the following website: https://wellesley.historyarchives.online/home.

Participant observations took place from March 2021 through August 2023 at public school concerts, awards ceremonies and graduations, and fundraising events, as well as in daily life at grocery stores, local merchants, and community gathering spots such as parks, coffee shops, and libraries. Notes were recorded either as observations were taking place when possible, or shortly thereafter when not possible.

Appendix B

Interview Protocol for Lifelong Residents

ID #:

Date @ Time:

Format:

Community Questions
1. How would you describe your town to someone who has never been here before? [*Prompt: economically, ethnically, religiously, racially, etc.*]
2. As someone who grew up in town, how do you think the community has changed through the years? [*Prompt: economically, ethnically, religiously, racially, etc.*]

Ethnic Ancestry/Childhood

3. Tell me about your family background [*Prompt: economically, ethnically, religiously, racially, etc.*]
   a. When did your family come to the US?
   b. When did your family come to town?
4. Growing up, how important was your ethnic or immigrant background?
   a. Did you celebrate any holidays specific to your background?
   b. Did you speak a language other than English at home?
   c. Did you eat ethnic-specific foods?
   d. Did you have other practices or traditions specific to your background?

Adult Family

5. Are you married or in a long-term relationship? [*If no, skip to question 6.*]
   a. [*If yes*] Tell me about that person.
   b. What is your spouse or partner's ethnic/racial/religious background?
6. Are there any aspects of your ethnic background that are still important to you today? [*If respondent cites holidays, language, foods, or practices in question 4, follow up to see if those are still relevant.*]

7. Are there different ethnic practices that are important in your adult household?
    a. [If yes] What are they? [Prompt: celebrations, language, food, dress, other traditions]
    b. How did they come about?

Children/School
8. Do you have children? [If no, skip to question 9.]
    a. [If yes] How old are they?
    b. If school age, are they in public, private, or parochial school?
9. How do you think your children's school experiences are different from yours as a kid in terms of academics? [If no kids] Tell me about your school experiences in terms of academics.
    a. Subject matter?
    b. Languages they can take?
    c. School trips?
10. What do you think about those kinds of curricular changes?
11. How do you think your children's school experiences are different from yours as a kid, in terms of ethnic/immigrant contact? [If no kids] Tell me about your school experiences in terms of ethnic/immigrant contact.
    a. Did you have friends of different ethnic backgrounds?
    b. [If yes] Have you stayed close to any of those friends? Why or why not?
    c. Does your child have friends of different ethnic backgrounds?
    d. [If yes] How has that impacted you? Have you gotten to know those families?
12. How do you think your children's extracurricular experiences (clubs, sports, etc.) are different from yours as a kid in terms of ethnic/immigrant contact? [If no kids] Tell me about your extracurricular activities in terms of ethnic/immigrant contact.
    a. Did you have friends of different ethnic backgrounds?
    b. [If yes] Have you stayed close to any of those friends? Why or why not?
    c. Does your child have friends of different ethnic backgrounds?
    d. [If yes] How has that impacted you? Have you gotten to know those families?

Professional Contact
13. Do you work outside of the home? [If no, skip to question 16.]
    a. [If yes] What do you do professionally?
14. How much contact do you have with people of different ethnic/religious racial backgrounds at work? [Prompt: as coworkers, supervisors, people you supervise, customers/clients]

15. How do you think these contacts affect you? [*Prompt: Have you developed any kind of relationships, friendships, etc.?*]

Neighborhood Contact

16. Do you have contact with people of different ethnic/religious/racial backgrounds in your neighborhood?
    a. Can you provide any examples?
17. How do you think these contacts affect you? [*Prompt: Have you developed any kind of relationships, friendships, etc.?*]

Friendships

18. Are your friends mostly of similar or different ethnic backgrounds from you, or does it vary?
    a. Can you give me any specifics?

Community Engagement

19. As a kid, do you remember the community celebrating any ethnic specific events? [*Prompt: Chinese New Year, Saint Patrick's Day, etc.*]
    a. [*If yes*] Did you participate?
    b. Did you participate in any ethnic activities that were not specific to your background?
20. Does the community celebrate any ethnic specific activities today?
    a. [*If yes*] Do you participate?
    b. Do you participate in any ethnic activities that are not specific to your background?

Community Organizations

21. Do you do any volunteer or civic or political work?
    a. [*If yes*] What kind? With what organizations?
22. Are there changes that you have seen in local institutions that you think are responding to changes in the ethnic/religious racial makeup of the town?
    a. In volunteer organizations?
    b. In schools?
    c. In local businesses?
    d. In town government?
    e. At the library?
    f. In religious organizations?

National Identity

23. What characteristics do you think make someone an American? [*Prompt: place of birth, language, race, religion, etc.*]

24. Across the country there has been a lot of discussion about immigration and whether it enriches the country or weakens the country. In recent times here in town, there has been a lot of discussion about changing Columbus Day to Indigenous People's Day. What do you think about these debates?
25. Is there anything that I haven't asked about that you think that I should know?

Demographics

[*Note: Do not record any identifying information.*]

Age:

Gender:

Race:

Ethnicity:

Religion:

Highest level of education:

Profession:

Marital status:

Children (ages):

= Appendix C =

Interview Protocol for Diverse Voices

ID #:

Date @ time:

Format: Zoom

Community Questions

1. How would you describe your town to someone who has never been here before? [*Prompt: (1) to friends who don't live here or to family back home; (2) economically, ethnically, religiously, racially, etc.*]
2. [*If respondent grew up here; otherwise skip to question 3.*] How do you think the community has changed through the years? [*Prompt: economically, ethnically, religiously, racially, etc.*]

Ethnic Ancestry/Childhood

3. Tell me about your family background [*Prompt: economically, ethnically, religiously, racially, etc.*]
   a. When did your family come to the US?
   b. When did your family come to town?
   [*If respondent grew up here; otherwise skip to question 5.*]
4. Growing up, how important was your ethnic or immigrant background?
   a. Did you celebrate any holidays specific to your background?
   b. Speak a language other than English at home?
   c. Did you eat ethnic-specific foods?
   d. Did you have other practices or traditions specific to your background?

Adult Family

5. Are you married or in a long-term relationship? [*If no, skip to question 6.*]
   a. [*If yes*] Tell me about that person.
   b. What is your spouse or partner's ethnic/racial/religious background?

6. Are there any aspects of your ethnic background that are still important to you today? [*If respondent cited holidays, language, foods, practices from question 4, follow up to see if those are still relevant.*]
7. Are there different ethnic practices that are important in your adult household?
    a. [*If yes*] What are they? [*Prompt: celebrations, language, food, dress, other traditions*] How did they come about?

Children/School

8. Where did you go to school for K-12?
9. Do you have children?
    a. [*If yes*] How old are they?
    b. If school age, are they in public, private, or parochial school?
    [*If respondent did not go to school in the US and has no children, skip to question 17.*]
    [*If respondent has children; otherwise skip to question 14.*]
10. What were/are your children's school experiences like in terms of academics?
    a. Subject matter?
    b. Languages they can take?
    c. School trips?
11. What were/are your children's school experiences like in terms of ethnic celebrations or holidays, i.e., those that are not federal holidays or Christian holidays?
12. How much do you think your children feel (felt) a sense of belonging in their school?
13. How much of a sense of belonging have you felt at your children's school?
    a. Have those feelings changed over time?
    [*If respondent went to school in the US, whether or not respondent has children; otherwise, skip to question 17.*]
14. What was your experience like in terms of ethnic celebrations or holidays?
15. How was your school experience in terms of academics?
    a. Subject matter?
    b. Languages they can take?
    c. School trips?
16. How much of a sense of belonging did you feel in your school growing up?

Professional Contact

17. Do you work outside of the home? [*If no, skip to question 19.*]
    a. [*If yes*] What do you do professionally?

18. How much of a sense of belonging have you felt in the workplace?
    a. Have these feelings changed over time?

Neighborhood Contact

19. Do you have contact with people of different ethnic/religious/racial backgrounds in your neighborhood?
    a. Can you provide any examples?
20. How much of a sense of belonging have you felt in the neighborhood?
    a. Have these feelings changed over time?

Friendships

21. Are your friends mostly of similar or different ethnic backgrounds from you, or does it vary?
    a. Can you give me any specifics?

Community Engagement

[If respondent grew up in town; otherwise, skip to question 23.]
22. As a kid, do you remember the community celebrating any ethnic specific events? [*Prompt: Chinese New Year, Saint Patrick's Day, etc.*]
    a. [*If yes*] Did you participate?
    b. Did you participate in any ethnic activities that were not specific to your background?
23. Does the community celebrate any ethnic-specific activities today?
    a. [*If yes*] Do you participate?
    b. Do you participate in any ethnic activities that are not specific to your background?

Community Organizations

24. Do you do any volunteer or civic or political work?
    a. [*If yes*] What kind? With what organizations?
25. How much of a sense of belonging have you felt in community organizations, either as a member of the organization or as a participant in events? [*Prompt: For example, would you feel comfortable speaking up in a meeting?*]
    a. Have these feelings changed over time?
26. Are there changes that you have seen in local institutions that you think are responding to changes in the ethnic/religious/racial makeup of the town?
    a. In volunteer organizations?
    b. In schools?
    c. In local businesses?
    d. In town government?
    e. At the library?
    f. In religious organizations?

27. Is there anything that I haven't asked about that you think that I should know?

Demographics

[*Note: Do not record any identifying information.*]

Age:

Gender:

Race:

Ethnicity:

Nativity:

If not born in the US, how long in the US?

How long in Wellesley?

Religion:

Highest level of education:

Profession:

Marital status:

Children (ages):

= Appendix D =

Interview Protocol for Organizational Leaders

ID #:

Date @ Time:

Format:

Organizational Background
  1. Can you begin by telling me a bit about your organization/committee?
     a. What is its mission and goals?
     b. Who is it meant to serve?
  2. What is your role in the organization/on the committee?
     a. How long have you had this role?
     b. Have you been involved with the organization in other ways? For how long, in total?

Composition
  3. Since you have been involved, or from what you know, have the people who participate in your organization changed in terms of ethnicity/race/religion, etc.?
     a. Volunteers?
     b. Clients?
     c. General community members?
     d. [*If yes*] In what ways? How have these changes impacted the organization?
  4. Do you think your organization has had to do different sorts of outreach to both potential clients and volunteers in recent years because of changes?

Mission/Goals

5. Since you have been involved, or from what you know, have the mission or goals of your organization/committee changed?
   a. Can you give me any examples?
   b. [*If yes*] Is it connected to ethnic/race/religious changes in volunteers/clients/community members?

Positives/Negatives

6. Some people think increasing immigration and diversity is a strength of our country, while other people think it is a challenge. How do you think changes in ethnicity/race/religion have impacted your organization, overall?
7. Have changes in the composition of the organization led to any tensions?
   a. Over goals?
   b. Programs?
   c. Budgeting?
8. Have changes in the composition of the organization led to any breakthroughs or positive developments?
   a. Greater involvement from the community?
   b. New ideas?
   c. More donations?
9. Is there anything else that I haven't asked about that you think I should know?

Demographics

[*Note: Do not record any identifying information.*]

Type of organization (civic, political, social service, education, other)

Size of organization (employees/volunteers)

Number of people served

Role in organization

Length of time at organization

Age

Race

Ethnicity

Profession (if other than organization)

Marital status

Children (ages)

Notes

Chapter 1: A Slowly Changing Town

1. WASP stands for White, Anglo-Saxon Protestant, a term popularized by sociologist E. Digby Baltzell, although the origination has never been definitively identified.
2. Dhingra 2020; Jiménez 2017; Lara-García 2021; Lemekh 2023; Matsumoto 2018; Warikoo 2022.
3. Feagin and O'Brien 2003.
4. Alba 2020.
5. Alba 2020.
6. Jiménez 2017.
7. For a full discussion of the methodology, see appendix A. The interview protocols for established residents, new residents, and organizational leaders can be found in appendixes B, C, and D, respectively.
8. Go 2024.

Chapter 2: A Brief History of Wellesley and a Brief History of Immigration Theory

1. Hinchliffe 1981.
2. Town of Needham, n.d.
3. Dorin 2014.
4. *Wellesley Townsman* 1922.
5. Hinchliffe 1981.
6. Cities, such as Los Angeles and New York, had already established zoning laws.
7. Hinchcliffe, n.d.
8. Geismer 2014; Prevost 2013; Rothstein 2017.
9. *Wellesley Townsman* 1927a.
10. Rothstein 2017.
11. Brown 2023a.
12. Geismer 2014.
13. Geismer 2014; Prevost 2013.
14. Town of Wellesley 2018.

15. Eaton 2001.
16. Geismer 2014.
17. Geismer 2014.
18. Geismer 2014.
19. Geismer 2014; DiAngelo 2021.
20. Bueker 2017; Eaton 2001; Holland 2012; Ispa-Landa 2013.
21. *Wellesley Townsman* 1966.
22. Dell 1966.
23. Berndt 1966.
24. All names used are pseudonyms.
25. Bueker 2017; Feagin and O'Brien 2003.
26. *U.S. News and World Report* 2022.
27. Alba 2020; Alba and Nee 2003; Gans 1997.
28. *Wellesley Townsman* 1938a, 1947a.
29. Blumenstock et al. 2023; Munshi 2020; Patel and Vella 2013; Poros 2011.
30. Although Christopher was technically third-generation and thus an established resident, his experience was much more in keeping with that of second-generation Americans. His father was born in Wellesley, but returned to Italy as a young child and did not come back until he was in his twenties. His father's nativity made his return migration possible. This kind of return, and even circular migration, was not particularly unusual for Italian migration flows during this period. See Viola (2023) for an in-depth analysis of the processes at work for these Italian "birds of passage."
31. *Wellesley Townsman* 1906, 1926a.
32. *Wellesley Townsman* 1938a, 1947a.
33. *Wellesley Townsman* 1935a.
34. *Wellesley Townsman* 1910.
35. Sleeper 1908.
36. *Wellesley Townsman* 1926b.
37. *Wellesley Townsman* 1927b.
38. *Wellesley Townsman* 1928.
39. Gamm 1999.
40. Levine and Harmon 1993.
41. Alba 2020; Rothstein 2017.
42. *Wellesley Townsman* 1960a.
43. *Wellesley Townsman* 1907.
44. *Wellesley Townsman* 1924a.
45. *Wellesley Townsman* 1943a, 1943b, 1946.
46. Van Even 2021.
47. Gordon 1964.
48. Portes and Zhou 1993.
49. Alba and Nee 2003.

Notes   179

50. Foner 2022, 2023.
51. Alba and Nee 2003; Du Bois 1903/2008.
52. Hamilton 2019.
53. Jiménez and Horowitz 2013; Jiménez 2017.
54. Blumin and Altschuler 2022.
55. Jiménez 2017; Foner 2022.
56. Diaz and Ore 2020; Bueker and Rothschild 2022.
57. Lemekh 2023; Matsumoto 2018.
58. Itzigsohn and Brown 2021.
59. Alba 2020; Omi and Winant 2015.
60. Feagin 2020; Omi and Winant 2015.
61. Dhingra 2020; Ostfeld and Yadon 2022; Warikoo 2022.
62. Asad 2023; LeBrón et al. 2022; Menjívar 2021.
63. Asad 2023; Itzigsohn 2009; Jack-Vickers 2024.
64. Itzigsohn 2009.
65. Dhingra 2020; Eng and Han 2019; Lee and Sheng 2024; Lee and Zhou 2015; Warikoo 2022.
66. Eng and Han 2019; Lee and Zhou 2015.
67. Dhingra 2020; Warikoo 2022.
68. Gordon 1964.
69. Dhingra 2020.
70. Jiménez 2017.
71. Alba and Nee 2003; Lee and Sheng 2024; Warikoo 2022.
72. Lee and Sheng 2024.
73. Jiménez 2017; Warikoo 2022.
74. Valdez and Golash-Boza 2017.
75. Alba 2020; Alba and Nee 2003.
76. Kasinitz and Waters 2024.
77. Bozorgmehr and Ketcham 2018; Safi 2024.
78. Golash-Boza 2006.
79. Eng and Han 2019, 62; LeBrón et al. 2022.
80. Gans 1997.
81. Gans 2014.
82. Portes and Zhou 1993.
83. Go 2024.
84. Alba 2020; Foner 2022, 2023; Hamilton 2019.
85. Alba 2020.
86. Alba 2006, 2020; Bonilla-Silva 2004; Gans 1999, 2012.
87. Kasinitz and Waters 2024.
88. Klarenbeek 2023.
89. Bashi 2004; Bashi Treitler 2016; Hannah-Jones 2024; Karimi and Wilkes 2024.
90. Robertson 2012.
91. Swyngedouw 2004.

Chapter 3: Neighborhoods, Schools, and Places of Worship: Setting the Stage for Contact

1. Allport 1954.
2. Pettigrew and Tropp 2008.
3. Boin et al. 2021.
4. Alba 2020.
5. Boin et al. 2021.
6. Kunst, Lefringhausen, Sam, et al. 2021; Kunst, Lefringhausen, Skaar, et al. 2021.
7. Doucerain 2019; Doucerain et al. 2013; Haugen and Kunst 2017.
8. Gordon 1964.
9. Alba 2020; Jiménez 2017.
10. Klarenbeek 2023.
11. Lee and Ramakrishnan 2022.
12. Curley 2010; Small 2006.
13. Geismer 2014; Prevost 2013.
14. *Wellesley Townsman* 1958a.
15. Klarenbeek 2023.
16. Zemba and Mehrotra 2023.
17. Alba 2006; Gans 1999, 2012.
18. Anderson 2012; Bueker 2021.
19. Ostfeld and Yadon 2022.
20. Alba 2020.
21. Alba 2020; Alba and Nee 2003; Eng and Han 2019; Jiménez 2008.
22. Eng and Han 2019, 103.
23. Jiménez 2008.
24. Alba 2005.
25. Bueker 2017, 2021; Ispa-Landa and Conwell 2015; Ostfeld and Yadon 2022.
26. Bueker 2017; Eaton 2001.
27. Bueker 2021; Feagin 2020; Go 2024; Omi and Winant 2015.
28. Khan 2021.
29. *Wellesley Townsman* 1908.
30. *Wellesley Townsman* 1912a.
31. *Wellesley Townsman* 1926b.
32. *Wellesley Townsman* 1936a, 1936b.
33. Go 2024.
34. *Wellesley Townsman* 1911.
35. *Wellesley Townsman* 1924b.
36. *Wellesley Townsman* 1948a.
37. *Wellesley Townsman* 1932a.

38. *Wellesley Townsman* 1958b.
39. *Wellesley Townsman* 1958c.
40. *Wellesley Townsman* 1960b.
41. *Wellesley Townsman* 1967a.
42. Gamm 1999.
43. *Wellesley Townsman* 1955a.
44. Tocqueville 1835/2012.
45. Putnam 2000.
46. Tocqueville 1835/2012, 119.
47. Alba 1981, 2014.
48. Bourdieu 1992; Klarenbeek 2023.
49. Du Bois 1903/2008; Eng and Han 2019.
50. Eng and Han 2019.
51. *Wellesley Townsman* 1969a.
52. Dhingra 2020; Warikoo 2022.
53. *Wellesley Townsman* 1912b.
54. *Wellesley Townsman* 1912c.
55. *Wellesley Townsman* 1920.
56. *Wellesley Townsman* 1945, 1953.
57. Pettigrew and Tropp 2008.
58. Allport 1954.
59. Klarenbeek 2023; Zemba and Mehrotra 2023.
60. Bourdieu 1992; Eng and Han 2019, 54.
61. Klarenbeek 2023; Zemba and Mehrotra 2023.

Chapter 4: Multidirectional Influences on Individuals

1. Jiménez 2017.
2. Waters 1990.
3. Matsumoto 2018.
4. Dhingra 2020.
5. Portes and Zhou 1993.
6. Bozorgmehr and Ketcham 2018; Dhingra 2020; Kasinitz and Waters 2024; Safi 2024; Warikoo 2022.
7. Jiménez 2017.
8. Batalova 2023.
9. Alba 2020; Alba and Nee 2003.
10. Jiménez 2008, 2019.
11. Boutyline and Soter 2021.
12. Lee and Ramakrishnan 2022.
13. Bueker 2017, 2021; Ispa-Landa and Conwell 2015; Ostfeld and Yadon 2022.
14. Du Bois 1903/2008; see also Alba 2006; Gans 1999.

182   Notes

15. Alba 2006; Alba and Nee 2003; Drouhot and Nee 2019; Omi and Winant 2015.
16. Lee and Ramakrishnan 2022; Lee and Zhou 2015; Tuan 1998.
17. Alba 2005; Ostfeld and Yaddon 2022.
18. Eng and Han 2019; Hannah-Jones 2024; Morning and Maneri 2022.
19. Feagin 2020.
20. Morning and Maneri 2022.
21. Omanović and Langley 2023.
22. Bonilla-Silva 2014.
23. Blumer 1969/1986; Goffman 1982; Weber 2009.
24. Hannah-Jones 2024; Karimi and Wilkes 2024; Ostfeld and Yadon 2022.
25. Alba 2014; Alper and Cooperman 2021; Gans 2014; McCarthy 2021.
26. Bogardus 1933; Gordon 1964.
27. *Wellesley Townsman* 1970a.
28. *Wellesley Townsman* 1976a.
29. *Wellesley Townsman* 1970b.
30. *Wellesley Townsman* 1972a.
31. *Wellesley Townsman* 1980a.
32. Alba 2014.
33. Ostfeld and Yadon 2022.
34. Alba and Nee 2003.
35. Alba 2020.
36. Alba 2020; Gans 2012; Starr and Freeland 2024.
37. Alba 2020; Gordon 1964.
38. Kasinitz and Waters 2024.
39. Waters 1990.
40. Gordon 1964.
41. Alba 2020; Gans 1992, 1997.
42. Allport 1954.
43. Alper and Cooperman 2021.
44. Bozorgmehr and Ketcham 2018; Kasinitz and Waters 2024; Safi 2024.
45. Dhingra 2020.
46. Alba and Nee 2003; Foner 2023.
47. Wellesley School Committee 2023, public comment at minute 14:30–14:45.
48. Bueker and Rothschild 2022; Diaz and Ore 2020; Foner 2023.
49. Gordon 1964.
50. Gans 1997.
51. Akresh 2007; Doucerain 2019.
52. Bueker and Rothschild 2022; Haugen and Kunst 2017; Levitt 2004.
53. Diaz and Ore 2020; Parzer and Astleithner 2018.
54. Kunst, Lefringhausen, Sam, et al. 2021.
55. Arellano 2012; Chen 2021; Diaz and Ore 2020.
56. Diaz and Ore 2020; Foner 2022, 2023; Parzer and Astleithner 2018; Somashekhar 2019.

57. *Wellesley Townsman* 1943a.
58. *Wellesley Townsman* 1972b.
59. *Wellesley Townsman* 1972c.
60. Marple 1976a.
61. Mortarelli 1976.
62. DiSchino 1976.
63. Marple 1976b.
64. Li 2009.
65. Allport 1954; Boin et al. 2021.
66. Crul 2024.
67. Gans 2014.
68. Jiménez 2017.
69. Ostfeld and Yadon 2022.
70. Brodkin 1998; Ignatiev 1995/2008; Staples 2019.
71. Hannah-Jones 2024; Karimi and Wilkes 2024; Ostfeld and Yadon 2022.
72. Jiménez 2017.
73. Asad 2023; Dhingra 2020; Itzigsohn 2009; Warikoo 2022.
74. Klarenbeek 2023.

Chapter 5: Community Organizations as Cause and Consequence of Change

1. Tocqueville 1835/2012.
2. Durkheim 1893/1984.
3. Ingram 2020.
4. Ramakrishnan and Bloemraad 2008; Graauw 2008; Graauw et al. 2013; Graauw and Vermeulen 2016.
5. Gans 2014.
6. Klarenbeek 2023.
7. Gans 2014.
8. Matsumoto 2018.
9. Chen 2021.
10. *Wellesley Townsman* 1931, 1938b, 1949, 1955b.
11. Gans 2014.
12. Diaz and Ore 2020; Parzer and Astleithner 2018.
13. *Wellesley Townsman* 1935b.
14. *Wellesley Townsman* 1940a.
15. *Wellesley Townsman* 1950a.
16. *Wellesley Townsman* 1960c.
17. *Wellesley Townsman* 1961.
18. *Wellesley Townsman* 1973a.
19. Diaz and Ore 2020; Foner 2022, 2023.
20. *Wellesley Townsman* 1932b.
21. *Wellesley Townsman* 1939a.

22. Chen 2021.
23. *Wellesley Townsman* 1959a, 1960d.
24. Diaz and Ore 2020.
25. *Wellesley Townsman* 1983a.
26. *Wellesley Townsman* 1962.
27. *Wellesley Townsman* 1973b; Diaz and Ore 2020.
28. *Wellesley Townsman* 1985a.
29. *Wellesley Townsman* 1964a, 1971a.
30. Gans 2014.
31. *Wellesley Townsman* 1965.
32. *Wellesley Townsman* 1971b.
33. *Wellesley Townsman* 1971c.
34. *Wellesley Townsman* 1977a.
35. Khan 2021.
36. Diaz and Ore 2020.
37. Bourdieu 1992; Klarenbeek 2023; Zemba and Mehrotra 2023.
38. *Wellesley Townsman* 1951.
39. *Wellesley Townsman* 1970c, 1972d.
40. *Wellesley Townsman* 1942.
41. *Wellesley Townsman* 1948b.
42. *Wellesley Townsman* 1979a.
43. *Wellesley Townsman* 1981.
44. *Wellesley Townsman* 1925.
45. *Wellesley Townsman* 1971d.
46. *Wellesley Townsman* 1972e.
47. *Wellesley Townsman* 1939b.
48. *Wellesley Townsman* 1938c.
49. Gans 2014; Graauw 2008; Graauw and Vermeulen 2016.
50. Gans 2014; Matsumoto 2018.
51. Gans 2014.
52. See Roger Waldinger's (1990, 1993, 1999) extensive body of research on entrepreneurship among immigrants; see also Banh and Liu 2020; Chen 2021.
53. Alba 2020.
54. *Wellesley Townsman* 1935c.
55. Gans 2014.
56. Malick 1991.
57. *Wellesley Townsman* 1938d.
58. *Wellesley Townsman* 1939c.
59. *Wellesley Townsman* 1938e.
60. *Wellesley Townsman* 1939d.
61. Nixon's 1968 presidential campaign stands as a critical juncture, a time when the Republicans began to identify the White working class as the "silent majority." This identification came to include the

"Reagan Democrats," and it has only gained strength under Donald Trump's takeover of the party. Lily Geismer (2014) follows the evolution of the Democratic Party in the greater Boston area from being the party of labor and the working class to the party of the educated elite of New England. By way of example, only 22 percent of Wellesley voters voted for the Trump-Vance ticket in 2024; the bulk of town residents supported Harris-Walz.

62. *Wellesley Townsman* 1977b.
63. *Wellesley Townsman* 1980b.
64. *Wellesley Townsman* 1988a.
65. *Wellesley Townsman* 1943c.
66. *Wellesley Townsman* 1952a.
67. *Wellesley Townsman* 1988a.
68. *Wellesley Townsman* 1988b.
69. *Wellesley Townsman* 1958d.
70. *Wellesley Townsman* 1959b.
71. *Wellesley Townsman* 1959c.
72. *Wellesley Townsman* 1963.
73. Alba 2020.
74. *Wellesley Townsman* 1967b.
75. *Wellesley Townsman* 1934.
76. *Wellesley Townsman* 1936c.
77. *Wellesley Townsman* 1940b.
78. Gans 2014.
79. Warikoo 2022.
80. Dhingra 2020.
81. *Wellesley Townsman* 1947b.
82. *Wellesley Townsman* 1952b.
83. *Wellesley Townsman* 1958e.
84. *Wellesley Townsman* 1980a, 1980c.
85. *Wellesley Townsman* 1979b, 1980d, 1983b.
86. *Wellesley Townsman* 1972f.
87. *Wellesley Townsman* 1973c.
88. *Wellesley Townsman* 1974a.
89. *Wellesley Townsman* 1974b.
90. *Wellesley Townsman* 1975a.
91. *Wellesley Townsman* 1975b.
92. *Wellesley Townsman* 1980e.
93. *Wellesley Townsman* 1984.
94. *Wellesley Townsman* 1985b.
95. *Wellesley Townsman* 1985c.
96. D. Brown 2020.
97. *Wellesley Townsman* 1936a.
98. *Wellesley Townsman* 1943d.

99. *Wellesley Townsman* 1943e.
100. *Wellesley Townsman* 1950b.
101. *Wellesley Townsman* 1955c.
102. *Wellesley Townsman* 1959d.
103. *Wellesley Townsman* 1964b.
104. *Wellesley Townsman* 1970d.
105. *Wellesley Townsman* 1974c.
106. *Wellesley Townsman* 1969b.
107. *Wellesley Townsman* 1976b.
108. *Wellesley Townsman* 1976c.
109. *Wellesley Townsman* 1976d, 1976e.
110. *Wellesley Townsman* 1978.
111. *Wellesley Townsman* 1987a.
112. *Wellesley Townsman* 1983c.
113. Durkheim 1893/1984; Ingram 2020; Tocqueville 1835/2012; see also Ramakrishnan and Bloemraad 2008.
114. Gans 2014.
115. Graauw et al. 2013; Ramakrishnan and Bloemraad 2008.
116. Klarenbeek 2023.

Chapter 6: Durable Institutional Changes Across the Community

1. May 2023.
2. May 2023; Tocqueville 1835/2012.
3. Graauw 2008; Graauw and Vermeulen 2016; May 2023; O'Connor 1997; Puleo 2007.
4. *Wellesley Townsman* 1964b.
5. Klarenbeek 2023.
6. Klarenbeek 2023.
7. Graauw, Gleeson, and Bloemraad 2013.
8. *Wellesley Townsman* 1936d.
9. *Wellesley Townsman* 1936e.
10. *Wellesley Townsman* 1936f.
11. *Wellesley Townsman* 1936g.
12. *Wellesley Townsman* 1936h.
13. *Wellesley Townsman* 1936i.
14. *Wellesley Townsman* 1936j.
15. *Wellesley Townsman* 1936k.
16. Great!Schools.org, n.d.
17. Dhingra 2020; Kasinitz et al. 2008; Lee and Zhou 2015; Tran et al. 2018; Warikoo 2022.

18. Jiménez and Horowitz 2013; Kasinitz et al. 2008; Lee and Zhou 2015; Warikoo 2022; Zhou and Gonzales 2019.
19. Portes and Zhou 1993; Tran et al. 2018.
20. Dhingra 2020; Warikoo 2022.
21. Dhingra 2020; Warikoo 2022.
22. Dhingra 2020; Warikoo 2022.
23. Lepore 2022.
24. *Wellesley Townsman* 1980f.
25. *Wellesley Townsman* 1985d.
26. Matsumoto 2018.
27. *Wellesley Townsman* 1987b.
28. *Wellesley Townsman* 1987c.
29. *Wellesley Townsman* 1982.
30. Matsumoto 2018.
31. May 2023.
32. Fleming 2020.
33. Blanck 2019; Etzioni 2000; Wynn 2016; Yeh 2008.
34. *Wellesley Townsman* 1955d.
35. *Wellesley Townsman* 1971e.
36. Yeh 2008.
37. Jiménez 2008.
38. *Wellesley Townsman* 1983d, 1983e.
39. Jin 2022.
40. Brown 2023b.
41. Crul 2024.
42. May 2023.
43. Alba 2020.
44. Schuman et al. 2012; Schuman et al. 2005; Schwartz and Schuman 2005.
45. Eason et al. 2021.
46. *Wellesley Townsman* 1983f.
47. Alba 1981, 1985, 2014.
48. B. Brown 2020.
49. Dhingra 2020; Warikoo 2022.
50. Brown 2023a.
51. Hannah-Jones 2024; Karimi and Wilkes 2024.
52. Alba 2020.
53. *The Swellesley Report* 2021.
54. May 2023.
55. Waters 1990.
56. Gans 1992.
57. Ostfeld and Yadon 2022.
58. Gans 2014.

Chapter 7: A Variegated Process: Three Paths to Change and the Road Ahead

1. Alba 2020.
2. Bueker and Rothschild 2022; Diaz and Ore 2020; Jiménez 2017.
3. Foner 2023; Jiménez 2017.
4. Dhingra 2020; Warikoo 2022.
5. Bozorgmehr and Ketcham 2018; Kasinitz and Waters 2024; Safi 2024; Valdez and Golash-Boza 2017.
6. Foner 2023; Jiménez 2017.
7. Alba 2020.
8. Alba 2020; Bonilla-Silva 2004; Gans 1999, 2012.
9. Bashi 2004; Bashi Treitler 2016; Karimi and Wilkes 2024.
10. Alba 2005; Ostfeld and Yaddon 2022.
11. Bueker 2017, 2021.
12. Dhingra 2020; Warikoo 2022.
13. Alba 2020.
14. Alba 2020.
15. Ostfeld and Yadon 2022.
16. Alba 2014; Gans 2014.
17. Alba 2020.

References

Akresh, Ilana Redstone. 2007. "Dietary Assimilation and Health Among Hispanic Immigrants to the United States." *Journal of Health and Social Behavior* 48(4): 404–17.

Alba, Richard. 1981. "The Twilight of Ethnicity Among American Catholics of European Ancestry." *Annals of the American Academy of Political and Social Science* 454(1): 86–97. https://doi.org/10.1177/000271628145400108.

Alba, Richard. 1985. *Italian Americans: Into the Twilight of Ethnicity*. Prentice-Hall.

Alba, Richard. 2005. "Bright vs. Blurred Boundaries: Second-Generation Assimilation and Exclusion in France, Germany, and the United States." *Ethnic and Racial Studies* 28(1): 20–49. https://doi.org/10.1080/0141987042000280003.

Alba, Richard. 2006. "Beyond Race: Recognizing Minority Status in Elite Contexts." *Ethnicities* 6(4): 550–54. https://doi.org/10.1177/146879680600600408.

Alba, Richard. 2014. "The Twilight of Ethnicity: What Relevance for Today?" *Ethnic and Racial Studies* 37(5): 781–85.

Alba, Richard. 2020. *The Great Demographic Illusion: Majority, Minority, and the Expanding American Mainstream*. Princeton University Press.

Alba, Richard, and Victor Nee. 2003. *Remaking the American Mainstream: Assimilation and Contemporary Immigration*. Harvard University Press.

Allport, Gordon. 1954. *The Nature of Prejudice*. Addison-Wesley.

Alper, Becka A., and Alan Cooperman. 2021. "10 Key Findings About Jewish Americans." Pew Research Center, May 11. https://www.pewresearch.org/short-reads/2021/05/11/10-key-findings-about-jewish-americans/.

Anderson, Elijah. 2012. "The Iconic Ghetto." *Annals of the American Academy of Political and Social Science* 642(1): 8–24. https://doi.org/10.1177/0002716212446299.

Arellano, Gustavo. 2012. *Taco USA: How Mexican Food Conquered America*. Simon & Schuster.

Asad, Asad. 2023. *Engage and Evade: How Latino Immigrant Families Manage Surveillance in Everyday Life*. Princeton University Press.

Banh, Jenny, and Haiming Liu. 2020. *American Chinese Restaurants: Society, Culture, and Consumption*. Routledge.

Bashi, Vilna. 2004. "Globalized Anti-Blackness: Transnationalizing Western Immigration Law, Policy, and Practice." *Ethnic and Racial Studies* 27(4): 584–606. https://doi.org/10.1080/01491987042000216726.

Bashi Treitler, Vilna. 2016. "Racialization and Its Paradigms: From Ireland to North America." *Current Sociology* 64(2): 213–27. https://doi.org/10.1177/0011392115614782.

Batalova, Jeanne. 2023. "Frequently Requested Statistics on Immigrants and Immigration in the United States." Migration Policy Institute, March 13. https://www.migrationpolicy.org/article/frequently-requested-statistics-immigrants-and-immigration-united-states.

Berndt, William. 1966. "Letter to the Editor." *Wellesley Townsman*, April 7, p. 18.

Blanck, Emily. 2019. "Galveston on San Francisco Bay: Juneteenth in the Fillmore District, 1945–2016." *Western Historical Quarterly* 50(2): 85–112. https://doi.org/10.1093/whq/whz003.

Blumenstock, Joshua Evan, Guanghua Chi, and Xu Tan. 2023. "Migration and the Value of Social Networks." Review of Economic Studies 92(1): 97–128.

Blumer, Herbert. 1986. *Symbolic Interactionism: Perspective and Method*. University of California Press. (Originally published in 1969.)

Blumin, Stuart M., and Glenn C. Altschuler. 2022. *The Rise and Fall of Protestant Brooklyn: An American Story*. Cornell University Press.

Bogardus, Emory S. 1933. "A Social Distance Scale." *Sociology & Social Research* 17: 265–71.

Boin, Jessica, Mirjana Rupar, Sylvie Graf, Sybille Neji, Olivia Spiegler, and Hermann Swart. 2021. "The Generalization of Intergroup Contact Effects: Emerging Research, Policy Relevance, and Future Directions." *Journal of Social Issues* 77(1): 105–31.

Bonilla-Silva, Eduardo. 2004. "From Bi-Racial to Tri-Racial: Towards a New System of Racial Stratification in the USA." *Ethnic and Racial Studies* 27: 931–50.

Bonilla-Silva, Eduardo. 2014. *Racism Without Racists*, 4th ed. Rowman & Littlefield.

Bourdieu, Pierre. 1992. *Language and Symbolic Power*. Polity Press.

Boutyline, Andrei, and Laura K. Soter. 2021. "Cultural Schemas: What They Are, How to Find Them, and What to Do Once You've Caught One." *American Sociological Review* 86(4): 728–58.

Bozorgmehr, Mehdi, and Eric Ketcham. 2018. "The Integration Paradox: Second Generation Muslims in the United States." In *Growing Up Muslim in Europe and the United States*, edited by Mehdi Bozorgmehr and Philip Kasinitz. Routledge.

Brodkin, Karen. 1998. *How the Jews Became White Folks and What That Says About Race in America*. Rutgers University Press.

Brown, Bob. 2020. "Mourning Wellesley's Dr. A. Karim Khudairi: A Reminder of How We Got Here." *The Swellesley Report*, April 26. https://theswellesleyreport.com/2020/04/mourning-wellesleys-dr-a-karim-khudairi-a-reminder-of-how-we-got-here/.

Brown, Bob. 2023a. "Wellesley Town Meeting Week #3: Equity Audit, Resolution Approved." *The Swellesley Report*, April 21. https://theswellesleyreport.com/2023/04/wellesley-town-meeting-week-3-equity-audit-resolution-approved-hardy-gets-a-buffer-oks-for-stormwater-fund-housing-upgrades/.

Brown. Bob. 2023b. "Community Makes Strong Case to Add Lunar New Year to School Calendar." *The Swellesley Report*, January 9. https://theswellesleyreport.com/2023/01/community-makes-strong-case-to-add-lunar-new-year-to-school-calendar/.

Brown, Deborah. 2020. "Wellesley's Chinese Community Helps Fight Covid-19." *The Swellesley Report*, May 14. https://theswellesleyreport.com/2020/05/wellesleys-chinese-community-helps-fight-covid-19/.

Bueker, Catherine S. 2017. *Experiences of Women of Color in an Elite US Public School*. Palgrave.

Bueker, Catherine S. 2021. "Racialized Geographies." *Contexts* 20(2): 42–47. https://doi.org/10.1177/15365042211012070.

Bueker, Catherine S., and Teal Rothschild. 2022. "Global by the Seaside." *Contexts* 21(2): 24–29. https://doi.org/10.1177/15365042221107658.

Chen, Yong. 2021. *Chop Suey, USA: The Story of Chinese Food in America*. Columbia University Press.

Crul, Maurice. 2024. "Integration into Diversity Theory Renewing—Once Again—Assimilation Theory." *Journal of Ethnic and Migration Studies* 50(1): 257–71.

Curley, Alexandra M. 2010. "Neighborhood Institutions, Facilities, and Public Space: A Missing Link for Hope VI Residents' Development of Social Capital?" *Cityscape: A Journal of Policy Development and Research* 12(1): 33–64.

Dell, A. 1966. "Letter to the Editor." *Wellesley Townsman*, April 7, p. 18.

Dhingra, Pawan. 2020. *Hyper-Education: Why Good Schools, Good Grades, and Good Behavior Are Not Enough*. New York University Press.

DiAngelo, Robin. 2021. *Nice Racism: How Progressive White People Perpetuate Racial Harm*. Beacon Press.

Diaz, Christina J., and Peter D. Ore. 2020. "Landscapes of Appropriation and Assimilation: The Impact of Immigrant-Origin Populations on US Cuisine." *Journal of Ethnic and Migration Studies* 48(5): 1–25. https://doi.org/10.1080/1369183X.2020.1811653.

DiSchino, Robert. 1976. "Speaking of Ethnic Contributions." *Wellesley Townsman*, June 24, p. 2.

Dorin, Joshua. 2014. "Wellesley's Railroad Stations." Wellesley History, March 31. https://wellesleyhistory.wordpress.com/2014/03/31/wellesleys-railroad-stations/.

Doucerain, Marina. 2019. "Moving Forward in Acculturation Research by Integrating Insights from Cultural Psychology." *International Journal of Intercultural Relations* 73: 11–24. https://doi.org/10.1016/j.ijintrel.2019.07.010.

Doucerain, Marina, Jessica Dere, and Andrew Ryder. 2013. "Travels in Hyper-Diversity: Multiculturalism and the Contextual Assessment of Acculturation." *International Journal of Intercultural Relations* 37(6): 686–99. https://doi.org/10.1016/j.ijintrel.2013.09.007.

Drouhot, Lucas G., and Victor Nee. 2019. "Assimilation and the Second Generation in Europe and America: Blending and Segregating Social Dynamics Between Immigrants and Natives." *Annual Review of Sociology* 45(1): 177–99. https://doi.org/10.1146/annurev-soc-073117-041335.

Du Bois, W. E. B. 2008. *The Souls of Black Folk*, edited by B. H. Edwards. Oxford University Press. (Originally published in 1903.)

Durkheim, Émile. 1984. *The Division of Labor in Society*. Free Press. (Originally published in 1893.)

Eason, Arianne, Terrence Pope, Kendra Becenti, and Stephanie Fryberg. 2021. "Sanitizing History: National Identification, Negative Stereotypes, and Support for Eliminating Columbus Day and Adopting Indigenous Peoples Day." *Cultural Diversity & Ethnic Minority Psychology* 27(1): 1–17. https://doi.org/10.1037/cdp0000345.

Eaton, Susan. 2001. *The Other Boston Busing Story: What's Won and Lost Across the Boundary Line*. Yale University Press.

Eng, David, and Shinhee Han. 2019. *Racial Melancholia, Racial Dissociation: On the Social and Psychic Lives of Asian Americans*. Duke University Press.

Etzioni, Amitai. 2000. "Toward a Theory of Public Ritual." *Sociological Theory* 18(1): 44–59.

Feagin, Joseph R. 2020. *The White Racial Frame: Centuries of Racial Framing and Counter-Framing*, 2nd ed. Routledge.

Feagin, Joseph R., and Eileen O'Brien. 2003. *White Men on Race: Power, Privilege, and the Shaping of Cultural Consciousness*. Beacon Press.

Fleming, Daniel T. 2020. "'A Day On, Not a Day Off': Transforming Martin Luther King Day (1993–1999)." *Journal of American Studies* 54(5): 951–80. https://doi.org/10.1017/S0021875819001464.

Foner, Nancy. 2022. *One Quarter of the Nation: Immigration and the Transformation of America*. Princeton University Press.

Foner, Nancy. 2023. "Immigration and the Transformation of American Society: Politics, the Economy, and Popular Culture." *Journal of Ethnic and Migration Studies* 50(1): 114–31. https://doi.org/10.1080/1369183X.2023.2236906.

Gamm, Gerald. 1999. *Urban Exodus: Why the Jews Left Boston and the Catholics Stayed*. Harvard University Press.

Gans, Herbert. 1992. "Comment: Ethnic Invention and Acculturation, a Bumpy-Line Approach." *Journal of American Ethnic History* 12(1): 42–52. http://www.jstor.org/stable/27501012.

Gans, Herbert J. 1997. "Toward a Reconciliation of 'Assimilation' and 'Pluralism': The Interplay of Acculturation and Ethnic Retention." *International Migration Review* 31(4): 875–92. https://doi.org/10.2307/2547417.

Gans, Herbert. 1999. "The Possibility of a New Racial Hierarchy in the Twenty-First Century United States." In *The Cultural Territories of Race: Black and White Boundaries*, edited by Michèle Lamont. University of Chicago Press and Russell Sage Foundation.

Gans, Herbert. 2012. "'Whitening' and the Changing American Racial Hierarchy." *Du Bois Review: Social Science Research on Race* 9(2): 267–79. https://doi.org/10.1017/S1742058X12000288.

Gans, Herbert. 2014. "The Coming Darkness of Late-Generation European American Ethnicity." *Ethnic and Racial Studies* 37(5): 757–65.

Geismer, Lily. 2014. *Don't Blame Us: Suburban Liberals and the Transformation of the Democratic Party*. Princeton University Press.

Go, Julian. 2024. "Reverberations of Empire: How the Colonial Past Shapes the Present." *Social Science History* 48: 1–18.

Goffman, Erving. 1982. *Interaction Ritual: Essays on Face-to-Face Behavior*. Pantheon Books.

Golash-Boza, Tanya. 2006. "Dropping the Hyphen? Becoming Latino(a)-American Through Racialized Assimilation." *Social Forces* 85(1): 27–55. https://doi.org/10.1353/sof.2006.0124.

Gordon, Milton M. 1964. *Assimilation in American Life*, 2nd ed. Oxford University Press.

Graauw, Els de. 2008. "Nonprofit Organizations: Agents of Immigrant Political Incorporation in Urban America." In *Civic Hopes and Political Realities: Community Organizations and Political Engagement Among Immigrants in the United States and Abroad*, edited by S. Karthick Ramakrishnan and Irene Bloemraad. Russell Sage Foundation.

Graauw, Els de, Sharon Gleeson, and Irene Bloemraad. 2013. "Funding Immigrant Organizations: Suburban Free Riding and Local Civic Presence." *American Journal of Sociology* 119 (1): 75–130.

Graauw, Els de, and Floris Vermeulen. 2016. "Cities and the Politics of Immigrant Integration: A Comparison of Berlin, Amsterdam, New York City, and

San Francisco." *Journal of Ethnic and Migration Studies* 42(6): 989–1012. https://doi.org/10.1080/1369183X.2015.1126089.

Great!Schools.org. n.d. "John D. Hardy Elementary." https://www.greatschools.org/massachusetts/wellesley/1723-John-D.-Hardy-Elementary-School/ (accessed November 25, 2024).

Hamilton, Tod G. 2019. *Immigration and the Remaking of Black America*. Russell Sage Foundation.

Hannah-Jones, Nikole. 2024. "The 'Colorblindness' Trap: How a Civil Rights Ideal Got Hijacked." *New York Times*, March 13. https://www.nytimes.com/2024/03/13/magazine/civil-rights-affirmative-action-colorblind.html?smid=nytcore-ios-share&referringSource=articleShare.

Haugen, Ida, and Jonas Kunst. 2017. "A Two-Way Process? A Qualitative and Quantitative Investigation of Majority Members' Acculturation." *International Journal of Intercultural Relations* 60: 67–82. https://doi.org/10.1016/j.ijintrel.2017.07.004.

Hinchcliffe, Beth. n.d. "History of Wellesley." Town of Wellesley, Massachusetts. https://wellesleyma.gov/472/History-of-Wellesley#:~:text=The%20land%20was%20good%20and,a%20small%2C%20quiet%20farming%20town.

Hinchliffe, Elizabeth M. 1981. *Five Pounds Currency, Three Pounds of Corn: Wellesley's Centennial Story*. Town of Wellesley.

Holland, Megan. 2012. "Only Here for the Day: The Social Integration of Minority Students at a Majority White High School." *Sociology of Education* 85(2): 101–20.

Ignatiev, Noel. 2008. *How the Irish Became White*. Routledge. (Originally published in 1995.)

Ingram, George. 2020. "Civil Society: An Essential Ingredient of Development." Brookings Institution, April 6. https://www.brookings.edu/articles/civil-society-an-essential-ingredient-of-development/.

Ispa-Landa, Simone. 2013. "Gender, Race, and Justification for Group Exclusion: Urban Black Students Bussed to Affluent Suburban Schools." *Sociology of Education* 86(3): 218–33.

Ispa-Landa, Simone, and Jordan Conwell. 2015. "'Once You Go to a White School, You Kind of Adapt': Black Adolescents and the Racial Classification of Schools." *Sociology of Education* 88(1): 1–19. http://www.jstor.org/stable/43186822.

Itzigsohn, José. 2009. *Encountering American Faultlines: Race, Class, and the Dominican Experience in Providence*. Russell Sage Foundation.

Itzigsohn, José, and Karida Brown. 2021. "The Sociology of W. E. B. Du Bois." *Sociological Forum* 36(2): 511–14. https://doi.org/10.1111/socf.12691.

Jack-Vickers Esther. 2024. "Exploring the Nexus of Integration and Discrimination: A Comprehensive Study of Racial Dynamics Faced by Nigerian Immigrants in the United States." *Journal of Race, Ethnicity, and Politics* 9(2): 1–24. https://doi.org/10.1017/rep.2024.7.

Jiménez, Tomas. 2008. "What Different Generations of Mexican Americans Think About Immigration from Mexico." *Generations* 32(4): 93–96. https://www.ingentaconnect.com/content/asag/gen/2008/00000032/00000004/art00016.

Jiménez, Tomas. 2017. *The Other Side of Assimilation: How Immigrants Are Changing American Life*. University of California Press.

Jiménez, Tomas. 2019. "Tracking a Changing America Across the Generations After Immigration." *Annals of the American Academy of Political and Social Science* 677(1): 119–30. https://doi.org/10.1177/0002716218765416.

Jiménez, Tomas R., and Adam L. Horowitz. 2013. "When White Is Just Alright: How Immigrants Redefine Achievement and Reconfigure the Ethnoracial Hierarchy." *American Sociological Review* 78(5): 849–71. https://doi.org/10.1177/0003122413497012.

Jin, Lily. 2022. "The Wellesley Public Schools' New Strategic Plan: Is It an Opportunity to Add Religious and Cultural Holidays to the Calendar?" *The Bradford*, November 3. https://whsbradford.org/the-wellesley-public-schools-new-strategic-plan-is-it-an-opportunity-to-add-religious-and-cultural-holidays-to-the-academic-calendar/.

Karimi, Aryan, and Rima Wilkes. 2024. "A Transnational Amendment to Assimilation Theory: Country of Origin's Racial Status Versus Transnational Whiteness." *Ethnic and Racial Studies* 47(3): 459–82. https://doi.org/10.1080/01419870.2023.2174810.

Kasinitz, Peter, John Mollenkopf, and Mary Waters. 2008. *Inheriting the City: The Children of Immigrants Come of Age*. Russell Sage Foundation.

Kasinitz, Peter, and Mary Waters. 2024. "Becoming White or Becoming Mainstream? Defining the Endpoint of Assimilation." *Journal of Ethnic and Migration Studies* 50(1): 95–113 https://doi.org/10.1080/1369183X.2023.2293298.

Khan, Shamus. 2021. *Privilege: The Making of an Adolescent Elite at St. Paul's School*. Princeton University Press.

Klarenbeek, Lea. 2023. "Relational Integration: From Integrating Migrants to Integrating Social Relations." *Journal of Ethnic and Migration Studies* 50(1): 233–56. https://doi.org/10.1080/1369183X.2023.2259038.

Kunst, Jonas R., Katharina Lefringhausen, David L. Sam, John W. Berry, and John F. Dovidio. 2021. "The Missing Side of Acculturation: How Majority-Group Members Relate to Immigrant and Minority-Group Cultures." *Current Directions in Psychological Science: A Journal of the American Psychological Society* 30(6): 485–94. https://doi.org/10.1177/09637214211040771.

Kunst, Jonas R., Katharina Lefringhausen, Sara W. Skaar, and Milan Obaidi. 2021. "Who Adopts the Culture of Ethnic Minority Groups? A Personality Perspective on Majority-Group Members' Acculturation." *International Journal of Intercultural Relations* 81: 20–28. https://doi.org/10.1016/j.ijintrel.2021.01.001.

Lara-García, Francisco. 2021. "Components of Context: Respecifying the Role of Context in Migration Research." *International Migration Review* 56(4): 992–1029. https://doi.org/10.1177/01979183211061506.

LeBrón, Alana, Amy Schulz, Cindy Gamboa, Angela Reyes, Edna Viruell-Fuentes, and Barbara Israel. 2022. "Mexican-Origin Women's Construction and Navigation of Racialized Identities: Implications for Health amid Restrictive Immigrant Policies." *Journal of Health Politics, Policy, and Law* 47(2): 259–91. https://doi.org/10.1215/03616878-9518665.

Lee, Jennifer, and Min Zhou. 2015. *The Asian American Achievement Paradox*. Russell Sage Foundation.

Lee, Jennifer, and Karthick Ramakrishnan. 2022. "A Year After Atlanta." Asian American Pacific Islander (blog), March 16. https://aapidata.com/blog/year-after-atlanta/.

Lee, Jennifer, and Dian Sheng. 2024. "The Asian American Assimilation Paradox." *Journal of Ethnic and Migration Studies* 50(1): 68–94. https://doi.org/10.1080/1369183X.2023.2183965.

References 195

Lemekh, Halyna. 2023. "Changing the Landscape of an American Town: Immigrantrification of a Korean Ethnoburb and Its Cultural and Economic Consequences." *Journal of International Migration and Integration* 24(3): 1039–65.

Lepore, Jill. 2022. "Why the School Wars Still Rage." *The New Yorker*, March 14. https://www.newyorker.com/magazine/2022/03/21/why-the-school-wars-still-rage.

Levine, Hillel, and Lawrence Harmon. 1993. *The Death of an American Jewish Community: A Tragedy of Good Intentions.* Touchstone Books.

Levitt, Peggy. 2004. "Salsa and Ketchup: Transnational Migrants Straddle Two Worlds." *Contexts* 3(2): 20–26. https://doi.org/10.1525/ctx.2004.3.2.20.

Li, Wei. 2009. *Ethnoburb: The New Ethnic Community in Urban America.* University of Hawai'i Press.

Malick, Deborah. 1991. "Schools Tepid to HRC." *Wellesley Townsman*, November 7, p. 1.

Marple, Max. 1976a. "3895 to 1815 Vote on Swimming Pool Issue Hands Town Meeting Third Slap in a Row." *Wellesley Townsman*, June 17, p. 1.

Marple, Max. 1976b. "Apologies for Implied Slight." *Wellesley Townsman*, June 24, p. 2.

Matsumoto, Noriko. 2018. *Beyond the City and the Bridge: East Asian Immigration in a New Jersey Suburb.* Rutgers University Press.

May, Paul. 2023. "Local Practices vs. National Models of Integration? The Management of Ethno-Religious Diversity in an Urban Context." *Ethnopolitics* 24(2): 159–78. https://doi.org/10.1080/17449057.2023.2265635.

McCarthy, Justin. 2021. "US Approval of Interracial Marriage at New Highs." Gallup, September 10. https://news.gallup.com/poll/354638/approval-interracial-marriage-new-high.aspx.

Menjívar, Cecilia. 2021. "The Racialization of 'Illegality.'" *Daedalus* 150(2): 91–105.

Morning, Ann, and Marcello Maneri. 2022. *An Ugly Word: Rethinking Race in Italy and the United States.* Russell Sage Foundation.

Mortarelli, Bruno. 1976. "Finds Referendum Remark Distasteful." *Wellesley Townsman*, June 24, p. 2.

Munshi, Kaivan. 2020. "Social Networks and Migration." *Annual Review of Economics* 12(August): 503–24. https://doi.org/10.1146/annurev-economics-082019-031419.

O'Connor, Thomas. 1997. *The Boston Irish: A Political History.* Back Bay Books.

Omanović, Vedran, and Ann Langley. 2023. "Assimilation, Integration, or Inclusion? A Dialectical Perspective on the Organizational Socialization of Migrants." *Journal of Management Inquiry* 32(1): 76–97. https://doi.org/10.1177/10564926211063777.

Omi, Michael, and Howard Winant. 2015. *Racial Formation in the United States.* Routledge.

Ostfeld, Mara, and Nicole Yadon. 2022. *Skin Color, Power, and Politics in America.* Russell Sage Foundation.

Parzer, Michael, and Franz Astleithner. 2018. "More than Just Shopping: Ethnic Majority Consumers and Cosmopolitanism in Immigrant Grocery Shops." *Journal of Ethnic and Migration Studies* 44(7): 1117–35.

Patel, Krishna, and Francis Vella. 2013. "Immigrant Networks and Their Implications for Occupational Choice and Wages." *Review of Economics and Statistics* 95(4): 1249–77. https://doi.org/10.1162/REST_a_00327.

Pettigrew, Thomas F., and Linda R. Tropp. 2008. "How Does Intergroup Contact Reduce Prejudice? Meta-Analytic Tests of Three Mediators." *European Journal of Social Psychology* 38(6): 922–34. https://doi.org/10.1002/ejsp.504.

Poros, Maritsa. 2011. "Migrant Social Networks: Vehicles for Migration, Integration, and Development." Migration Policy Institute, March 30. https://www.migrationpolicy.org/article/migrant-social-networks-vehicles-migration-integration-and-development.

Portes, Alejandro, and Min Zhou. 1993. "The New Second Generation: Segmented Assimilation and Its Variants." *Annals of the American Academy of Political and Social Science* 530(1): 74–96. https://doi.org/10.1177/0002716293530001006.

Prevost, Lisa. 2013. *Snob Zoning: Fear, Prejudice, and Real Estate*. Beacon Press.

Puleo, Stephan. 2007. *The Boston Italians: A Story of Pride, Perseverance, and Paesani, from the Years of the Great Immigration to the Present Day*. Beacon Press.

Putnam, Robert. 2000. *Bowling Alone: The Collapse and Revival of American Community*. Simon & Schuster.

Ramakrishnan, S. Karthick, and Irene Bloemraad, eds. 2008. *Civic Hopes and Political Realities: Immigrants, Community Organizations, and Political Engagement*. Russell Sage Foundation.

Robertson, Roland. 2012. "Globalisation or Glocalisation?" *Journal of International Communication* 18(2): 191–208. https://doi.org/10.1080/13216597.2012.709925.

Rothstein, Richard. 2017. *The Color of Law: A Forgotten History of How Our Government Segregated America*. Liveright.

Safi, Mirna. 2024. "Immigration Theory Between Assimilation and Discrimination." *Journal of Ethnic and Migration Studies* 50(1): 173–202. https://doi.org/10.1080/1369183X.2023.2207250.

Schuman, Howard, Amy Corning, and Barry Schwartz. 2012. "Framing Variations and Collective Memory: 'Honest Abe' Versus 'the Great Emancipator.'" *Social Science History* 36(4): 451–72.

Schuman, Howard, Barry Schwartz, and Hannah D'Arcy. 2005. "Elite Revisionists and Popular Beliefs: Christopher Columbus, Hero or Villain?" *Public Opinion Quarterly* 69(1): 2–29.

Schwartz, Howard, and Barry Schuman. 2005. "History, Commemoration, and Belief: Abraham Lincoln in American Memory, 1945–2001." *American Sociological Review* 70(2): 183–203.

Sleeper, William T. 1908. "Wellesley Fresh Air Excursions." *Wellesley Townsman*, July 31, p. 4.

Small, Mario L. 2006. "Neighborhood Institutions as Resource Brokers: Childcare Centers, Inter-Organizational Ties, and Resource Access Among the Poor." *Social Problems* 53(2): 274–92.

Somashekhar, Mahesh. 2019. "Ethnic Economies in the Age of Retail Chains: Comparing the Presence of Chain-Affiliated and Independently Owned Ethnic Restaurants in Ethnic Neighbourhoods." *Journal of Ethnic and Migration Studies* 45(13): 2407–29.

Staples, Brent. 2019. "How Italians Became 'White.'" *New York Times*, October 12.

Starr, Paul and Edward Freeland. 2024. "'People of Color' as a Category and Identity in the United States." *Journal of Ethnic and Migration Studies* 50(1): 47–67.

The Swellesley Report. 2021. "Wellesley to be Part of the Stop the Hate Rally Route." *The Swellesley Report*, March 27. https://theswellesleyreport.com/2021/03/wellesley-to-be-part-of-the-stop-hate-rally-route-march-27th/.

Swyngedouw, Eric. 2004. "Globalisation or 'Glocalisation'? Networks, Territories, and Rescaling." *Cambridge Review of International Affairs* 17(1): 25–48. https://doi.org/10.1080/0955757042000203632.

Tocqueville, Alexis de. 2012. *Democracy in America*, 4 vols., edited by Eduardo Nolla and translated from the French by James T. Schliefer. Liberty Fund. (Originally published in 1835.)

Town of Needham Massachusetts. n.d. "History." https://www.needhamma.gov/1092/History#:~:text=Needham%20was%20incorporated%20in%201711,River%20through%20the%2018th%20cenury.

Town of Wellesley. 2018. "Wellesley Housing Production Plan." May 14. https://wellesleyma.gov/DocumentCenter/View/10781/Wellesley-Housing-Needs-v6.

Town of Wellesley. 2024. "School Districts." Approved January 2024. https://wellesleyps.org/wp-content/uploads/2024/02/Elementary-School-Districts-Map_School-Committee-Approved_Jan-2024.pdf.

Tran, Van, Jennifer Lee, Oshin Khachikian, and Jess Lee. 2018. "Hyper-Selectivity, Racial Mobility, and the Remaking of Race." *Russell Sage Foundation Journal of the Social Sciences* 4(5): 188–209. https://doi.org/10.7758/RSF.2018.4.5.09.

Tuan, Mia. 1998. *Forever Foreigners or Honorary Whites? The Asian Ethnic Experience Today*. Rutgers University Press.

US Census Bureau. 1970. "1970 Census of Population. Characteristics of the Population. Massachusetts." Washington: US Department of Commerce. https://usa.ipums.org/usa/resources/voliii/pubdocs/1970/Population/Vol1/1970a_ma-01.pdf.

US Census Bureau. 1980. "1980 Census of Population. Characteristics of Population. Number of Inhabitants. Massachusetts. Washington: US Department of Commerce. https://www2.census.gov/prod2/decennial/documents/1980a_maABC-01.pdf.

US Census Bureau. 1990. "1990 Census of Population. General Population Characteristics. Massachusetts." Washington: US Department of Commerce. https://www2.census.gov/library/publications/decennial/1990/cp-1/cp-1-23.pdf.

US Census Bureau. 2000. "Massachusetts: 2000. Summary Population and Housing Characteristics." Washington: US Department of Commerce. https://www2.census.gov/library/publications/2002/dec/phc-1-23.pdf.

US Census Bureau. 2010. "Massachusetts: 2010. Population and Housing Unit Counts." Washington: US Department of Commerce. https://www2.census.gov/library/publications/decennial/2010/cph-2/cph-2-23.pdf.

US Census Bureau. 2020. "QuickFacts. Wellesley CDP, Massachusetts." Washington: US Department of Commerce. https://www.census.gov/quickfacts/fact/table/wellesleycdpmassachusetts/PST045223.

U.S. News and World Report. 2022. "Wellesley Public Schools." https://www.usnews.com/education/k12/massachusetts/districts/wellesley-107051#:~:text=Students%20at%20Wellesley%20Public%20Schools,Hawaiian%20or%20other%20Pacific%20Islander.

Valdez, Zulema, and Tanya Golash-Boza. 2017. "Towards an Intersectionality of Race and Ethnicity." *Ethnic & Racial Studies* 40(13): 2256–61. https://doi.org/10.1080/01419870.2017.1344277.

Van Even, Catherine. 2021. "An Early History of Boston's Chinatown." National Park Service, updated December 22. https://www.nps.gov/articles/000/boston-chinatown.htm.

Viola, Lorella. 2023. "Narratives of Italian Transatlantic (Re)migration, 1897–1936." *Frontiers in Sociology* 22(8): https://doi.org/10.3389/fsoc.2023.1239585.

Waldinger, Roger. 1990. *Ethnic Entrepreneurs: Immigrant Business in Industrial Societies.* Sage.

Waldinger, Roger. 1993. "The Ethnic Enclave Debate Revisited." *International Journal of Urban and Regional Research* 17(3): 444–52. https://doi.org/10.1111/j.1468-2427.1993.tb00232.x.

Waldinger, Roger. 1999. *Still the Promised City? African Americans and New Immigrants in Post-industrial New York.* Harvard University Press.

Warikoo, Natasha K. 2022. *Race at the Top: Asian Americans and Whites in Pursuit of the American Dream in Suburban Schools.* University of Chicago Press.

Waters, Mary C. 1990. *Ethnic Options: Choosing Identities in America.* University of California Press.

Weber, Max. 2009. "Class, Status, Party." In *Inequality and Society: Social Science Perspectives on Social Stratification,* edited by Jeff Manza and Michael Sauder. W. W. Norton.

Wellesley School Committee. 2023. Wellesley School Committee meeting, December 12, 2023. Wellesley Public Media. https://videoplayer.telvue.com/player/LGze1WqTsE8jwTKC−4xu4kSh8jPjdoJ/playlists/2773/media/841933.

Wellesley Townsman. 1906. "Drowning Accident." *Wellesley Townsman,* July 6, p. 8.

Wellesley Townsman. 1907. "Chinese Young Women at Wellesley." *Wellesley Townsman,* September 13, p. 4.

Wellesley Townsman. 1908. "Church News." *Wellesley Townsman,* January 17, p. 9.

Wellesley Townsman. 1910. "Wellesley Outings." *Wellesley Townsman,* July 29, p. 9.

Wellesley Townsman. 1911. "About Town." *Wellesley Townsman,* January 13, p. 6.

Wellesley Townsman. 1912a. "Dr. Ravi's Marlboro Address." *Wellesley Townsman,* October 18, p. 11.

Wellesley Townsman. 1912b. "About Town." *Wellesley Townsman,* July 19, p. 7.

Wellesley Townsman. 1912c. "A Boy's Gratitude." *Wellesley Townsman,* July 26, p. 7.

Wellesley Townsman. 1917. "War Recipes." *Wellesley Townsman,* August 17, p. 7.

Wellesley Townsman. 1920. "Girl Scout Week." *Wellesley Townsman,* November 5, p. 5.

Wellesley Townsman. 1922. "History of Wellesley." *Wellesley Townsman,* July 14, p. 17.

Wellesley Townsman. 1924a. "Chinese Gather at Merry Mount." *Wellesley Townsman,* August 8, p. 8.

Wellesley Townsman. 1924b. "Wellesley Congregational Church." *Wellesley Townsman,* November 28, p. 8.

Wellesley Townsman. 1925. "Italian Books at the Main Library." *Wellesley Townsman,* July 10, p. 2.

Wellesley Townsman. 1926a. "Village Church Notes." *Wellesley Townsman,* March 26, p. 4.

Wellesley Townsman. 1926b. "Our Jewish Neighbors." *Wellesley Townsman,* September 17, p. 2.

Wellesley Townsman. 1927a. "English House, Wellesley Hills." *Wellesley Townsman,* February 18, p. 6.

Wellesley Townsman. 1927b. "Wellesley People Celebrate New Year's Day." *Wellesley Townsman,* September 30, p. 1.

References

Wellesley Townsman. 1928. "To Celebrate Rosh Hashona." *Wellesley Townsman,* September 2, p. 5.
Wellesley Townsman. 1931. "Wellesley Local News." *Wellesley Townsman,* November 13, p. 2.
Wellesley Townsman. 1932a. "Hills Congregational Church." *Wellesley Townsman,* October 7, p. 4.
Wellesley Townsman. 1932b. "Wellesley on Chop Suey Diet." *Wellesley Townsman,* March 25, p. 2.
Wellesley Townsman. 1934. "Wellesley Local." *Wellesley Townsman,* March 16, p. 5.
Wellesley Townsman. 1935a. "Rental." *Wellesley Townsman,* November 15, p. 2.
Wellesley Townsman. 1935b. "First National Stores." *Wellesley Townsman,* May 3, p. 4.
Wellesley Townsman. 1935c. "Wellesley Local Brevities." *Wellesley Townsman,* October 25, p. 3.
Wellesley Townsman. 1936a. "Summer Institute Offers Public Evening Forums." *Wellesley Townsman,* July 10, p. 1.
Wellesley Townsman. 1936b. "Next Week in Wellesley's Churches." *Wellesley Townsman,* November 13, p. 5.
Wellesley Townsman. 1936c. "Italian Evening Classes." *Wellesley Townsman,* February 21, p. 1.
Wellesley Townsman. 1936d. "School Districts." *Wellesley Townsman,* August 28, p. 1.
Wellesley Townsman. 1936e. "Changes Announced in School Organization." *Wellesley Townsman,* November 20, p. 1.
Wellesley Townsman. 1936f. "To Supt. of Schools and School Committee." *Wellesley Townsman,* November 27, p. 2.
Wellesley Townsman. 1936g. "1937 Models." *Wellesley Townsman,* December 11, p. 4.
Wellesley Townsman. 1936h. "Letter to the Editor." *Wellesley Townsman,* November 27, p. 2.
Wellesley Townsman. 1936i. "Editorial Comment." *Wellesley Townsman,* December 4, p. 2.
Wellesley Townsman. 1936j. "To All Wellesley Parents." *Wellesley Townsman,* December 4, p. 2.
Wellesley Townsman. 1936k. "Letter to the Editor." *Wellesley Townsman,* December 11, p. 4.
Wellesley Townsman. 1938a. "Local Man to Wed Saturday in Connecticut." *Wellesley Townsman,* May 27, p. 2.
Wellesley Townsman. 1938b. "Chinese Dinner at Village Church to Be Last of Series." *Wellesley Townsman,* February 25, p. 1.
Wellesley Townsman. 1938c. "Wellesley Summer Playgrounds to Close for Season Today." *Wellesley Townsman,* August 19, p. 2.
Wellesley Townsman. 1938d. "To Form Branch of Italo-American Voters League." *Wellesley Townsman,* September 16, p. 12.
Wellesley Townsman. 1938e. "Political Advertisement." *Wellesley Townsman,* November 4, p. 9.
Wellesley Townsman. 1939a. "Fred Kennedy's Grill." *Wellesley Townsman,* December 15, p. 7.
Wellesley Townsman. 1939b. "Otto . . . " *Wellesley Townsman,* September 15, p. 7.
Wellesley Townsman. 1939c. "Italians and Democrats." *Wellesley Townsman,* October 2, p. 2.

References

Wellesley Townsman. 1939d. "Editorial Comment." *Wellesley Townsman,* November 11, p. 4.
Wellesley Townsman. 1940a. "Star Market." *Wellesley Townsman,* May 17, p. 11.
Wellesley Townsman. 1940b. "Classes Offered in Music and Italian Language." *Wellesley Townsman,* March 22, p. 4.
Wellesley Townsman. 1942. "John Doherty Colonial Funeral Home." *Wellesley Townsman,* May 28, p. 8.
Wellesley Townsman. 1943a. "Otto . . . " *Wellesley Townsman,* November 11, p. 8.
Wellesley Townsman. 1943b. "Otto . . . " *Wellesley Townsman,* March 25, p. 1.
Wellesley Townsman. 1943c. "Send Thanks for Help to the Cause of China." *Wellesley Townsman,* December 9, p. 8.
Wellesley Townsman. 1943d. "Activities at Wellesley College." *Wellesley Townsman,* April 15, p. 7.
Wellesley Townsman. 1943e. "Activities at Wellesley Colleges." *Wellesley Townsman,* October 21, p. 2.
Wellesley Townsman. 1945. "To Observe Boy Scout Week." *Wellesley Townsman,* February 9, p. 8.
Wellesley Townsman. 1946. "Wellesley College." *Wellesley Townsman,* April 25, p. 18.
Wellesley Townsman. 1947a. "William H. Danforth Jr. Weds Belmont Girl." *Wellesley Townsman,* August 7, p. 3.
Wellesley Townsman. 1947b. "Neighborhood News." *Wellesley Townsman,* October 30, p. 2.
Wellesley Townsman. 1948a. "Unitarian Wayside Pulpit Extends New Year's Greetings." *Wellesley Townsman,* September 30, p. 9.
Wellesley Townsman. 1948b. "J. S. Waterman." *Wellesley Townsman,* January 1, p. 4.
Wellesley Townsman. 1949. "High School Highlights." *Wellesley Townsman,* May 5, p. 15.
Wellesley Townsman. 1950a. "Wellesley Hills Market." *Wellesley Townsman,* May 25, p. 13.
Wellesley Townsman. 1950b. "Prof. Owen Lattimore One of Six Experts on Problems of East and Southeast Asia to Speak Here." *Wellesley Townsman,* October 19, p. 13.
Wellesley Townsman. 1951. "Services at Temple Israel, Natick." *Wellesley Townsman,* April 12, p. 13.
Wellesley Townsman. 1952a. "Mr. Alper Urges Truman to Veto Immigration." *Wellesley Townsman,* June 5, p. 16.
Wellesley Townsman. 1952b. "Jewish Community Group Meets Wednesday." *Wellesley Townsman,* January 24, p. 2.
Wellesley Townsman. 1953. "'Tap-Out' Ceremony Features Boy Scout Spring Camporee." *Wellesley Townsman,* May 21, p. 8.
Wellesley Townsman. 1955a. "In Appreciation." *Wellesley Townsman,* October 20, p. 14.
Wellesley Townsman. 1955b. "Church School Opens at the Unitarian Church This Sunday." *Wellesley Townsman,* September 29, p. 15.
Wellesley Townsman. 1955c. "Henri Aubert at Bardwell February 10th." *Wellesley Townsman,* February 3, p. 9.
Wellesley Townsman. 1955d. "Grossman's Lumber Yard." *Wellesley Townsman,* September 15, p. 21.
Wellesley Townsman. 1958a. "Forum Here to Discuss 'Integration and Our Suburbs.'" *Wellesley Townsman,* November 6, p. 2.

Wellesley Townsman. 1958b. "A Most Hearty Welcome." *Wellesley Townsman*, September 18, p. 26.
Wellesley Townsman. 1958c. "Calls Attention to Services of Jewish Faith." *Wellesley Townsman*, September 25, p. 16.
Wellesley Townsman. 1958d. "Robert E. Segal to Talk on Suburban Homes for Minority Groups." *Wellesley Townsman*, March 13, p. 2.
Wellesley Townsman. 1958e. "Wellesley Public Schools to Host Mental Health Institute." *Wellesley Townsman*, October 2, p. 18.
Wellesley Townsman. 1959a. "Smorgasbord Dinners at the Beaconsfield." *Wellesley Townsman*, October 15, p. 16.
Wellesley Townsman. 1959b. "Selectmen Endorse Fair Housing Practices." *Wellesley Townsman*, October 15, p. 2.
Wellesley Townsman. 1959c. "Forum to Discuss 'Integration and Our Suburbs.'" *Wellesley Townsman*, November 6, p. 2.
Wellesley Townsman. 1959d. "'Diary of Anne Frank' Now at Playhouse." *Wellesley Townsman*, August 20, p. 17.
Wellesley Townsman. 1960a. "To the Editor." *Wellesley Townsman*, April 28, p. 12.
Wellesley Townsman. 1960b. "Civil Defense Forms Council of Religious Groups." *Wellesley Townsman*, April 7, p. 11.
Wellesley Townsman. 1960c. "A&P." *Wellesley Townsman*, March 31, p. 9.
Wellesley Townsman. 1960d. "Halls for Rent." *Wellesley Townsman*, June 16, p. 1.
Wellesley Townsman. 1961. "Wellesley Supermarket." *Wellesley Townsman*, February 9, p. 8.
Wellesley Townsman. 1962. "Newcomers Enjoy an Oriental Meal." *Wellesley Townsman*, January 18, p. 2.
Wellesley Townsman. 1963. "Fair Housing Meeting Hears Discrimination." *Wellesley Townsman*, April 4, p. 32.
Wellesley Townsman. 1964a. "Classifieds." *Wellesley Townsman*, April 9, p. 17.
Wellesley Townsman. 1964b. "Communication." *Wellesley Townsman*, February 6, p. 18.
Wellesley Townsman. 1965. "The Night Owl." *Wellesley Townsman*, October 14, p. 9.
Wellesley Townsman. 1966. "St. Andrew's Church Announcements." *Wellesley Townsman*, April 7, p. 21.
Wellesley Townsman. 1967a. "Church Services." *Wellesley Townsman*, June 1, p. 5.
Wellesley Townsman. 1967b. "Realtors, Clergy & Fair Housing Officers Discuss Local Conditions." *Wellesley Townsman*, December 7, p. 20.
Wellesley Townsman. 1969a. "St. Paul's Basketeers Hold Tryouts Nov. 1." *Wellesley Townsman*, Oct. 23, p. 21.
Wellesley Townsman. 1969b. "'The Two of Us,' Warm, Human Drama." *Wellesley Townsman*, January 30.
Wellesley Townsman. 1970a. "Miss Walter Is Bride of Matthew King." *Wellesley Townsman*, September 24, p. 13.
Wellesley Townsman. 1970b. "Beth Elohim." *Wellesley Townsman*, November 19, p. 19.
Wellesley Townsman. 1970c. "Counters (and Kibitzers!)" *Wellesley Townsman*, March 19, p. 1.
Wellesley Townsman. 1970d. "Temple Beth Elohim." *Wellesley Townsman*, December 17, p. 23.
Wellesley Townsman. 1971a. "BU Introduces Exotic Languages." *Wellesley Townsman*, September 30, p. 14.

202   References

Wellesley Townsman. 1971b. "Tutoring in Japanese and Chinese Available." *Wellesley Townsman*, June 29, p. 13.

Wellesley Townsman. 1971c. "Chinese Lessons." *Wellesley Townsman*, November 4, p. 20.

Wellesley Townsman. 1971d. "Library Has New Cassettes for the Blind." *Wellesley Townsman*, September 9, p. 7.

Wellesley Townsman. 1971e. "The Head of the Chinese Dragon." *Wellesley Townsman*, October 14, p. 1.

Wellesley Townsman. 1972a. "Church Services." *Wellesley Townsman*, April 20, p. 12.

Wellesley Townsman. 1972b. "Political Advertisement." *Wellesley Townsman*, October 26, p. 3.

Wellesley Townsman. 1972c. "Political Advertisement." *Wellesley Townsman*, November 2, p. 21.

Wellesley Townsman. 1972d. "Brecks." *Wellesley Townsman*, January 13, p. 8.

Wellesley Townsman. 1972e. "New Encyclopaedia at Free Library." *Wellesley Townsman*, May 18, p. 4.

Wellesley Townsman. 1972f. "Charles River District Doctors Hear Acupuncture Warning." *Wellesley Townsman*, November 9, p. 13.

Wellesley Townsman. 1973a. "Wellesley Supermarket." *Wellesley Townsman*, October 4, p. 3.

Wellesley Townsman. 1973b. "New Shop Caters to Everyday Gourmet Chef." *Wellesley Townsman*, September 6, p. 12.

Wellesley Townsman. 1973c. "Acupuncture Clinic Opens in Boston." *Wellesley Townsman*, July 19, p. 13.

Wellesley Townsman. 1974a. "Advertisements." *Wellesley Townsman*, September 12, p. 2.

Wellesley Townsman. 1974b. "Acupuncture & Pain Therapy Associates of Wellesley." *Wellesley Townsman*, October 10, p. 2.

Wellesley Townsman. 1974c. "Jews on Campus to Observe Two-Week Memorial Service." *Wellesley Townsman*, April 11, p. 13.

Wellesley Townsman. 1975a. "Automotive Acupuncture Is Preventive Medicine." *Wellesley Townsman*, January 9, p. 11.

Wellesley Townsman. 1975b. "Dr. Lennig Chang Studies Acupuncture Effectiveness." *Wellesley Townsman*, September 4, p. 22.

Wellesley Townsman. 1976a. "McCue-Corkin Wedding." *Wellesley Townsman*, October 21, p. 7.

Wellesley Townsman. 1976b. "Four Week Series to Focus on Holocaust in Germany." *Wellesley Townsman*, April 22, p. 24.

Wellesley Townsman. 1976c. "Car Wash Earns $114 for Library's Holocaust Series." *Wellesley Townsman*, April 29, p. 8.

Wellesley Townsman. 1976d. "Hills Librarian Praised for Holocaust Program." *Wellesley Townsman*, June 10, p. 2.

Wellesley Townsman. 1976e. "Worlds and Words of Thanks to Special Hills Librarian." *Wellesley Townsman*, August 12, p. 2.

Wellesley Townsman. 1977a. "Continuing Education." *Wellesley Townsman*, September 15, p. 2.

Wellesley Townsman. 1977b. "Political Advertisement." *Wellesley Townsman*, February 24, p. 9.

Wellesley Townsman. 1978. "Temple Fire, Act of Religious Prejudice." *Wellesley Townsman,* May 18, p. 2.
Wellesley Townsman. 1979a. "A Patient's Day at the Charles River Hospital." *Wellesley Townsman,* May 24, p. 9.
Wellesley Townsman. 1979b. "Discussion Series Begins in January." *Wellesley Townsman,* December 20, p. 5.
Wellesley Townsman. 1980a. "Mixed Marriages Discussion Group." *Wellesley Townsman,* April 24, p. 6.
Wellesley Townsman. 1980b. "Democrats." *Wellesley Townsman,* August 21, p. 9.
Wellesley Townsman. 1980c. "Courses." *Wellesley Townsman,* October 16, p. 10.
Wellesley Townsman. 1980d. "Family Life Discussions." *Wellesley Townsman,* September 4, p. 19.
Wellesley Townsman. 1980e. "Nutritional Educational Series." *Wellesley Townsman,* September 11, p. 13.
Wellesley Townsman. 1980f. "'Fiddler' Cast Gets a History Lesson." *Wellesley Townsman,* April 24, p. 9.
Wellesley Townsman. 1981. "Changes in Society Keep Up Demands on Mental Health Agency." *Wellesley Townsman,* July 23, p. 7.
Wellesley Townsman. 1982. "School Board." *Wellesley Townsman,* July 22, p. 6.
Wellesley Townsman. 1983a. "Good Beginning at Bates." *Wellesley Townsman,* June 23, p. 5.
Wellesley Townsman. 1983b. "Help & Support." *Wellesley Townsman,* March 3, p. 15.
Wellesley Townsman. 1983c. "Religion." *Wellesley Townsman,* October 27, p. 45.
Wellesley Townsman. 1983d. "School Start Date Irks Jewish Parents." *Wellesley Townsman,* July 21, p. 27.
Wellesley Townsman. 1983e. "Parents Not Irked." *Wellesley Townsman,* July 28, p. 5.
Wellesley Townsman. 1983f. "Peter Amalfi." *Wellesley Townsman,* December 8, p. 6.
Wellesley Townsman. 1984. "Acupuncture Lecture." *Wellesley Townsman,* February 2, p. 17.
Wellesley Townsman. 1985a. "Symbolic Foods for Passover." *Wellesley Townsman,* April 4, p. 44.
Wellesley Townsman. 1985b. "Wellesley Acupuncture Group." *Wellesley Townsman,* March 28, p. 6.
Wellesley Townsman. 1985c. "Acupuncture for Dogs and Cats." *Wellesley Townsman,* October 31, p. 35.
Wellesley Townsman. 1985d. "Fall Musical to Be Staged by St. John's Players." *Wellesley Townsman,* October 24, p. 25.
Wellesley Townsman. 1987a. "Stepping Up Synagogue Security." *Wellesley Townsman,* November 19, p. 21.
Wellesley Townsman. 1987b. "Wellesley Schools Must Face Questions." *Wellesley Townsman,* January 14, p. 4.
Wellesley Townsman. 1987c. "The Grinchess Who Stole Christmas." *Wellesley Townsman,* December 17, p. 5.
Wellesley Townsman. 1988a. "Bush and Dukakis Supporters Face Off on Israel." *Wellesley Townsman,* October, 13, p. 14.
Wellesley Townsman. 1988b. "Wellesley Women Support Soviet Refusniks." *Wellesley Townsman,* April 7, p. 2.

Wynn, Jonathan R. 2016. "On the Sociology of Occasions." *Sociological Theory* 34(3): 276–86.
Yeh, Chiou-Ling. 2008. *Making an American Festival: Chinese New Year in San Francisco's Chinatown*. University of California Press.
Zemba, Stephanie, and Meeta Mehrotra. 2023. "'What's Your Accent, Where Are You From?': Language and Belonging Among Older Immigrants." *Journal of Aging Studies* 67: 101189. https://doi.org/10.1016/j.jaging.2023.101189.
Zhou, Min, and Roberto G. Gonzales. 2019. "Divergent Destinies: Children of Immigrants Growing Up in the United States." *Annual Review of Sociology* 45(1): 383–99. https://doi.org/10.1146/annurev-soc-073018-022424.

Index

Tables and figures are listed in **boldface**.

A Better Chance (ABC) program, 17, 19, 49
acupuncture in Wellesley, 120–21
Alba, Richard, 6, 19, 30, 31, 146, 157, 161–62
Allport, Gordon, 39–40, 62, 78
Americanization programs in Wellesley, 23
anti-Semitism in Wellesley: first contacts with Jews in early 20th century and, 23; foreignness of Judaism and, 23–24, 36; Holocaust and, 6, 123, 160; housing segregation and, 24, 25, 42, 118, 124; Jewish organizations and, 113, 116; periodic incidents of, 113, 123, 154, 158–59; town resolution condemning, 152
Asian residents of Wellesley: Black/non-Black color line and, 70; children's extracurricular activities, 60; inclusion of holidays on school calendar, 143–44; multigenerational households, 28; organizations, 113; as percentage of population, 4, **4**; provisional feelings of acceptance, 68–69; racialization of, 32, 36; range of nationalities, 28; school redistricting conflict and, 131–32. *See also* Chinese residents of Wellesley; Indian residents of Wellesley
assimilation: American diet and, 86; and ethnic retention, interaction of, 33–34, 74, 92–94, 157–59; honor and belonging and, 162, 163; loss of culture and, 74; and mainstream reformation, 2–3, 84–87; mixing of food traditions and, 81–87; moral elevation and, 162, 163; perceptions from inside *vs.* outside of group, 41; and racialization, 3; and reform of mainstream, 34; visually distinct groups and, 160. *See also* neo-assimilation; variegated assimilation
assimilation theories, 29–32; data collection issues in, 33, 34–35; unification of, in variegated assimilation theory, 32–34

Black Americans: changes in Black identity and, 31; and housing discrimination in Wellesley, 117–18; racialization of, 32, 45, 49, 69
Black Lives Matter, 132, 140, 152
Black residents of Wellesley: feelings of not belonging, 59; as percentage of population, 4, **4**; racialization of, 59, 66, 69, 160–61; reasons for small number of, 45

Black/non-Black line: as barrier to group interactions, 45–56; as bright and sticky boundary, 48–49, 70; and church attendance, 54; and definition of diversity, 100; movement in, 31; replacement of Black/White line, 45, 70, 160
Bonilla-Silva, Eduardo, 71
Boston: Jewish migration from, 24; school desegregation in, 17
bridges: building of, by ethnic groups, 7, **8**, 29, 52, 54, 77, 99, 101, 102, 111, 153, 155–56; failure to build, 64; organizations as, 29; and two-way cultural influence, 113, 123–24

changes prompted by ethnic groups: de-Christianization of public square, 125, 149–50, **150**; gaining knowledge and strength for, 126, 153–54; influences on, from micro- to macro-levels, 157–60; perceived as zero-sum game, 146–47; public events, internationalization of, 150–51; school activities and events featuring ethnic groups, 137–38; school calendar, addition of ethnic holidays to, 125, 143–48; school calendar changes, opposition to, 145–46, 162–63; school communications in multiple languages, 140–41, **141**; in school curricula, 132–37; school redistricting conflict and, 127–32; schools' accommodation of ethnic religious needs, 138–40, 141–42; as significant and ongoing, 153, 155–56, 157; tensions over, 127; town meeting resolutions and, 151–53; unequal integration and, 127
Chiang Kai-shek, Madame. *See* Soong, Mayling
Chinese Exclusion Act of 1882, 27–28, 87, 116, 158
Chinese residents of Wellesley: areas of settlement, 28–29; businesses in early 20th century, 27; changes to school and, 29, 102–3, 125, 138, 143–46; children's superior school performance, 132–33; and Chinese Language School, 55, **56**, 97; and definition of "mainstream," 36; delay in political engagement by, 153–54; demographics of current residents, 28, 29, 36; demographics of early arrivals, 26; "double consciousness" and, 59; ethnic retention, and influence on mainstream, 97–98, 136–37; first arrivals, 26; health and well-being contributions, 120–21; immigration activism by, 116; language as barrier for, 43, 58–59, 62–64; language retention, 28; limited mainstream contact in 20th century, 39; Mandarin language and, 105–6, 108, 113, 118–19, 136–37; multigenerational households, 28, 36; normative inversion sought by, 119; organizations, 29, 113; as percentage of population, 28; period of arrival, 5–6, 19, 27–28; political engagement by, 126, 154; racialization of, 25–27, 36; reasons for PTO avoidance, 58–59, 97; religious practices, and relational assimilation, 79, 80; retention of traditional foods, 82, 83; retreat from assimilation (ethnic reactivity), 92; school curricula conflict and, 132–37; town "Tolerance Pledge" and, 29
Chinese Service Bureau, 26, 116, 122
Chin's Village, 87, 143, 151, 166
churches as setting for group interactions, 50–55; interfaith outreach, 51–53 54–55; outreach to immigrants, 51, 54–55, **56**; past role in maintaining homogeneity, 52–54
civil discourse training, 163
civil engagement in Wellesley, 55–56
civil rights groups in Wellesley, 117–18

Index   207

colorblindness, White pretense of, 71–72, 163
Columbus Day: Italian American views on, 93, 147–48, 163; removal as town holiday, 143, 147–48, 155, 163
community organizations in Wellesley: anti-racism/bias groups, 98; and civic assimilation, 97, 99, 100; ethnic foods and, 103–5; ethnic groups' influence on, 110, 123–24; ethnic organizations, 99, 110–13; ethnic political groups, influence of, 114–16, 126; fair housing groups, 117–18; functions of, 99; holiday celebration de-Christianization, 101–2; hybrid groups promoting inclusion, 113; immigrant-serving groups, 98–99; and immigration activism, 116–17; language classes offered by, 105–6; multilingual resources adopted by, 108–9; range of groups, 98; reformation of mainstream and, 97–103, 159; as setting for assimilation of new groups, 98; significant influence of, 123–24; tensions caused by ethnic influence, 113–14; and variegated assimilation, 159
contact theory (Allport), 39–40
Council of Religious Groups, 52
Council on Aging, 109, 110
COVID-19 pandemic: and anti-Asian hate, 29, 68, 97–98, 140, 152, 159, 160, 163; and Chinese contributions to health, 121; and High School ranking, 133
cultural change: danger of assumptions about, 35; neo-assimilation and, 31
cultural omnivorism, 86, 103, 106

DEI. *See* diversity, equity, and inclusion
demographic changes, US, effects of, 161–62
diversity, equity, and inclusion (DEI): backlash against, 140, 145, 146; equity audit funded by town, 151, 152; established parents' objection to curriculum based on, 134–36; town resolutions supporting, 151–52; Trump administration and, 140; in Wellesley Public Schools, 140
diversity and equality, as dueling concepts, 71
diversity and multiculturalism in Wellesley: and "color-blind" rhetoric, 70–71, 162–63; effects of, 2–3, 6; increase of, **2**, 3, **4**, 4–5, 19–20; as increasingly welcomed, 19, 37; and interest in learning languages, 106; *vs.* Massachusetts and United States, 4–5, **5**; pushback against, 109; school redistricting and, 130–32; as under-studied, 2, 5–6; young peoples' preference for, 67
Du Bois, W.E.B., 59
Durkheim, Emile, 98

Eason, Arianne, 147
educated elite, national influence of, 3–4
education: elite college access as issue in Wellesley, 161–62; public, on immigrants' countries of origin, 121–23. *See also* schools
Eng, David, 59
equality and diversity, as dueling concepts, 71
ethnic retention: assimilation and, 33–34, 74, 92–94, 157–59; mainstream reformation and, 2–3, 65–66, 70, 101–3; and multilingual resources in community organizations, 108; and variegated assimilation, 6, **7**, 157–59
extracurricular activities as setting for group interactions, 55–61, 63; children's activities, 59–61, 63; parent teacher organizations (PTOs), 58–59; variegated assimilation and, 60; volunteer organizations and clubs, 56–58, 63

208   Index

Fair Housing Act of 1968, 15
Feagin, Joe, 3, 71
Federal Housing Administration (FHA), 14–15
Floyd, George, 161
Foner, Nancy, 31
food: Chinese, move from exotic to everyday, 103–5; ethnic, and appropriative assimilation, 104; important cultural functions, 81, 83; Italian, penetration of mainstream, 104–5; Jewish, penetration of mainstream, 104; as point of entry into new culture, 86; and relational assimilation, 81–87
footpaths between individuals: and better group relations, 7, 40; development into ladders, 7, 49, 101, 103, 113; development through contact, 7, **8**, 40, 44, 95; failure to build, 64; food and, 81; mainstream reformation through, 66, 81; micro-level incidents that block, 81; multidirectional flow along, 79, 89, 158; new residents' conscious building of, 66, 69, 99; political interaction and, 89, 126; racialization and, 49, 66, 81; religion and, 52, 54, 69; settings for creation of, 40, 111, 123–24; unifying event, US need for, 164
Frank, Barney, 116

Gamm, Gerald, 24
Gans, Herbert, 99, 103, 157
Geismer, Lily, 15, 17, 185n61
glocal factors in assimilation, 6–7, **8**, 19–20, 37–38; definition of, 38; immigration policies and, 39; interaction of ethnic groups and, 71, 163–64; neo-assimilation and, 39, 51, 67; Nixon's visit to China and, 106, 120; relational assimilation and, 96; as under-studied, 37; variegated assimilation and, 6–7, **8**, 19–20, 37–38, 157–60

Go, Julian, 35
Gordon, Milton, 30, 32, 40, 81

Han, Shinhee, 59
Hardy, John D. (Elementary School), 28, **42**, 127–32, **130**
health and well-being, ethnic groups' contributions to, 119–21
Heckler, Margaret, 115–17
history of Wellesley, 13–19; early industries and residents, 13–14; growth under restrictive housing laws, 14–16; settlement, 13; voluntary school integration, 16–19; zoning laws, 14, 16
honors and belonging, assimilation and, 162
housing in Wellesley: affordable housing, 15–16, 118; fair housing groups, 117–18; high cost of, as issue, 118; restrictive housing laws, 14–16, 41–42, 118
Hunnewell: H. H., 13; Elementary School, **42**, 127; Topiary, **21**

identity, relational assimilation and, 91–95, 96
Immigration Act of 1924, 30
Immigration and Nationality Act of 1965 (Hart-Celler Act), 5, 19, 28, 30, 43, 48, 130, 133, 158
immigration policy, Wellesley activism on, 116–17
Indian residents of Wellesley: changes to school and, 29, 33, 89, 102–3, 125, 138, 139, 143–46; provisional feelings of acceptance, 79–80; religious practices, relational assimilation and, 79–80; retention of traditional foods, 82–84
individual interactions: and emulation of ethnic groups, 94–95; and mainstream reformation, 7; relational assimilation in, 66–71. *See also* bridges
interaction of ethnic groups in Wellesley: Black/non-Black color line in, 45–56; churches as setting

Index   209

for, 50–55; decreasing segregation and, 61–62; demographic traits conducive to, 40–41; easy integration of non-threatening individuals, 100; extracurricular activities as setting for, 55–61, 63; glocal factors influencing, 71; improved intergroup relations and, 39–40; language as barrier to, 43, 58–59, 62–64; as limited in most of 20th century, 39; memories of past exclusion as barrier to, 64; neighborhoods as setting for, 41–46; perceptions of diversity as subjective in, 43–48, 57–58, 63, 67–68, 70–71, 100; personality traits conducive to, 40; primary and secondary transfer effects of, 40; as relatively positive, 95–96; schools as setting for, 46–50; town government as setting for, 61–63; various settings for, 40, 63
intermarriage: relational assimilation in, 72–73; and religious practices, 74–76
Israel-Gaza war, and group relations, 163–64
Italian residents of Wellesley: appeal of Italian culture in early 20th century and, 20, **21**, 36; areas of settlement, 22, 43; assimilation process for, 35–36; Catholicism and, 36; on changing experience of Jewish identity, 92; church-based social groupings, 53–54; circular migration to and from Italy, 178n30; discrimination experienced by, 155; ethnic retention in, 23; isolation of children at school, 39; Italian language and, 20–22, 105, 108, 118, 136; limited mainstream contact in 20th century, 39; organizations to promote interests and culture, 111, **112**; period of arrival, 5–6, 13, 20; political influence of, 114–15, 148, 154–55; racialization of, 36, 39; retention of traditional foods, 81–82; retreat from assimilation (ethnic reactivity), 92, 93; school redistricting and, 127–29; segregation by school district, 41; social class and professions, 20–23, 35; views on Columbus Day, 93, 147–48, 163; Waldensian sect, 36, 51
Italo-American Educational Club, 110–12, **112**, 115, 118, 148, 166

Jewish Community Group, 55, 111–12, 119
Jewish residents of Wellesley: areas of settlement, 25; assimilation process for, 35–36; changes to school activities and events and, 137–38; on changing experience of Jewish identity, 91; children's superior performance in school, 133; color line, move across, 35; de-Christianization of public space and, 125, 139, 149–50; delay in political engagement by, 154; early newspaper reports on holiday celebrations, 23–24; early restrictive housing practices and, 15; engagement with local government, 61, 62; fair housing activism, 117–18; fear of losing public recognition of holidays, 162, 164; health and well-being contributions, 119–20; and Hebrew/Yiddish language, 105, 106; immigration activism by, 116–17; inclusion of holidays on school calendar, 25, 142, 143–44; increases in, 4–5, 24, 35; interfaith outreach and, 52, 54–55; intermarriage with Christians, 72, 74–76; Jewish flight from Boston and, 24; limited mainstream contact in 20th century, 39; number of families in 1963, 117; organizations, 111–13; period of arrival, 5–6; political engagement by, 126; political influence of,

115–16; public education on Holocaust, 122–23; racialization of, 23–24, 36; and relational assimilation, 75–79; retention of traditional foods, 83; school accommodations for religious needs, 139–40, 141–42; segregation by school district, 42–43; small early community, 23; surface-level inclusion in mid-20th century, 24–25; temples, 24. *See also* anti-Semitism in Wellesley

Jiménez, Tomas, 9, 66, 94

Juliani, Felix, 115, 126

Kasinitz, Philip, 33

Klarenbeek, Lea, 37

ladders: building of, by ethnic groups, **8**, 49, 115, 124, 131, 148, 149, 153, 155–56, 159; footpaths' development into, 7, 49, 101, 103, 113; organizations as, 29, 37

Langley, Ann, 71

language: bilingualism in relational assimilation, 89; heritage language classes, 118–19; increased language learning with diversity, 105–6; mainstream, ethnic influence on, 106–8; as measure of assimilation, 106

Latino immigrants, racialization of, 31–32

Latino residents of Wellesley, 4, **4**

Lee, Jennifer, 33

Manieri, Marcello, 71

Massachusetts: affordable housing laws, 16; diversity *vs.* Wellesley, 4–5, **5**; housing discrimination policies, 15; MBTA Communities Law, 16

McCarran-Walter Immigration Bill, 116

melting pot metaphor, 2

METCO. *See* Metropolitan Council for Educational Opportunity

methodology, 8–11; analysis, 10–11; data sources beyond interviews, 9–10, 166; interview protocols, 167–76; subjects and interviews, 8–9, 165

Metropolitan Council for Educational Opportunity (METCO): and integration of Wellesley schools, 17–18, 49; and racialization of Black Americans, 45, 49, 69; residents' views on, 18–19

missionaries (missionary), 25, 50–51, 122

moral elevation, assimilation and, 162, 163

Morning, Ann, 71

multiculturalism. *See* diversity and multiculturalism in Wellesley

Muslim residents of Wellesley: de-Christianization of public square and, 149; in organizations, 57, 58, 98, 164; push to add holidays to school calendar, 140, 145, 146; school accommodation of religious needs, 140

national public service, required, 164

Nee, Victor, 30, 31, 33

neighborhoods as setting for group interactions, 41–46; racial/ethnic segregation by school districts and, 41–43, **42**; residents' acceptance of gradually-increasing diversity, 43–46; restrictive housing laws and, 41–43

neo-assimilation: definition of, 6, 30–31; glocal nature of, 39, 51, 67; multidirectional change in, 6, 30–31; organizations and, 99; and racialization, interaction of, 6, 32–33, 34, 48, 157–59; scholarship on, 31

New Deal housing programs, 14–15

Nixon, Richard M., 106, 120, 184–85n61

normative inversion, 80, 119

O'Brien, Eileen, 3

Omanov, Vedran, 71

parent teacher organizations (PTOs): Chinese residents' reasons for avoiding, 58–59, 63–64, 97; mainstream reformation through assimilation and, 2, 102, 105, 125; multilingual resources added to, 109; as setting for groups interactions, 58–59, 102–3
polarization, political, impact of, 12, 19–20, 159, 161–62
politics in Wellesley: Democrat's current dominance, 185n61; interaction and relational assimilation in, 87–89; party realignment, 114–16, 184–85n61; town government as setting for group interaction, 61–63; town "Tolerance Pledge" and, 29; turn from conservative to progressive dominance, 114
Portes, Alejandro, 30, 34
Putnam, Robert, 55

race: factors affecting significance of, 160; steps to eliminate inequality, 161
racialization: assimilation and, 3, 66, 160–61; challenges to White middle-class norms and, 32; definition of, 6, 31; glocal nature of, 39; mainstream reformation and, 3, 59, 66, 69–70, 125; and neo-assimilation, interaction of, 6, 32–33, 34, 48, 157–59; theories of, 31–32; ubiquity in US, 160; and variegated assimilation, 6, 7, 34, 157–59; White pretense of colorblindness and, 70–71, 162–63
racism in Wellesley: COVID and anti-Asian hate, 29, 68, 97–98, 140, 152, 159, 160, 163; racial incidents, 113, 158–59; restrictive housing laws and, 14–16, 41–42, 118. *See also* anti-Semitism in Wellesley
relational assimilation in Wellesley: changes in both ethnic group and mainstream, 96; color line restructuring and, 67, 70; definition of, 37, 65; effect on identity, 91–95, 96; established residents' feelings of enrichment from, 89–91; ethnic retention and, 66–67, 70; food and, 81–87; glocal influences on, 96; in individual interactions and friendships, 66–71; in intermarriage, 72–73; invisibility of, in some cases, 67–68, 70; new residents' provisional feelings of acceptance by Whites, 68–69; opening of barriers between groups and, 67–68; political interaction and, 87–89; religion and, 73–81; and variegated assimilation, 96
religion in Wellesley: change over time in, 4–5; feared loss of, with assimilation, 74; high levels of religiosity, 50; mainstream's protection from loss, 80; relational assimilation and, 73–81; school calendar's addition of ethnic religious holidays, 125, 143–48

schools: activities, changes prompted by ethnic groups, 137–38; Black and Latino students bused from Boston, 19; calendar, addition of ethnic holidays to, 125, 143–48; celebrations of Asian holidays, 143; Columbus day removed as holiday, 143, 147–48, 155, 163; culturally responsive teaching and, 89; de-Christianization of holidays, 138–39, 146; DEI policies, 140; integration, residents' views on, 18–19; integration through voluntary program, 16–19, 49; Italian children's isolation in, 39; multiple languages for official communications, 140–41, **141**; percentage of Chinese students in, 28; policies accommodating ethnic religious needs, 138–40, 141–42; racial/ethnic segregation by districts, 41–43, **42**; racialization of Black children, 49; redistricting, ethnic groups' conflict over, 127–32

schools, curricula: changes prompted by ethnic groups, 132–37; languages of ethnic groups, addition of, 136–37; objections to DEI and "woke" curriculum, 134–36, 145

schools as setting for group interactions, 46–50; increased diversity in schools and, 46–48; private and parochial schools, 49–50, 63

Scouting, group interactions in, 60–61, 63

segmented assimilation theory, 30, 34

Servicemen's Readjustment Act (GI Bill), 15, 24

Sheng, Dian, 33

Soong, Mayling (Madame Chiang Kai-shek), 26, **27**, 87, 122, 158

Sprague, Isaac (Elementary School), 22, 41–42, **42**, 110, 114, 127–32, **128**

St. Paul's Church, 53–54, 59

straight-line assimilation theory, 30, 40

Students for Fair Admission v. Harvard (2023), 161

Swyngedouw, Erik, 38

Temple Beth Elohim, 24, 52–54, 72, 107, 112, 115–18, 120, 122–23, 126, 138

Tocqueville, Alexis de, 55–56, 98, 126

Trump, Donald J.: and DEI programs, 140; demonization of China, 160; demonization of immigrants, 161; designation of English as official language, 109, 141

variegated assimilation in Wellesley, 70, 90, 157–59; civic integration and, 125; ethnic retention and, 60, 80; multiple paths to, 96, 103, 159; organizations and, 99; religion and, 74, 142; responses to discrimination and, 81; schools and, 50

variegated assimilation theory: definition of, 6, **7**, 34; glocal factors in, 6–7, **8**, 19–20, 37–38, 157–60; inclusion of other theories within, 32–34; influence as multidirectional and ongoing in, 6–7, 34, 157

Village Church, 1, 36, 51, 52, 55

Waters, Mary, 33, 74–75

WCLS. *See* Wellesley Chinese Language School

weather events: glocal context and, 163–64; and perception of ethnic groups, 19–20, 160, 161

Wellesley, Massachusetts: businesses, schools, and notable buildings, 1; demographics of, 1–2, 4, **4**; racial attitudes, national influence of, 3–4; residents' wealth as barrier to ethnic interaction, 164

Wellesley Chinese Language School (WCLS), 55, **56**, 97, 108, 113, 118–19, 121, 126, 136–37, 144, 145, 151, 152–53, 154

Wellesley College, 13, 16, 20, 26, **27**, 39, 105–6, 122–23, 158

Wellesley Country Club, 24–25, 52, 71

Wellesley Hills Congregational Church, 23, 53, 103, 123

Wellesley Townsman: on acupuncture, 120–21; annual "welcome" letter to College students, 52; apology to Italian residents for accusatory article, 88; on appeal of Italian culture, 20; on Chinese Service Bureau lectures, 26; as data source, 10, 166; de-Christianization of public square and, 149–50; early coverage of China, 25–26; early coverage of Chinese in Wellesley, 26, 27; on ethnic food, 82, 103, 104, 105; ethnic groups' influence on mainstream language and, 106–8; ethnic holidays coverage, 142, 143–44; fair housing debate in, 117; Holocaust and, 122, 123; immigration debate in, 87, 116; on interfaith outreach, 51, 55; intermarriage announcements in, 72; on Jewish holidays, 23–24, 25; on Jewish organizations, 111–12; on Jewish Shabbat requirements, 141; on language classes, 105; liquor license debate and, 87–88; local sports coverage, 59; political debates in, 114, 115–16; and school desegregation, 17; school redistricting coverage, 127, 128, 129; on Scouting, 60–61

White identity, 31. *See also* Black/non-Black line

White residents of Wellesley: claims to be colorblind, 70–71, 162–63; as percentage of population, 4, **4**

Zhou, Min, 30, 34